The Professional Caterer Series

(Volume 4)

The Professional Caterer Series

Volume 4

Meat and Games - Sauces and Bases
Execution, Display and Decoration
for Buffets and Receptions

Denis Ruffel
assisted by
Roland Bilheux and Alain Escoffier
under the direction of
Pierre Michalet

Translated by Anne Sterling

A copublication of
CICEM (Compagnie Internationale
de Consultation *Education* et *Media*)
Paris

and

**Van Nostrand Reinhold
New York**

Introduction to the 4 Chapters

This volume completes the series " Professional Caterer " by Denis Ruffel.
The selection of dishes and buffet menus culminates the prestigious collection of classic preparations personalized by Chef Ruffel.

Chapter 1 – Elaborate Meat Dishes

The elaborate meat dishes encompasses buffet show-pieces prepared with pork, beef, veal, lamb and game. This completes the series of elaborate dishes described in Volume 3 (Fish and Poultry in Aspic, Lobsters), all of which are a highlight on any buffet.

Chapter 2 – Stocks, Glazes, and Aspics

Stocks form the foundation of classic French cuisine. They should be made with quality ingredients, following precise recipes. A delicious stock is the sign of a serious, dedicated chef.

of the Professional Caterer Volume 4

The sample menu combinations demonstrate how the various dishes presented in this series can be combined to create menus for any occasion. The detailed outline for each event is a useful tool for the professional caterer to help organize the planning and preparation.

Chapter 3 – Sauces

Often made with the stocks described in the previous chapter, there are many basic sauces with countless derivatives. Denis Ruffel presents a large selection grouped in families.

Chapter 4 – Sample Menu Combinations for Buffet Receptions

Knowing how to cook is just the beginning for the professional caterer. He must also know how to create different menu combinations and organize receptions from A to Z.

Aside from his role as chef, the caterer orchestrates the event. Denis Ruffel outlines the step-by-step planning of 16 different buffet receptions.

Table of Contents

Introduction to the Chapters 4

Chapter 1 - Elaborate Meat Dishes 9

A Choice of Different Meats 10
A Variety of Sauces 11
A Selection of 14 Elaborate Meat Dishes 12
Sliced Decorated Ham 14
Cubed Ham with Pineapples and Cherries 22
Pork Loin with Exotic Fruits 30
Pork Sirloin with Sweet and Sour Sauce 38
Stuffed Suckling Pig 46
Beef Tenderloin " Périgueux " 54
Braised Beef " Bourgeoise " 62
Prime Rib with Young Vegetables 70
Breast of Veal with Dried Fruits 78
Leg of Lamb with Mint 86
Noisette of Venison 94
" Dodines " of Wild Boar 102
Hare " à la Royale " 110
Pheasant Ballotine " en Volière " 118

Chapter 2 - Stocks, Glazes and Aspics 127

Introduction 128
White Veal Stock 130
White Poultry Stock 134
Brown Veal Stock 136
Brown Stock " Estouffade " 138
Demi-glaze and Meat Glaze 142
Rabbit Stock 144
Duck Stock 147
Game Stock 150
Sweetbread Stock 152
Pigeon Stock 156
Lamb Stock 158
Guinea Hen Stock 162
Meat Juice and Deglazing 164
Fish Stock 166
Aspic and Clarified Stock 170
Meat Aspic 174
Poultry Aspic 177
Fish Aspic 178
Court-bouillon and Poaching Liquid 180
Consommé 181

Chapter 3 - Sauces 183

Introduction 184
Liaisons 186
Bechamel Sauce, Parmesan Sauce, Sauce
    Crème 188
Fish Sauces 190
Sauces for Meat and Poultry 194
Cold Emulsified Sauces 198
Hot Emulsified Sauces 200
Quiche Custards 202
Chaud-Froid Sauces 204
Vinaigrette Sauces 206
Compound Butters, Mousses, Cream-based
    Spreads 208
Other Sauces 210

Chapter 4 - Planning Buffet Receptions 213

The Services Offered to the Client by the Caterer 214
Equipment Rental 216
Billing Procedure 218
Sixteen Sample Menu Combinations 219
Introduction to the Sample Menu Combina-
   tions 220
A+ Annual Bridge Club Party 222
A++ Engagement Party 228
A+++ Board of Directors Meeting 234
A++++ Golden Anniversary 240
B+ Baptism 246
B++ Informal Wedding Reception 252
B+++ Designer Clothing Boutique Inaugura-
   tion 258
B++++ Public Relations on a " Bateau Mouche " 264
C+ Awards Ceremony 270
C++ Officers Reserve Ball 276
C+++ Chamber of Commerce Reception 282
C++++ Formal Wedding Reception 288
D+ Reception at City Hall 294
D++ Annual Business School Ball 300
D+++ New Car Model Promotion 306
D++++ Factory Opening 312

Preparations in the 4 volumes classified by food cost   318

Chapter 1
Elaborate Meat Dishes

These elaborate meat dishes along with the fish and poultry in aspic and lobsters described in volume 3, are the showpieces of the buffet table. A caterer's ability is often judged on the finesse in taste and decoration of these impressive presentations.

Denis Ruffel presents 14 of his specialities. Each dish is a treat for the palate as well a delight to the eye.

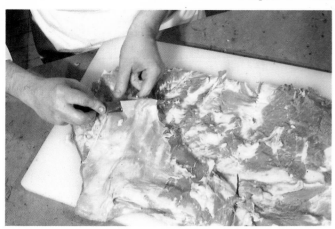
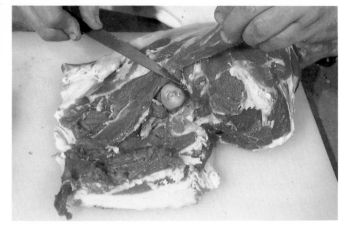

Choice of Meats

This chapter on elaborate meat dishes completes the collection of fancy buffet centerpieces in Volume 3 of The Professional Caterer which includes chapters on Poultry in Aspic, Fish and Lobsters.

The selection here offers a wide range of impressive meat presentations using many different cuts of meat, cooked and decorated in a variety of ways which can add dimension to a buffet menu.

Pork

These presentations are very straight forward with a size and style to suit any occasion. The food cost of these items is relatively low.

Five different dishes are described.

Beef

Beef dishes are always appreciated for their wonderful flavor. The cuts of beef used here allow the chef to create presentations that are succulent as well as attractive.

The food cost will vary with the cut of meat used.

Three different dishes are described.

Veal

The dish presented can be offered to the customer at a reasonable price due to the choice of stuffing ingredients. A moist texture is achieved through careful cooking. A slice of this breast of veal is attractive as well.

Lamb

It is difficult to resist this wonderful leg of lamb, cooked medium-rare so its meat remains rosy and moist. It is enhanced by a refreshing mint-scented glaze.

The small garnishes that accompany this dish marry perfectly with the taste of the lamb.

Game

When game is in season, these presentations will help the caterer take full advantage of these delicious meats and offer variety to the buffet menu.

The garnishes as well feature seasonal ingredients that compliment the full flavor of the game.

Characteristics in Common

All of the meats are cooked in advance (24-48 hours minimum).

The meats are portioned, reassembled then glazed with a sauce and/or aspic.

The garnishes are chosen to marry with the flavor of the dish and enhance the presentaton.

The meats used in each dish are of prime quality and the decorations highlight the taste and shape of the meat.

There is a presentation to suit every occasion, ranging from simple to very elaborate, using a variety of techniques, ingredients and bases. All the dishes are easy to prepare.

All of these elaborate meat dishes deserve a place of prominence on the buffet and are appropriate as a centerpiece around which other dishes are arranged.

The cooking methods differ according to the meat used. They are poached, roasted or braised. Before cooking they are thoroughly trimmed. In some cases they are boned and stuffed.

When necessary they are tied securely with kitchen twine to maintain a neat shape during cooking which ensures an attractive slice.

The taste of many meats, especially game, are improved by marinating before cooking. The time needed to marinate the meat must be planned on in advance.

Allow ample time to properly portion and garnish the dish. Slicing or cutting the meat in cubes requires time as well as skill.

The final glazing of the meat should be done with great care for an impeccable presentation.

Choosing a Sauce

These elaborate dishes are appropriate for serving many people at a large buffet. Depending on the occasion and number of people, the caterer can propose several different meat centerpieces to suit everyone's taste.

It is important to choose dishes that are appropriate for the occasion and that feature the ingredients that are best in each season.

The sauces and garnishes can vary to adapt a dish to the season and occasion.

The imagination of the chef should play a key role in creating new combinations. However, it is important that the flavor and texture of the three elements-meat, garnish and sauce are always in perfect harmony.

The meat should be cooked well in advance and thoroughly chilled so that it will slice neatly and be easier to arrange and glaze.

The sauces included in this chapter are varied and imaginative.

When choosing a sauce, keep in mind the texture and flavor of the meat.

Gelatin is added to the sauces so that they will coat the meats evenly and not melt during the reception. The amount of gelatin needed varies according to the temperature.

The garnishes can be coated with the same sauce as the meat or simply brushed with a clear glaze of aspic.

It is indispensible to brush a final coat of clear aspic over the meat and garnishes to seal in the freshness and make the dish shine.

11

A Beautiful Selection
of 14 Elaborate Meat Dishes

Each dish presented in this chapter is described in detail: introduction and advice, recipe for the meat and its garnishes, procedure, decoration and platter presentation. A "procedure diagram" outlines the work step-by-step to facilitate the preparation of the dish.

Pork: *Sliced Decorated Ham*

Pork: *Cubed Ham with Pineapple and Cherries*

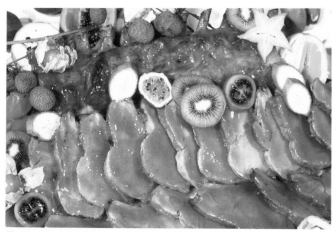

Pork: *Pork Loin with Exotic Fruits*

Pork: *Pork Sirloin with Sweet and Sour Sauce*

Pork: *Stuffed Suckling Pig*

Veal: *Breast of Veal with Dried Fruits*

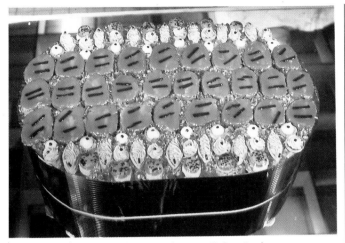

Beef: *Beef Tenderloin " Perigueux " in Aspic*

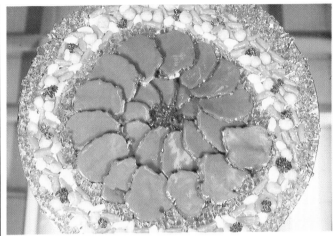

Beef: *Braised Beef " Bourgeoise "*

Beef: *Prime Ribs with Spring Vegetables*

Lamb: *Leg of Lamb with Mint*

Game: *Noisettes of Venison*

Game: *" Dodines " of Wild Boar*

Game: *Saddle of Hare " à la Royale "*

Game: *Pheasant Ballotine " en Volière "*

Sliced Decorated Ham

Introduction

Due to its lovely shape and color and succulent flavor, ham is a popular choice for elaborate presentations. The size allows the caterer to offer up to 60 portions of meat from a single dish. In general a good-sized ham will serve 40-50 guests on a buffet.

The " purée Matignon " is a flavorful mixture that holds the slices in place and counteracts the saltiness of the ham.

Equipment

Cutting board, large stockpot, small round wire rack, saucepan with lid, wooden spoon, boning knife, paring knife, vegetable peeler, chef's knife, thermometer, measuring cup, food processor, drum sieve, plastic scraper, thin-bladed knife, meat slicing knife, triangular spatuala, platter, paper frills, decorative skewers, small wooden skewers, bowls, pastry brush

Ingredients

York ham weighing 5-6.5 kilos (11-13 lbs)

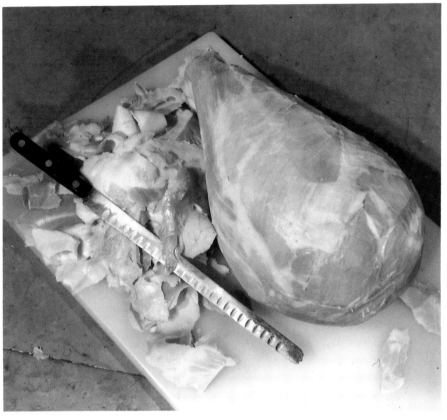

Cooking liquid

30 liters (about 35 quarts) water
150 grams (5 oz) coarse salt
1 bouquet garni (30 stems parsley,
2 branches thyme, 2 bay leaves)
30 black peppercorns
20 coriander seeds
1 clove

Purée Matignon

40 grams (1 1/2 oz) clarified but-
    ter
150 grams (5 oz) young, fresh car-
    rots
150 grams (5 oz) onions
60 grams (2 oz) celeriac
120 grams (4 oz) boiled ham
1 bouquet garni (5 parsley stems,
1 branch thyme, 1/4 bay leaf,
    leek)
1.5 deciliters (2/3 cup) madeira

Decoration

1 L (1 qt) aspic for glazing, flavored
    with madeira, port, or sherry
7 firm, red tomatoes
Green portion of 1 leek
2 L (2 qt) firm aspic, chopped

Preparing the Ham Before Poaching

If you are not using a pre-cooked ham:

Remove the aitchbone.

This is the flat bone that joins the central bone or femur at the base of the ham.

This operation allows for more thorough desalting at the center of the ham. Reserve the bone for the poaching liquid.

Desalt the ham

Put the ham in a large recipient and soak it in cold water for six hours, with the tap running in a thin stream to continually rinse the ham.

Place the round grill with "feet" on the bottom of the stockpot to keep the ham from sitting on the bottom of the pot.

Tie the ham with kitchen twine, with a large loop of twine at one end.

Set a rod (the metal bars used for forming candies is ideal) over the top of the pot and tie the twine around the rod so the ham is suspended in the liquid.

Add the water and seasonings and poach the ham for about 30 minutes per kilo (2 lbs), maintaining the cooking liquid at a temperature of 75 °C (165 F).

Check the cooking liquid from time to time and add hot water if necessary to maintain the volume and temperature.

The ham is done when the center registers 65 °C (150 F) on a meat thermometer.

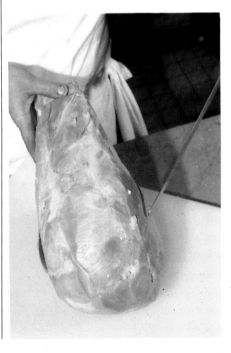

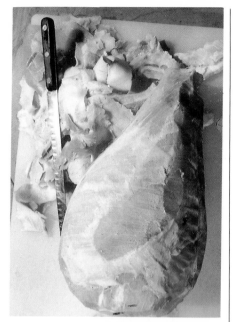

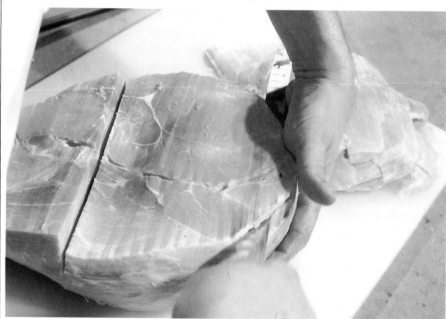

Cooling the Ham

Generally the ham cools in the cooking liquid.

If the ham has overcooked, however, remove it from the hot liquid and wrap it in damp handtowels so it will not dry out.

The cooled ham must then rest in the refrigerator for 2-3 days before slicing.

Trimming the Ham

Trim a slice from the bottom of the ham so it will sit perfectly flat and be stable.

This slice can be used for the purée Matignon.

Using a long thin-bladed slicing knife, remove the skin and trim the 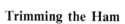 fat, maintaining the smooth, even form of the ham.

16

Slicing the Ham

Cut the ham in slices about 2 mm (about 1/8 inch) thick with the long slicing knife.

Turn each slice over and stack them neatly so the ham can be reassembled in its original form.

The larger slices in the center should be cut in 2 or 3 pieces so that each portion is about the same.

Leave a large portion of the ham uncut to serve as a base as shown.

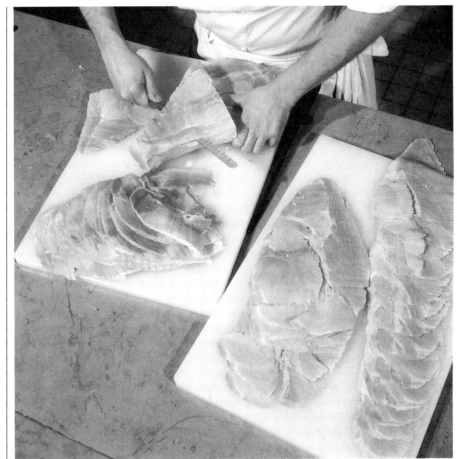

Making the Purée Matignon

Wash and peel the carrots, onions and celeriac. Cut the vegetables and ham into small dice.

Cook these ingredients in butter in a covered pan over low heat, until softened, about 4-5 minutes.

Deglaze with the madeira, continue to cook, covered until the vegetables are very well done.

Remove the cover and evaporate the liquid.

Purée the vegetables and ham in a food processor.

Press this mixture through a fine-meshed drum sieve to obtain a perfectly smooth purée.

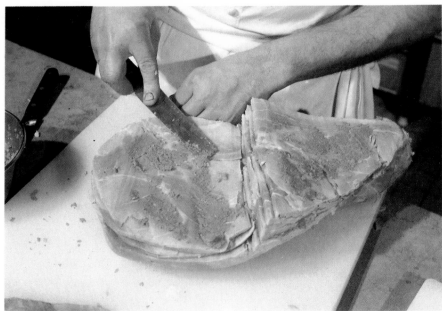

Assembling the Ham

Starting with the last slice removed, spread a thin layer of purée Matignon on each slice and replace them one by one on the base to reconstruct the ham.

Cover the assembled ham in plastic wrap and place it in the refrigerator to thoroughly chill.

The ham can be prepared to this point 24-48 hours in advance.

The Choice of Ham

In France a top choice for this dish is the York ham which is available from specialty charcuteries.

It is a very delicious ham which is cured with dry salt instead of brine and lightly smoked. The special preparation of this ham is protected by its name.

This ham is available with or without the aitchbone attached and is cooked on the bone (femur) with the fat and skin.

It is possible to purchase the ham cured but not cooked in which case it must be desalted for 6 hours under cold running water before cooking. It is then poached in a flavorful liquid at 75 °C (165F) for approximately 30 minutes per kilo (2 pounds).

The ham should not rest on the bottom of the pot while cooking. It can be tied with kitchen twine and suspended in the liquid.

A small round wire rack with "feet" can be set in the bottom of the pot to make sure the ham does touch the bottom.

Another good choice is a boned ham cooked in a mold. This ham is boned, salted then placed in a two-sided metal mold shaped like a ham.

It is cooked and cooled then unmolded.

The molded, boneless ham is very easy to slice as the meat is very firm. Although not as delicious as the York ham, it is a good choice for these elaborate dishes.

The preparation of the molded ham is quite lengthy so orders must be placed well in advance.

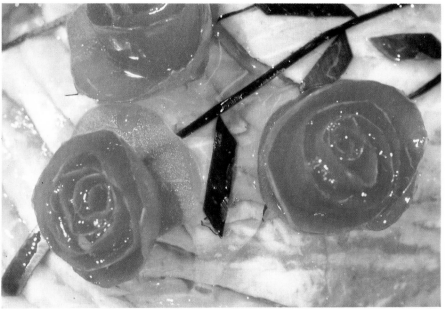

Preparing the Decoration

The decoration must be applied at the last moment.

The Aspic: Melt the aspic.

The Tomatoes: Choose beautiful, round, firm, red tomatoes to make the roses.

Wash them, then cut away the skin in a spiral with a very sharp knife. Twist the spiral of skin to form a rose.

The Leek: Wash the green portion of several leaves of leek. Blanch them in rapidly boiling water then refresh them in ice water to stop the cooking and fix the color.

Cut leaf shapes and long strips to form the stems of the roses.

Glazing and Decorating the Ham

Stir the aspic over ice until slightly thickened, taking care not to form air bubbles.

Brush two coats of aspic on the ham using a soft-bristled pastry brush.

Decorate the ham with the tomato roses, stems and leaves as shown. Hold the roses in place with skewers if necessary.

Glaze the decorations twice with aspic. Remove the skewers.

Place the ham on the platter and spoon a thin layer of chopped aspic on the platter.

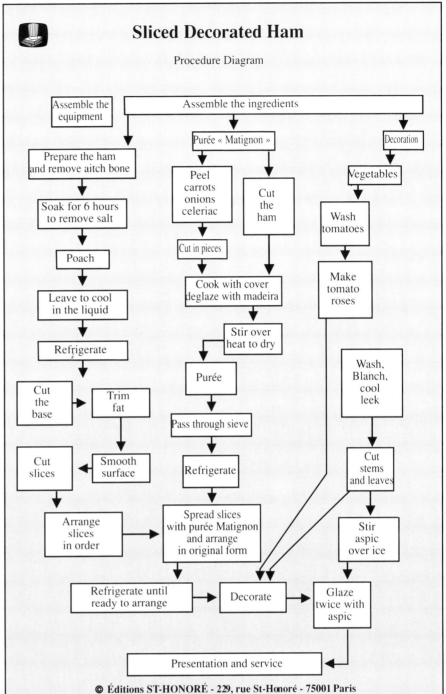

Sliced Decorated Ham

Procedure Diagram

Assemble the equipment → Assemble the ingredients

Prepare the ham and remove aitch bone → Soak for 6 hours to remove salt → Poach → Leave to cool in the liquid → Refrigerate → Cut the base → Trim fat → Smooth surface → Cut slices → Arrange slices in order

Purée « Matignon » → Peel carrots onions celeriac → Cut in pieces → Cook with cover deglaze with madeira → Stir over heat to dry → Purée → Pass through sieve → Refrigerate

Cut the ham → Cook with cover deglaze with madeira

Spread slices with purée Matignon and arrange in original form

Decoration → Vegetables → Wash tomatoes → Make tomato roses

Wash, Blanch, cool leek → Cut stems and leaves → Stir aspic over ice

Refrigerate until ready to arrange → Decorate → Glaze twice with aspic → Presentation and service

© Éditions ST-HONORÉ - 229, rue St-Honoré - 75001 Paris

21

Cubed Ham with Pineapple and Cherries

Introduction

For this preparation, it is necessary to use a ham that has been cooked in a mold.

As previously explained, this ham is completely boned then pressed into a two-sided metal mold that is shaped like a ham. It is important to carefully replace the top half of the mold so that the final product has an attractive, uniform shape with no gaps or holes. Once cooked and cooled, this boned ham is ideal for cutting into bite-sized cubes and re-assembled for this stunning display.

The cooled ham is first cut into thick even slices that are then cut into strips and then into neat cubes. You must work very methodically and keep each layer intact so the ham can be reconstructed into its original shape. A delicious purée of goose liver is used to secure each layer of

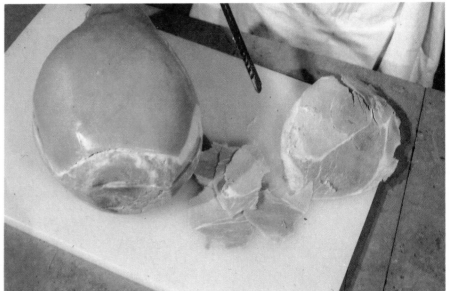

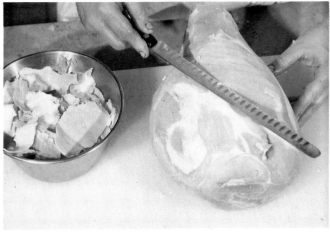

cubes into place. The colorful decoration harmoniously combines golden pineapples, deep red cherries and black cloves, it is held in place by a light sweet and sour glaze flavored with pineapple.

The platter is augmented with small brochettes of ham with pineapple and cherries, which facilitates the service and provides supplementary portions.

Small barquettes filled with goose liver puree, topped with pineapple and cherries also garnish the platter.

All the elements are glazed with aspic and arranged on a platter coated with chopped aspic.

Equipment

Cutting board, paring knife, slicing knife, fine-bladed knife, palette knife, mixing bowls, spatula, triangular scraper, sauté pan, measuring cup, whisk, conical sieve, small boat-shaped molds, oval pastry cutters, small wooden skewers, pastry bag and star tip, pastry scraper, vegetable peeler, pastry brush, platter, cloth or paper ribbon

Recipe

Principal Ingredients

1 5-6 kg (1 10-13 lb) boned ham, cooked in a mold

Assembly Ingredients

250 g (1/2 lb) goose liver purée

Decoration

1 fresh pineapple, or 1 can of 8 slices
300 g (10 oz) cherries
1/2 l (2 cups) red wine
3 strips of pared orange zest
Cloves
1 L (1 qt) aspic

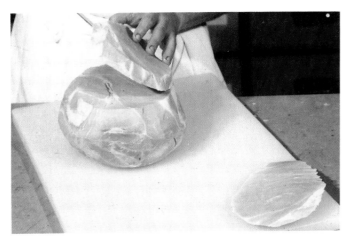
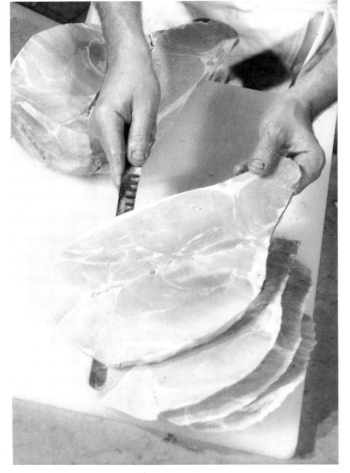

Glaze Ingredients

2 dl (3/4 cup) pineapple syrup
5 cl (1/4 cup) wine vinegar
1.5 dl (2/3 cup) dry white wine
 (sauvignon)
1 1/4 l (5 cups) reduced brown stock
Roux (optional)
8 leaves (16 g (1/2 oz)) gelatine per
 1 L (1 qt) sauce
Salt, pepper

Garnish

Small boat-shaped tartelettes in
 basic pie pastry
Goose liver purée
Pineapple sections
Cherries

Aspic for glazing
Firm aspic, chopped, for decorating
 the platter

Preparing the Ham

To prepare the ham cooked in the mold, follow the procedure described on preceding pages for the sliced ham.

Cutting the Ham into Dice

Cut a thick flat slice from the bottom of the ham which will serve as a solid base for the presentation. Using a well-sharpened knife, trim the sides and remove the skin and trim the fat to give the ham a smooth surface, being careful to maintain the shape.

Cutting the ham is a delicate and dangerous procedure. Care must be taken to make perfectly even cubes which will allow the ham to be reassembled neatly and easily. It is recommended to use a well-sharpened long thin slicing knife as shown.

Each slice, about 2 cm (3/4 in) thick, is systematically transferred to a cutting board and stacked in the order in which they are removed from the ham. Thus the last slice to be cut will be the first to be replaced on the base.

Assembling the Ham

The goose liver purée is softened and beaten until smooth. It is spread between the layers of ham to hold them together. Stack several slices together as shown and cut them into even cubes.

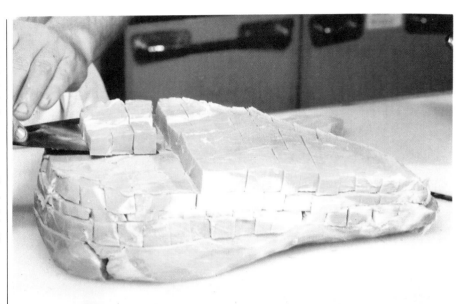

Spread a thin layer of liver purée on the base. With a spatula, replace a small stack of cubes on the base, keeping the slices in the right order so each cube will be returned to its proper place.

Coat the sides of these cubes with liver purée then proceed with another "block" of cubes, pressing them to stick them together.

Continue to coat each block of ham cubes with liver purée and replace them in order until the ham is completely reassembled. To simplify the procedure, the following is recommended:

• Lay out each slice separately on the cutting board in the order in which it was removed. (The slices can be numbered to keep them in the right order.)

• Cut each slice into cubes just before replacing it on the base.

• Replace one slice at a time, trying to avoid placing the cuts or "seams" in one layer directly atop the seams of the lower layer; staggering the seams will give the structure more stability.

• Do not invert the slices; use the palette knife to position the cubes. After each layer has been positioned, double-check the placement of each cube and make sure the form of the ham is being maintained.

Chilling the Ham

The assembled ham is thoroughly chilled to harden the liver purée so that it can be decorated and glazed without falling apart.

Preparing the Decoration

The Pineapple

Choose fresh ripe pineapples and remove the skin and core. Cut into even slices 5 mm (about 1/4 in) thick and poach in a light syrup (250-300 g sugar per 1 l water (1 1/4-1 1/2 cups sugar per quart water)). Chill for 24 hours in the syrup. Drain thoroughly before using.

Canned pineapple can also be used. In this case, drain the slices thoroughly, dry on a hand towel or paper towels so that no juice will render out which would dilute the aspic.

The Cherries

Drain the cherries in syrup, then poach them in red or white wine flavored with orange zest. Let them cool in the liquid for 12-24 hours. Fresh cherries can be used as well. Poach them and let cool in the liquid.

The wine for poaching should not be too dry, which would draw out the acidic flavor of the cherries.

26

Preparing the Garnishes

The boat-shaped molds (barquettes) are lined with basic pie pastry one day in advance, then blind-baked just before filling. So that the pastry remains crisp, pipe the goose-liver purée into the cooled barquettes at the last minute. Arrange the cherries and pieces of pineapple on top of the purée and chill to harden the purée before glazing with aspic. The small brochettes of pineapple and cherries can be made in advance and

kept chilled until ready to garnish the platter.

Decorating the Ham

Cut each slice of drained pineapple into 6-8 pieces. For a more delicate presentation and to keep the sweet flavor in the right proportion to the salty, cut each piece of pineapple in half to make thin, petal-like pieces.

Arrange the pineapple and cherries in an attractive pattern as shown, augmenting the design with the cloves. Add the small brochettes around the edge to finish the decoration.

Chill the decorated ham until ready to glaze.

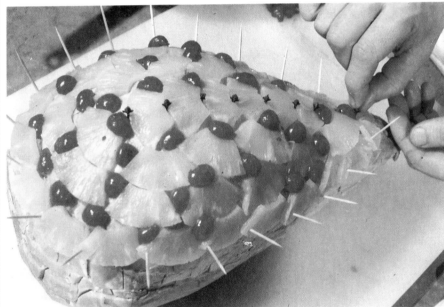

27

Making the Sauce

In a heavy saucepan, reduce the poaching syrup from the pineapple

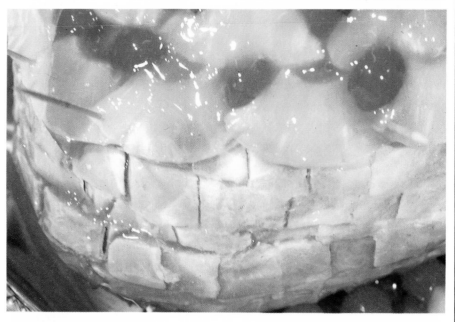

to a light caramel. Deglaze the caramel with vinegar, dissolving all the caramel. Add the white wine and reduce by half. Add the reduced stock and reduce by half.

If necessary, add a little cooked roux to obtain a sauce with a light coating consistency.

Taste and adjust the seasoning if necessary. Add the softened gelatin and stir to melt completely.

Pass the sauce through a fine-meshed sieve to make it perfectly smooth and homogenized and set aside to cool.

Glazing the Ham

Stir the strained sauce over ice until it thickens slightly. Using a soft-bristled pastry brush, coat the chilled, decorated ham with the sauce. It is often necessary to brush on two coats of glaze to obtain a smooth finish.

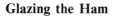

It is recommended that the first coat of sauce be a little thick to cover well. The second coat should be thinned with a little white wine or pineapple juice to add a smooth finish.

Chill the ham to set the sauce before glazing with aspic.

The small brochettes and filled barquettes are also brushed with two coats of sauce and chilled before being glazed with aspic.

Arranging the Ham on the Platter

Just before transfering the ham to the platter, brush one or two coats of clear aspic to make it shine. Place the ham on the platter and arrange the garnishes in an attractive pattern around the ham. Fill the spaces around the ham and garnishes with finely chopped aspic. The edge of the platter can be lined with leaves of lettuce or another decoration if desired.

Cubed Ham with Pineapple and Cherries

Procedure Diagram

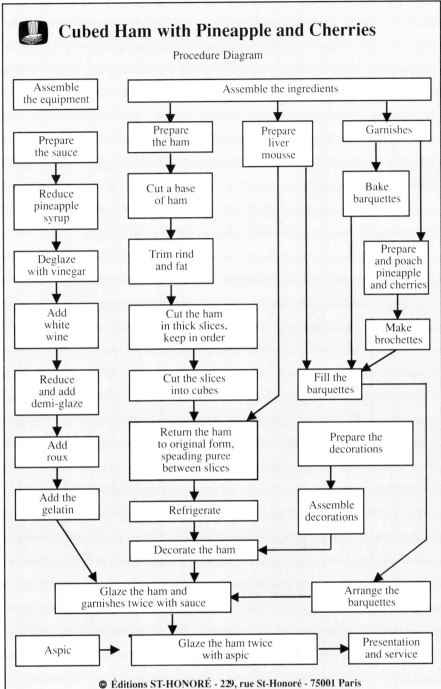

- Assemble the equipment
- Assemble the ingredients
- Prepare the sauce → Reduce pineapple syrup → Deglaze with vinegar → Add white wine → Reduce and add demi-glaze → Add roux → Add the gelatin
- Prepare the ham → Cut a base of ham → Trim rind and fat → Cut the ham in thick slices, keep in order → Cut the slices into cubes → Return the ham to original form, speading puree between slices → Refrigerate → Decorate the ham
- Prepare liver mousse → Fill the barquettes
- Garnishes → Bake barquettes → Prepare and poach pineapple and cherries → Make brochettes → Fill the barquettes
- Prepare the decorations → Assemble decorations
- Glaze the ham and garnishes twice with sauce
- Arrange the barquettes
- Aspic → Glaze the ham twice with aspic → Presentation and service

© Éditions ST-HONORÉ - 229, rue St-Honoré - 75001 Paris

Pork Loin with Exotic Fruits

Introduction

The reasonable price of pork allows the caterer to offer interesting dishes at affordable prices.

The size and form of the pork loin is ideal for elaborate dishes such as the one described here.

A hint of curry adds a delicious flavor that marries well with the fruit garnish.

The pork, which is cooked well done, must be basted often during the lengthy cooking time to keep it moist.

It is therefore of prime importance to follow the guidelines for searing and basting the meat.

Equipment

Cutting board, vegetable peeler, boning knife, paring knife, slicing knife, cleaver, roasting pan, measuring cup, spouted spoon, tongs, skimmer, kitchen scissors, conical sieve, ladle, large pot, whisk, mixing bowls, pastry brush, stainless steel sheet pans, cooling racks, platter

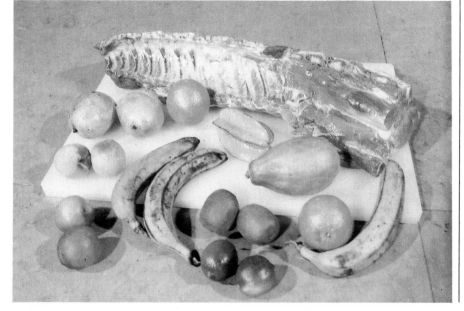

Ingredients

Main Ingredient
1 rack of pork 4-4.5 kilos (9-10 lbs)

Aromatics and Seasonings
60 g (2 oz) clarified butter
5 cl (1/4 cup) oil
Salt, pepper and curry powder
300 g (10 oz) carrots
300 g (10 oz) onions
60 g (2 oz) garlic
75 g (2 1/2 oz) celery
Bouquet garni (1 leaf leek, 6 parsley
    stems, 2 sprigs thyme, 1 bay leaf)

For basting: 5 cl (1/4 cup) dry white
    wine
2 L (about 2 qts) brown stock

Garnishes
Assorted Exotic Fruits
Firm aspic, chopped

Glaze Ingredients
Cooked roux
15 g (1/2oz) gelatin per liter (qt) of
    sauce
1.5 L (1.5 qt) aspic

Procedure

Trimming and Boning the Pork

Using a well-sharpened boning knife, slice down between the ribs about 2-3 cm (1") and scrape along the bones to expose them.

Trim away excess fat from around the meat.

Remove the chine, which is the flat bone at the base of the rack. Since this bone is part of the animal's vertabrae, there are knobby bones along the length the chine. Cut around these bones to free the chine.

Tying up the Pork Loin

Tie kitchen twine securely between each rib to give the roast a uniform shape for even cooking and a neat final product.
Add salt and pepper.

Cooking the Pork Loin

Heat the oil and butter in the roasting pan over high heat. Add the pork, and lightly brown it on all sides.

Turn the meat over without piercing the surface which would release juices and cause the meat to dry out.

Add the aromatic vegetables, then place the pan in the oven (220 °C (425 F) for 30 minutes to brown the vegetables.

Remove the meat and deglaze the pan with dry white wine.

Return the meat to the pan. The deglazing juices will provide a moist environment for the pork to finish cooking in without drying out.

Add the bouquet garni. Return the pan to the oven for 15-20 minutes. Baste the meat several times and stir the vegetables a little to prevent them from burning.

Add the brown stock and return to the oven to finish cooking for about 1 hour at 200 °C (375 F).

Baste the meat frequently with the pan juices.

Check the doneness of the meat by inserting a skewer to the center which should feel warm when touched to the lower lip.

The juices that flow from the hole should be clear, indicating that the pork is well done.

Cooling and Storing

Drain the meat on a cooling rack. When it is no longer hot, put the meat, unwrapped in the refrigerator to cool.

When thoroughly cooled, cover in plastic wrap to keep it from drying out and store in the refrigerator.

The meat should chill for at least 24 hours to ensure easy slicing and can be stored for 3-4 days.

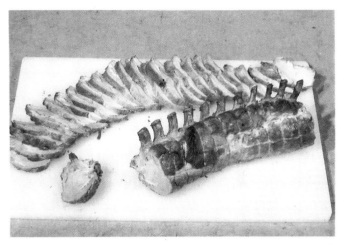

Making the Sauce

Strain the cooking juices and skim off the fat that rises to the surface.

Chill then remove the hardened fat on the surface. (If the juices are being stored for a short while, the layer of fat can be left to protect the surface and keep the liquid fresh.)

To thicken the sauce, heat the degreased juices and whisk in enough pre-cooked roux to achieve a light coating consistency.

Soften the gelatin and stir it in until completely melted.

Finishing the Dish

Remove all remaining bones from the cooled pork. Cut in even slices about 1 cm (3/8") thick.

This can be done with a serrated knife.

Careful slicing is important; slices too thick are unattractive and hard to eat, slices too thin fall apart.

Stir the sauce over ice to thicken slightly.

Using a soft-bristled pastry brush, coat each slice of pork with sauce (one side and around the edges).

Lay them on a rack and chill to set. Brush on a second coat for a smooth finish. Chill to set.

Stir the aspic over ice to thicken slightly.

Brush a coat of aspic on the slices of pork to protect them and make them shine.

The Braising Liquid

The pork is basted with brown veal stock and white wine during cooking.

This liquid, which absorbs flavor from the pork and the aromatic vegetables, is strained and the fat is removed.

It is thickened, gelatin is added, then this sauce is brushed on the slices of meat to give a shiny finish.

The Garnish

Exotic fruits are a delicious accompaniment to pork.

Not only are they colorful, but they provide an exciting variety of shapes and refreshing flavors, which are very pleasing to customers.

There are many exotic fruits to choose from. The combination pictured here is but one example of the variety.

Many are readily available while others must be purchased from a specialty purveyor.

Examples of exotic fruits (from top to bottom)

Tamarillos	Mango	Passion fruit
Star fruit	Custard apple	Papaya
Kiwi	Persimmon	Loquat
Custard apple	Zalaca	Plantain
(assortment)	Tamarillos	Apple

The price of some exotic fruits is quite high, however, with such a large variety to choose from, an assortment can be chosen to accomodate the cost of the dish.

Arranging on the Platter

Arrange the slices in an attractive pattern on the platter.

Set the exotic fruits around the meat and platter, making the most of the various colors and shapes to achieve a well balanced and eye-pleasing presentation.

Fill the spaces around the meat and fruits with firm aspic that has been chopped or cut in small cubes.

This simple decoration glistens and adds an elegant touch.

Store the dish in the refrigerator until ready to serve.

If the dish is to be transported, the elements can be packaged separately and arranged on the platter at the last minute.

Presentation

The arrangement of the meat and fruits on the platter will depend on the occasion, number of guests and the imagination of the chef.

For a particularly impressive presentation, a portion of the loin can be left uncut and used as a support for the remaining slices which are arranged around it.

It is recommended to cut some of the fruits into attractive pieces that can be served with the meat and leave some of them whole to garnish the platter with colorful " bouquets ".

The fruits should be placed so that the colors and shapes are in perfect harmony with the meat and size and shape of the platter.

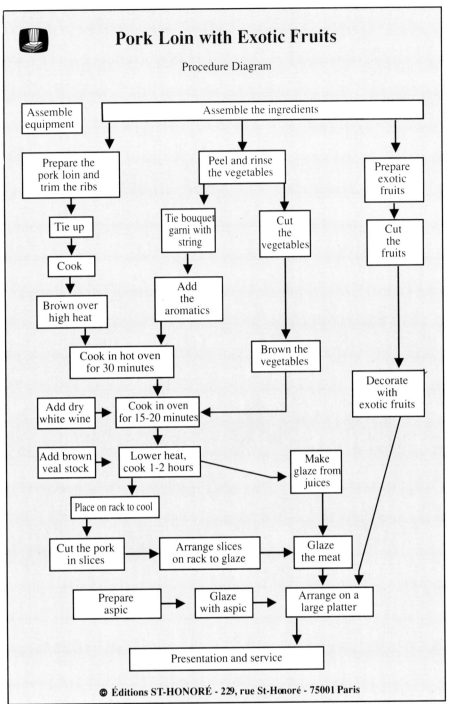

Pork Loin with Exotic Fruits

Procedure Diagram

Assemble equipment

Assemble the ingredients

Prepare the pork loin and trim the ribs

Peel and rinse the vegetables

Prepare exotic fruits

Tie up

Tie bouquet garni with string

Cut the vegetables

Cut the fruits

Cook

Brown over high heat

Add the aromatics

Cook in hot oven for 30 minutes

Brown the vegetables

Decorate with exotic fruits

Add dry white wine → Cook in oven for 15-20 minutes

Add brown veal stock → Lower heat, cook 1-2 hours → Make glaze from juices

Place on rack to cool

Cut the pork in slices → Arrange slices on rack to glaze → Glaze the meat

Prepare aspic → Glaze with aspic → Arrange on a large platter

Presentation and service

© Éditions ST-HONORÉ - 229, rue St-Honoré - 75001 Paris

Pork Sirloin with Sweet and Sour Sauce

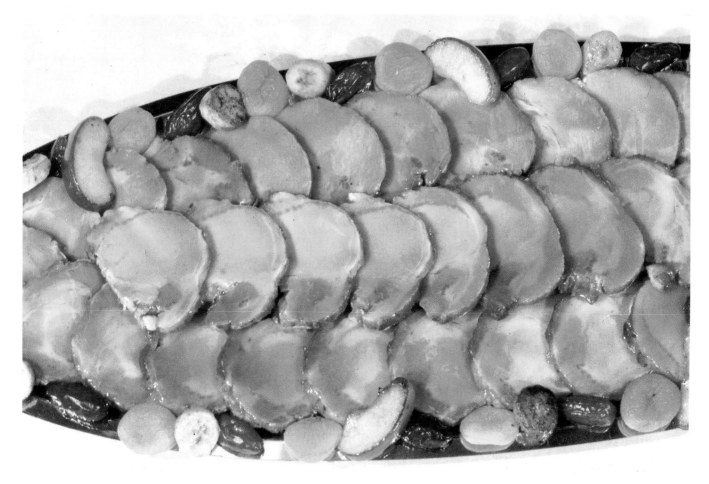

Introduction

This recipe, like the preceding one, features pork which is less expensive than other meats. This cut also requires close attention to the cooking so that the meat does not dry out.

The first step is to purchase prime quality meat. The sirloin roast comes from the tender end of the loin. The boned sirloin provides very neat slices as well.

For this dish, the meat is cooked in two stages. First the tied roast is gently poached. It is drained and dried on clean handtowels then finished in the oven.

The meat looks a little dull after poaching. In the oven it roasts to a lovely golden brown. This method of cooking ensures meat that is moist and flavorful.

Equipment

Cutting board, fish poacher or large pot, meat thermometer, chef's knife, paring knife, vegetable peeler, scissors, kitchen twine, handtowels, stainless steel baking sheets, cooling rack, roasting pan, two-tined fork, saucepan, measuring cup, large bowls, conical sieve, spatula, pastry brush, platter

Ingredients

Main Ingredient
Pork sirloin roast, 3.5-4 kg (8-9 lbs)

Aromatics and Seasonings
For poaching: 6-7 L (about 7 qts) light stock or water
300 g (10 oz) carrots
300 g (10 oz) onions
80g (2 1/2 oz) garlic, unpeeled
Bouquet garni (8 parsley stems, 1 sprig thyme, 1 bay leaf, 1 leek leaf)
15 g (1/2 oz) salt per liter (qt) water
Tied in cheesecloth: 10 peppercorns, 10 coriander seeds

For roasting: 30g (1oz) clarified butter,
3 cl (2 tbls) oil

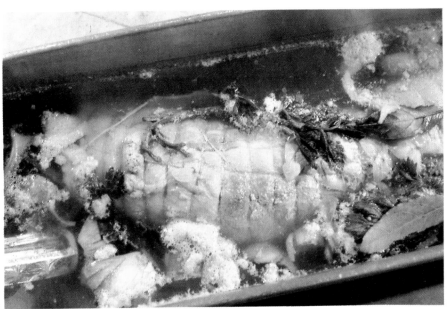

Fruit Garnish
20 large prunes
1 tea bag
20 dried apricots
20 fresh dates
4 bananas
3 Red Delicious apples
50g (1 1/2oz) clarified butter

Sauce Ingredients
100g (1/2 cup) sugar
5cl (1/4 cup) white wine vinegar
4 strips of orange zest
80 coriander seeds
3 dl (1 1/4 cups) dry white wine
2 L (4 qts) demi-glaze
Cooked roux
15 g (1/2 oz) gelatin per liter (qt) sauce
Aspic for glazing

Procedure

Preparing the Pork

Choose a lean, evenly formed sirloin roast which will provide attractive slices.

Tie the roast neatly with kitchen twine so it holds its shape during cooking.

Tying the roast compacts the meat slightly which makes the meat easier to slice. Leave a loop of twine to attach to the handle of the pot.

Preparing the Aromatics

Peel and wash the vegetables and cut into medium dice. Secure the bouquet garni in kitchen twine and tie the spices in cheesecloth.

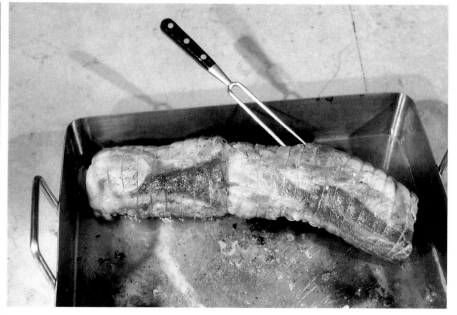

Cooking the Pork

The first step is to poach the meat in stock or salted water.

Add the vegetables to the stockpot with the stock or salted water.

Suspend the meat in the liquid by tying the end of the twine around the handle of the pot. It should not touch the bottom of the pot. Here the pork is poached in a fish poacher and rests on the rack on the bottom.

Bring the liquid to a simmer and maintain an even temperature (85 °C (185 F)) for 1 1/2 hours.

Lift the meat out, without piercing it, and drain it well on a handtowel.

The second step is to brown the meat in the oven.

Heat the butter and oil in the roasting pan.

Over high heat, brown the meat on all sides, turning the meat over without piercing it.

Finish cooking the meat in the oven (230 °C (450 F)), basting often. Test the doneness of the meat with a skewer (warm to the touch, juices run clear).

Reserve the pan juices for the sauce.

Cooling and Slicing the Meat

Drain the pork on a cooling rack.

When the meat is cool, cover it with plastic wrap or aluminum foil and refrigerate 48 hours.

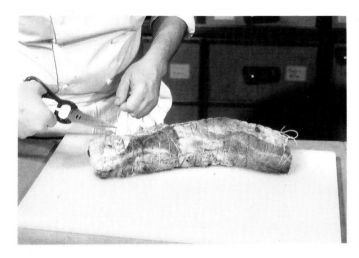 

Remove the kitchen twine from the roast.

With a well-sharpened knife, cut even slices 8 mm (1/3 ") thick.

Slices too thick are unattractive and difficult to eat and slices too thin tend to fall apart.

Arrange the slices on a rack and chill before coating with sauce.

The sweet and sour sauce that is used to glaze each slice is a pretty color as well delicious. The meat and sauce are in perfect harmony with the fruit garnish.

Several roasts can be prepared for a large reception or a single roast can be nicely arranged on a platter to serve fewer guests.

Since the food cost is not high, this dish is ideal for moderately priced menus.

The choice of fruits can vary to make the most of seasonal specialties.

Shape and color should always be considered so that the final presentation is as attractive as possible.

To better organize the work involved, the meat can be cooked up to 48 hours in advance.

Although the dish is best if assembled the day of the event, it will hold up satisfactorily, arranged on the platter, one day in advance.

Preparing the Garnish

The Apricots
Soak them in hot water. Poach them gently if necessary.

The Prunes
Poach the prunes in an infusion of tea, which gives them a delicious flavor. Cool and remove the pits.

The Dates
Fresh or dried dates may be used. Choose large, plump dates.
Remove the pits.

The Apples
Peel and cut the apples in medium slices. Sauté them in a little clarified butter or brown them in the oven on a no-stick baking sheet.

The Bananas
Peel the bananas and cut into medium slices. Sauté in a little clarified butter to brown them without overcooking.

Set the prepared fruits aside in the refrigerator until ready to assemble the dish.

Making the Sauce

Make a caramel in a heavy saucepan.

Combine the sugar, vinegar, orange zest, and coriander seeds and cook over medium heat until golden brown.

Deglaze the pan with the dry white wine and bring to a boil to eliminate the acidity of the wine.

Add the demi-glaze and reduce the sauce over medium heat.

Whisk in a little cooked roux to achieve a light coating consistency.

Soften the gelatin and, off the heat, stir it into the hot sauce until it is completely melted.

Glazing with Sauce

Stir the sauce over ice until it thickens slightly.

Use a soft-bristled pastry brush to coat each slice of chilled meat and the fruits with sauce.

Chill to set and glaze a second time for a smooth finish.

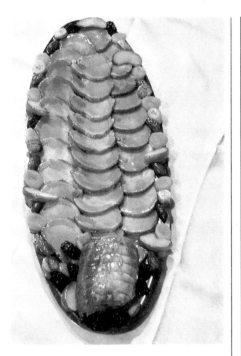

Adding an Aspic Finish

Melt the aspic then stir it over ice to thicken slightly.

Brush two coats of aspic on the slices of meat and fruit garnish.

Chill to set. The aspic keeps the sauce from drying out and adds a shiny finish.

Presentation

Arrange the slices of meat on the platter in an attractive pattern.

Decorate with the glazed fruit garnish, using the shapes and colors to make a lovely presentation.

Fill in the spaces around the meat and fruit with chopped aspic.

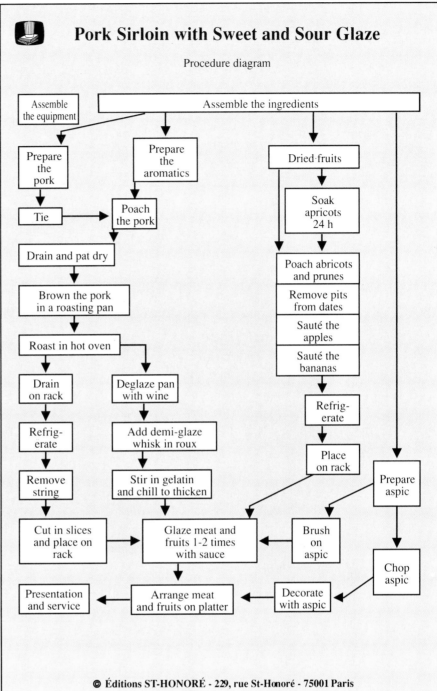

Pork Sirloin with Sweet and Sour Glaze

Procedure diagram

Assemble the equipment

Assemble the ingredients

Prepare the pork → Tie → Poach the pork

Prepare the aromatics

Dried fruits → Soak apricots 24 h

Poach abricots and prunes

Remove pits from dates

Sauté the apples

Sauté the bananas

Refrigerate

Place on rack

Drain and pat dry

Brown the pork in a roasting pan

Roast in hot oven

Drain on rack → Refrigerate → Remove string

Deglaze pan with wine → Add demi-glaze whisk in roux → Stir in gelatin and chill to thicken

Prepare aspic → Chop aspic

Cut in slices and place on rack → Glaze meat and fruits 1-2 times with sauce ← Brush on aspic

Presentation and service ← Arrange meat and fruits on platter ← Decorate with aspic

© Éditions ST-HONORÉ - 229, rue St-Honoré - 75001 Paris

Stuffed Suckling Pig

Introduction

The dramatic presentation of whole suckling pig is always the highlight on the buffet table.

This dish provides a substantial number of portions so is appropriate only for large receptions.

The final presentation is impressive enough to be presented on a platter on its own. If you choose to add garnishes, select simple ones such as cornichons (small sour pickles), cherry tomatoes, or olives which do not detract from the pig.

The stuffing is delicious and moist due to a combination of veal and pork.

Suckling pig is an expensive item. However, the dramatic presentation and large number of portions makes it a popular choice for large events.

Organizing the Work

Making this dish is not complicated if close attention is paid to each step of the preparation.

The most delicate operation is the boning of the pig. The method described here ensures a neatly boned pig that can be easily closed around the stuffing and reshaped in its original form.

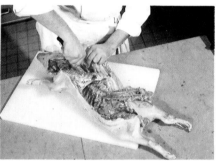

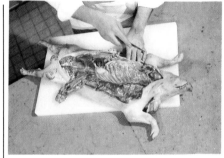

Equipment

Cutting board, chef's knife, boning knife, paring knife, vegetable peeler, palette knife, trussing needle, kitchen twine, scissors, meat grinder (optional), spatula, roasting pan, pastry brush, large bowls, plates, platter.

Ingredients

Main Ingredient 1 suckling pig 4.5-5 kg (about 10 lbs)

For cooking: 100 g (3 1/2 oz) clarified butter
5 cl (1/4 cup) oil

Stuffing Ingredients 1.5 kg (3 lb 5 oz) ground pork (67%) and veal (33%)
30 g (1 oz) shelled pistachios
1 bunch chervil
1 bunch chives
25 g (scant 1 oz) truffles
1 thin sheet of barding fat
200 g (7 oz) boiled ham
250 g (9 oz) pimento stuffed green olives
Salt, pepper

Glaze ingredients 1.5 L (1.5 qt) chaud-froid (1/3 mayonnaise, 2/3 aspic)
1.5 L (1.5 qt) aspic

Garnish Green or black olives.

Procedure

Boning the Pig

Place the pig on its back on a large cutting board. The pig will be boned through the stomach cavity which was cut open when the animal was cleaned.

Pass the knife behind the ribs, working down toward the spinal column, scraping along the bones to free the flesh without cutting through the skin.
Cut around the spine and neck to free the bones and remove in one piece.
Cut around the shoulder blades and hip bones and remove.

The boned pig can be stuffed right away or refrigerated.

Cut even strips of boiled ham, about 1 cm (3/8 ") on each side.
Drain the pimento-stuffed olives.

Stuffing the Suckling Pig

Lay the boned pig on its back on a cutting board.

To facilitate the stuffing procedure, sew each end (under the throat and between the legs) together a little so the filling will not ooze from the ends.

Sprinkle the interior with a little salt and freshly ground pepper. Spread an even layer of the mixture with chopped herbs over the interior of the pig.

Arrange alternating rows of ham strips and olives over this layer of stuffing.

Cover with a thick layer of the ground meat mixed with pistachios.

Place the "ballotine" of truffled meat in the center.

Making the Stuffing

The stuffing is a delicious combination of pork (67%) and veal (33%).

Pass the meats through the fine disk of a meat grinder (or order ground meats from the butcher). Season the meat (1 tsp salt per 500 g (1 lb) meat) then divide it into three parts:

- 800 g (1 lb 12 oz) of meat is blended with 30g (1oz) shelled, skinned pistachios. (Remove skins by blanching the nuts briefly then rubbing off the skins.)

- 500 g (1 lb) of meat is blended with the chopped herbs (chives and chervil).

- 250 g (1/2 lb) is blended with 25 g (1 oz) chopped truffles. This last portion of meat is rolled in a thin sheet of barding fat to form a sausage-shaped "ballotine" the same length as the interior of the pig and about 3-4 cm (1 1/2 ") in diameter. Chill until ready to use.

With the help of a second person, close the pig around the stuffing, bringing the edges together to give the pig its original form. Sew together the opening with a trussing needle and kitchen twine. Tie the pig neatly, like a roast, so that it maintains its shape during cooking.

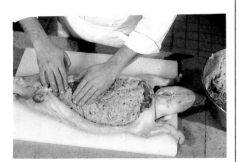

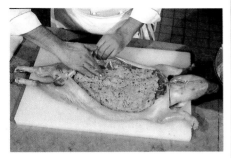

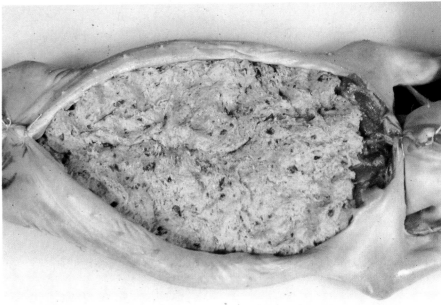

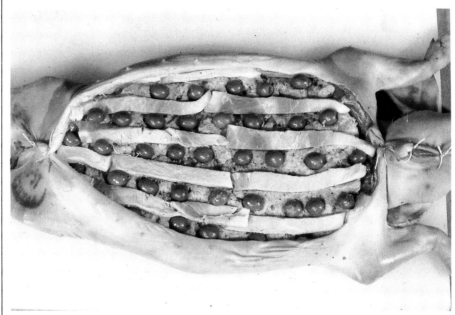

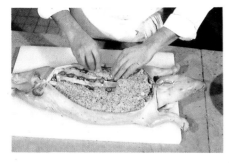

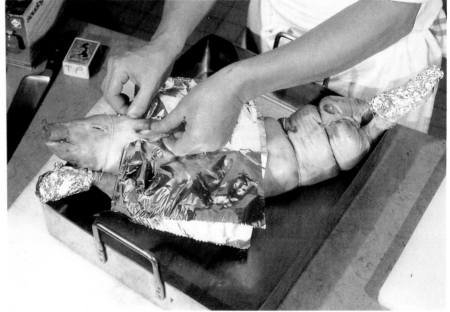

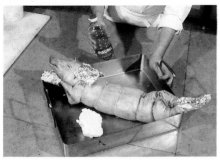

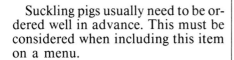

Suckling pigs usually need to be ordered well in advance. This must be considered when including this item on a menu.

The pig can be boned, stuffed, and cooked and refrigerated up to 4 days in advance.

This allows the caterer to choose a relatively calm moment in the kitchen to prepare this dish which requires time, space and attention to detail.

Cooking

Certain precautions should be taken for cooking the stuffed suckling pig.

Wrap the feet and ears in several thicknesses of aluminum foil to keep them from becoming too brown in the oven.

To prevent the fragile skin from cracking during cooking, it is important to baste frequently (with water or stock).

This will also keep the meat and stuffing moist.

Melt a little clarified butter in a roasting pan large enough to hold the pig. Place the pig in the pan and brown in a hot oven (230 °C (450 F)) for 1/2 hour.

Lower the heat to 200 °C (375 F) and continue to cook 1 1/2-2 hours, basting frequently.

Check the doneness with a skewer plunged into the center of the meat for a few seconds; it should feel warm to the touch and the juices running from the hole should be clear.

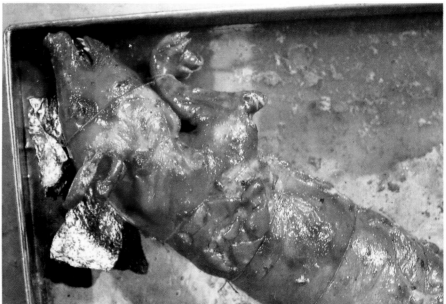

Cooling

Transfer the cooked pig immediately to a cooling rack to drain and

cool evenly on all sides.

As soon as it is cool, place it in the refrigerator. When the pig is completely chilled, cover it in foil or plastic wrap and keep in the refrigerator for up to 3 days.

Note: Wipe off the skin with a clean handtowel or paper towel so the skin is clean and smooth so that the glaze will adhere properly.

Slicing the Cooked Pig

Place the pig on a cutting board and cut slices from the center portion.

The head and rear portion are left intact for the presentation. (The amount of the animal left intact depends on the type of presentation and number of slices needed.)

As with all the elaborate meat dishes, the slices should not be too thick or too thin. Arrange the slices on a rack and chill before glazing.

Glazing

The head and rear portion are glazed with a chaud-froid sauce made by stirring cold liquid aspic (2/3) into mayonnaise (1/3).

This sauce is stirred over ice to thicken slightly then brushed on the

The slices are coated only with clear aspic.

Chill after the first coat and brush on a second coat to make a perfect finish.

pig with a soft-bristled brush. A second coat is necessary to ensure a smooth finish.

When set, a final glaze of clear aspic is carefully brushed on to keep the chaud-froid from drying out and make the dish shine.

Presentation and Service

Arrange the uncut portions and slices of suckling pig on a large platter to make an impressive display that is easy to serve.

The stuffed suckling pig needs very little garnish. A few simple additions

of color such as cherry tomatoes, small sour pickles (cornichons) and olives is enough.

The platter can be further embellished with chopped aspic.

Note: Since this dish provides a large number of portions, the platter should be large enough to accomodate the size of the pig and the slices that are arranged for easy service.

A large base can be carved in a decorative shape from styrofoam, covered with aluminium foil and chaud-froid sauce if a suitable platter is not available.

For a very fancy presentation, leaves and flowers can be made with bread or noodle dough and baked to a golden brown and arranged around the edge of the platter.

Stuffed Suckling Piq

Procedure diagram

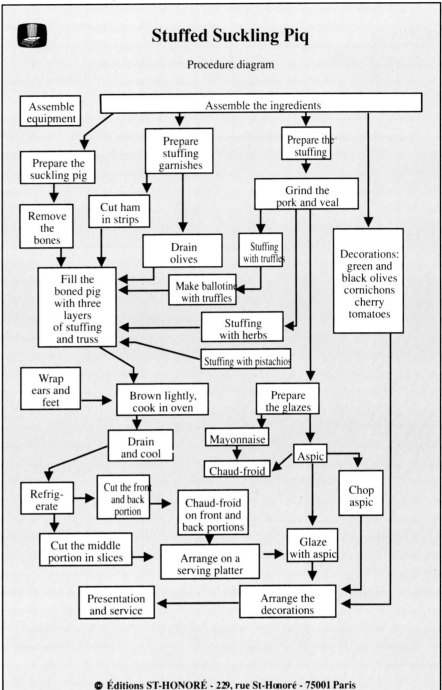

Flowchart:

- Assemble the ingredients
- Assemble equipment
- Prepare the suckling pig
  - Remove the bones
- Prepare stuffing garnishes
  - Cut ham in strips
  - Drain olives
- Prepare the stuffing
  - Grind the pork and veal
  - Stuffing with truffles
  - Decorations: green and black olives cornichons cherry tomatoes
- Make ballotine with truffles
- Fill the boned pig with three layers of stuffing and truss
  - Stuffing with herbs
  - Stuffing with pistachios
- Wrap ears and feet
- Brown lightly, cook in oven
- Prepare the glazes
  - Mayonnaise
  - Chaud-froid
  - Aspic
  - Chop aspic
- Drain and cool
- Refrigerate
  - Cut the front and back portion
  - Chaud-froid on front and back portions
  - Glaze with aspic
- Cut the middle portion in slices
- Arrange on a serving platter
- Arrange the decorations
- Presentation and service

© Éditions ST-HONORÉ - 229, rue St-Honoré - 75001 Paris

Beef Tenderloin " Perigueux " in Aspic

Introduction

This very elegant dish combines succulent tenderloin with foie gras and truffles. The sauce is named for the city of Perigueux in the southwest where truffles are found.

It is recommended to choose a small tenderloin (untrimmed weight: about 3 kg (6.5 lbs)) so that the slices are of a manageable size for a stand-up buffet. This is important because the filling of foie gras makes the slices more fragile.

The tenderloin must be thoroughly trimmed of nerves and fat.

The " chain " of meat that is loosely attached along the length of the meat is removed to ensure neat, even slices.

Count on about 35 % loss in weight from trimming.

A trimmed tenderloin can be ordered from the butcher. In this case, specify that it should not be tied, as it will be tied after it is filled. Order the meat in advance of the event so that the cooked meat chills thoroughly for 1-2 days before being sliced.

The foie gras used to line the interior of the filet can be slices of fresh terrine " en bloc ".

 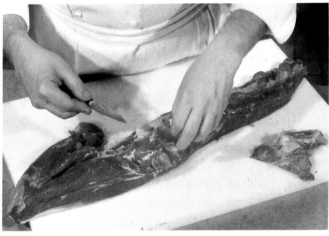

This is a superior product with a superb melting quality made from whole lobes of foie gras and cooked gently in a water bath (described in Volume 2 of this series). A less expensive and perfectly acceptable alternative is good quality canned purée of foie gras.

The sauce is a delicate blend of madeira, demi-glaze and truffle essence. It is set with a little gelatin. (The amount of gelatin needed depends on the natural gelatin in the demi-glaze and the temperature.)

A julienne of truffles decorates the slices providing a contrast of color and wonderful flavor.

The platter can be decorated with an elegant assortment of garnishes: pastry barquettes with foie gras, mini-aspics with foie gras and truffles, quail eggs in chaud-froid with truffles and mushrooms with foie gras.

To give this dish a more prominent place on the buffet table, a base can be carved in an appropriate shape from styrofoam and covered with foil and chaud-froid.

The high food cost of this elaborate dish is justified by the perfect marriage of luxurious ingredients.

Equipment

Cutting board, paring knife, slicing knife, chef's knife, kitchen twine, large roasting pan, stainless steel baking sheets, cooling rack, saucepan, pot, pastry bag and star tip, plastic scraper, whisk, spatula, small round cutter, barquettes molds, barquette cutter, measuring cup, pastry brush, conical sieve, small molds (for aspics), large platter.

Ingredients

Main Ingredients

1 untrimmed beef tenderloin (3 kg (6.5 lbs))
150-200 g (6 oz) foie gras (" en bloc " or purée)
Salt and freshly ground pepper
30 g (1 oz) clarified butter
4 cl (1/6 cup) oil

" Perigueux " Sauce

1/2 L (2 cups) madeira
1 L (4 cups) demi-glaze
5 cl (1/4 cup) truffle juice
Cooked roux 15g (1/2 oz) gelatin per liter (qt) of sauce
Aspic for glazing

Garnishes

Barquettes with Foie Gras
Basic pie pastry
Purée of foie gras
Truffles
Aspic

Aspics with Foie Gras and Truffles
Aspic
Purée of foie gras
Truffles
Small rounds of bread, toasted

Quail Eggs in Chaud-froid with Truffles
Quail eggs
Vinager Chaud-froid (mayonnaise and aspic)
Truffles
Aspic
Small rounds of bread, toasted

Mushrooms with Foie Gras
Mushrooms
Purée of foie gras
Butter
Lemon
Truffles
Aspic

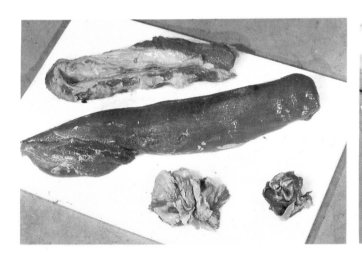 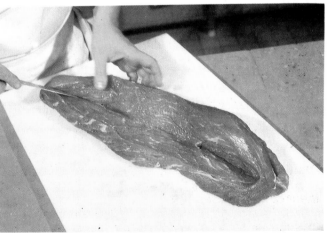

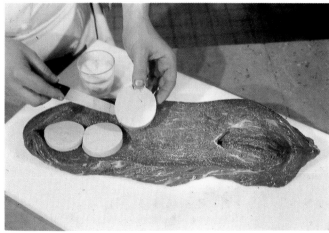

Procedure

Preparing the Tenderloin

Remove the chain of meat that is loosely attached to the tenderloin. (Once trimmed this tender meat can be used to make brochettes.)

Using a well-sharpened paring knife, trim away all nerves and fat. Be very careful not to cut into the meat or pierce it as you trim.

Butterfly the trimmed tenderloin as shown. Fold the small end over so the meat is uniform.

Season with salt and freshly ground pepper. Slice the foie gras (1 cm 3/8 ") thick and place it neatly down the center of the butterflied meat.

If necessary, smooth the foie gras with a palette knife to make the filling even from one end to the other.

Close the meat around the foie gras making sure none of the filling is exposed which would melt if it comes in contact with the heat.

The tenderloin can be wrapped in a thin sheet of barding fat if necessary.

Tying up the Tenderloin

First wrap the kitchen twine around the meat lengthwise then tie it like a roast at intervals of 5 cm (2 in).

Wrap the twine around the ends a second time, crossing over as shown, to secure the meat evenly.

Lastly, tie a short lengths of twine around the meat so that the meat is tied at intervals of 2.5cm (1 in).

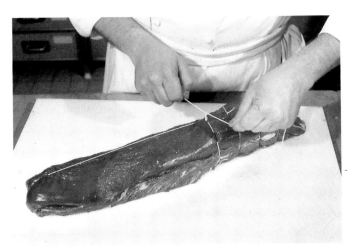

Cooking

Melt the clarified butter with oil in the roasting pan over high heat.

Sear the meat on all sides. Roll the meat, using the strings to turn it so that it is not pierced which would release juices and cause the meat to dry out.

(230 °C (450 F)) to finish cooking (15-20 minutes depending on the size).

Turn the meat and baste it every five minutes. Be careful not to pierce the meat as it is turned.

Transfer the cooked tenderloin to a cooling rack to drain. Deglaze the roasting pan with reduced demi-glaze and reserve the liquid for the sauce.

When the meat is cool, refrigerate until completely chilled.

Cover in plastic wrap and refrigerate for up to 2 days.

Count about 5 minutes to brown it evenly and thoroughly.

Place the tenderloin in a hot oven

Making the " Perigueux " Sauce

Reduce the madeira by 1/2.

Strain the deglazing juices and add to the madeira. Reduce by 1/3.

Add the truffle juice. Taste and season if necessary with salt and pepper.

Whisk in enough cooked roux to achieve a light coating consistency.

Soften the gelatin, then stir it into the hot sauce until it completely melts.

Strain the sauce through a conical sieve and set aside.

Slicing and Glazing the Tenderloin

Carefully remove the kitchen twine from around the meat.

Cut the tenderloin into even slices that are thin enough to be attractive and easy to eat but thick enough to hold the delicate foie gras filling in place.

Place the slices on a cooling rack and chill before glazing.

If the Perigueux sauce is set, melt it gently in a water bath until liquid but still cool. Stir the sauce over ice until it thickens slightly. Coat the slices with sauce using a soft-bristled pastry brush.

Decorate with thin slices of truffle then chill to set.

Brush on a final glaze of aspic and chill until ready to arrange on the platter.

Preparing the Garnishes

Pastry Barquettes with Foie Gras

Cut out the pastry using the cutter that corresponds to the small barquette molds you are using. Press the pastry into the molds and refrigerate.

Blind bake the barquettes then cool thoroughly.

Stir the foie gras purée to a smooth consistency then pipe it into the barquettes using a pastry bag and star tip. Decorate with truffles then chill to set the purée.

Glaze the chilled barquettes with aspic.

Reserve in the refrigerator until ready to arrange on the platter.

Aspics with Foie Gras and Truffles

Pour a little aspic into the bottom of each mold and chill to set.

Place a small cube of foie gras (or purée) on the layer of aspic.

Sprinkle a little chopped truffle over the foie gras. Pour in aspic to cover then chill to set.

Dip the aspics briefly in warm water to release them from the molds. Turn them out onto small rounds of toasted bread.

Chill until ready to use.

Quail Eggs with Chaud-froid

Poach the eggs in water with vinegar added. (Do not salt the water.)

Transfer the cooked eggs to ice water to stop the cooking and cool them quickly.

Drain on towels and pat dry then brush on a glaze of chaud-froid.

Pipe a rosette of foie gras into each mushroom, decorate with truffle then refrigerate to set the foie gras.

Brush on a glaze of aspic to make them shine and protect the filling.

Chill until ready to arrange on the platter.

Presentation

Choose a platter that is large enough to accomodate the slices and the various garnishes or carve one out of styrofoam which can be custom designed to coordinate with the theme of the occasion.

Arrange the slices in an attractive pattern that will also be easy to serve. Decorate the platter with the elaborate garnishes, using the variety of

Decorate with truffles then glaze with aspic.

Place the eggs on small rounds of toasted bread.

Chill until ready to use.

Mushrooms with Foie Gras

Trim the mushrooms, wash them in a large basin of cold water to remove all the sand then rub with lemon so they will not darken.

Combine a little water, a squeeze of lemon, a little butter, salt and pepper in a saucepan and bring to a boil.

Add the mushrooms, cover and cook over high heat, shaking the pan so the mushrooms cook evenly.

Drain the mushrooms, pat dry and chill.

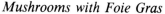

shapes to make an impressive display.

The platter can be further augmented with chopped aspic.

Beef Tenderloin " Perigueux " in aspic

Procedure diagram

```
Assemble                    Assemble the ingredients
equipment

                                              Prepare the garnishes
         Trim fat and nerves
         from tenderloin              Foie gras           Stuffed
                                      barquettes          quail
                                                          eggs
   Butterfly      Foie gras
   and fill with  purée                 Cook        Aspics    Mushrooms
   foie gras
                                        Chill       Aspic     Cook
         Close and tie
         the tenderloin
                                    Reduce          Refrigerate
                                    madeira
   Sear in roasting pan
                                                    Finish garnish
                              Deglaze               preparation
   Cook in hot oven           the pan
                              Add madeira,
   Drain on rack,             reduce, add           Glaze
   refrigerate                truffle juice          with aspic

   Remove                     Season to taste,      Refrig-
   strings                    add gelatin           erate

   Slice      Refrigerate     Pass through strainer  Arrange
   beef                                              the
                              Chop         Decorate  garnishes
   Arrange on a rack          aspic for    with
   and glaze slices           decoration   chopped aspic
   with sauce
                              Arrange on
   Glaze the                  presentation platter
   slices with aspic

                  Presentation and service
```

© Éditions ST-HONORÉ - 229, rue St-Honoré - 75001 Paris

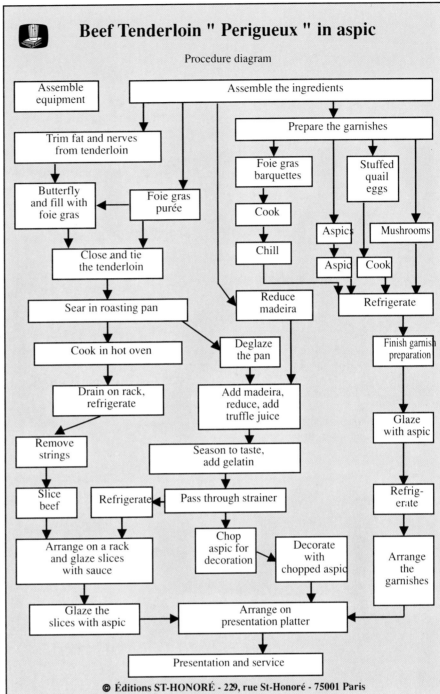

Braised Beef " Bourgeoise "

Introduction

This dish is a refined version of an old-fashioned French classic. The term " bourgeoise " denotes " homestyle " and specifically refers to the modest vegetables that the meat is cooked with.

Equipment

Cutting board, stainless steel hotel pan for marinade, paring knife, chef's knife, vegetable peeler, kitchen twine, frying pan, pot for braising, colander, large bowl, skimmer, ladle, cooling racks, stainless steel baking sheets, pastry brush, saucepan, spatula, whisk, conical sieve, measuring cup, stockpot

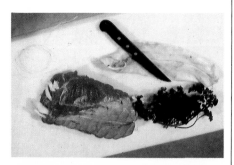

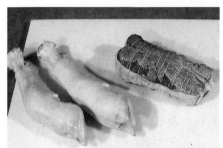

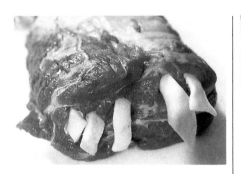

Ingredients

Main Ingredients

- Beef suitable for braising weighing 1.5-2 kg (about 3-4 lbs)
- 6 thin strips of fat back (about 250 g (1/2 lb) 4 cm (1 3/4 ") longer than the meat
- 75 g (2 1/2 oz) chopped parsley
- 3 cl (2 tbls) cognac
- Salt, pepper
- Barding fat For cooking: 40g (1/2 oz) clarified butter 3 cl (2 tbls) peanut oil

Marinade Ingredients

330 g (10 oz) carrots
(2007 oz) onions
60 g (2 oz) shallots
40g (1/2 oz) garlic
Bouquet garni (8 stems parsley, 1 bay leaf, 2 sprigs thyme, 1 leek green 20 g (4 tsps) salt
Tied in cheesecloth: 12 peppercorns, 12 coriander seeds

Liquid Ingredients

5 cl (1/4 cup) cognac
5 cl (1/4 cup) olive oil
7.5 dl (3 cups) full-bodied red wine
2.5 dl (1 1/4 cups) dry white wine
1.5 L (5 cups) demi-glaze
2 calves'feet

For the Sauce:

Cooked roux,
8 g (1/4 oz) gelatin per liter (qt)

For glazing: 1.5 L (3 cups) aspic

Garnish Ingredients

1 kg (2 lbs) carrots
750 g (1 1/2 lbs) turnips
400 g (14 oz) pearl onions
125 g (4 oz) butter
Salt, pepper, sugar, water

Decoration

1.5 L (3 cups) firm aspic, chopped

Procedure
Preparing the Strips of Fat
Cut the strips of fat. For this rec- ipe, prepare six strips 5 mm (1/5 ") across and 4 cm (1 3/4 ") longer than the meat.

Note: The marinating time can be shortened by heating the liquids and pouring them over the meat. This activates the marinating process more quickly but could also spoil the meat if not properly cooked shortly after being marinated. Although the results are not as good as with a classic marinade, this method can be used in emergencies.

Draining the Beef and Vegetables

Drain the meat thoroughly (up to 1 hour) so that it will brown properly.

Drain the vegetables in a colander and reserve the liquid which will be added to the pot when the meat is braised.

Searing the Beef

Heat the clarified butter and oil in a frying pan.

Sear the meat, turning it over to brown it on all sides.

Drain the meat on a cooling rack. Deglaze the pan with a little wine and add this liquid to the strained marinade.

Tie the meat like a roast to give it an even form.

The Marinade Ingredients

Peel the vegetables and cut into 1 cm (3/8 ") dice.
Secure the bouquet garni in kitchen twine.
Wrap the pepper and coriander in cheesecloth.
Measure the remaining ingredients; salt, cognac, red and white wine.

Marinating the Meat

Put the meat in a stainless steel bowl with the vegetables. Pour over the marinade, cover with plastic wrap and refrigerate for at least 48 hours.
Turn the meat occasionally so that it marinates evenly.

Remove the stems from the parsley (reserve for the bouquet garni). Wash, dry and chop finely. Marinate the strips of fat in the cognac with the parsley for 1-1 1/2 hours.

Preparing the Beef

If the meat has not been trimmed by the butcher, remove the nerves and fat with a paring knife.

Insert the marinated strips of fat using a larding needle which threads the strips through the meat. Hold the end of the strip and pull the larding needle out. The strips should be evenly spaced as they not only add moisture to the meat but make an attractive pattern in the slices. (Count on about 6 strips of fat for a piece of beef weighing 1.5 kg (3 lbs).)

Wrap the sheet of barding fat around the meat.

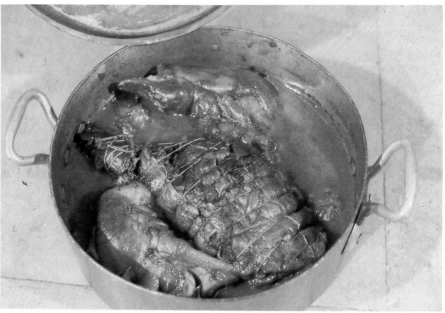

Cooking

Heat a little oil in the braising pot, add the drained vegetables and cook over medium heat to brown.

Add the strained marinade liquid, bring to a boil and skim all impurities that rise to surface.

Add the calves' feet and demi-glaze.

Place the seared meat in the pot and cook for 2-2 1/2 hours at 200 F (375 F). Turn the meat from time to time being careful not to prick the meat which would release juices and cause the meat to dry out.

Check the doneness by pressing on the meat with your fingers.

Cooling

When the meat is done, remove from the oven and let the meat cool in the braising liquid.

Thoroughly drain on a rack, then refrigerate until ready to assemble the dish.

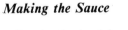

Making the Sauce

Strain the braising liquid and discard the aromatics.

Skim the fat from the surface, bring to a boil and skim any foam that rises to the surface. This important step ensures a good tasting sauce.

Whisk in a little cooked roux to achieve a light coating consistency.

Soften the gelatin in cold water. Off the heat, stir it into the hot sauce until it melts completely.

If not using right away, store in the refrigerator.

Drain each vegetable in a sieve then refrigerate until ready to assemble the dish.

Preparing the Garnish

Cut the carrots and turnips into even shapes about the size and the shape of a clove of garlic.

This operation, called " turning " (the vegetables are " turned " as they are trimmed into oval shapes) provides attractive pieces of vegetables that are the same size and cook evenly.

Peel and rinse the pearl onions.

Each vegetable is cooked separately in water with an addition of butter, sugar, salt and pepper.

Start the cooking with the pan covered.

Remove the cover and continue to cook over medium heat to reduce the liquid and glaze the vegetables.

Slicing and Glazing the Meat

Carefully remove the kitchen twine without damaging the meat.

Remove the barding fat.

Cut thin slices about 3 mm (1/8 ") thick and arrange on a rack and chill before glazing.

If the sauce is set, melt it gently in a water bath until liquid but still cool.

If necessary, stir the sauce over ice until it thickens slightly to a light coating consistency.

Brush a coat of sauce on each slice with a soft-bristled pastry brush.

Chill and apply another coat if necessary to achieve a smooth surface.

Summary

Several cuts of meat would be appropriate for this dish. The cut shown is particular to French butchering. It is called the " aiguillette " and comes from the heel of round. A small piece cut from the heel or eye-of-round could be used for this dish.

These braising cuts are less expensive and are delicious when prepared properly.

Braising the meat gently for a long time allows the meat to absorb the delicious flavors of the cooking liquid and vegetables.

Bring the aspic to the right coating consistency (same technique as the sauce) and glaze the slices of meat and the vegetable garnishes.

The lengthy cooking also tenderizes this tough cut of beef.

Presentation

Arrange the slices of meat in an attractive pattern on the platter.

Garnish with the vegetables and decorate simply with chopped aspic and sprigs of parsley.

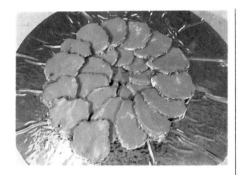

Calves' feet are added to the pot to contribute gelatin which improves the texture of the meat and the sauce.

Furthermore, the meat is larded with strips of fat that add moisture from the inside and barding fat wrapped around the outside adds additional moisture.

The trimmed and larded meat is then marinated with wine flavored with aromatics which breaks down the meat fibers a little in preparation for braising and also adds a wonderful flavor.

This marinade makes up part of the braising liquid along with a reduced veal stock or " demi-glaze ". The full-flavored braising juice is strained after the meat is cooked. It is degreased, then lightly thickened with roux. Gelatin is added so that the sauce will set when brushed on the slices of meat.

The pot or casserole that the meat is braised in should be just large enough to hold all the ingredients comfortably.

An appropriate vegetable garnish, including carrots, turnips, and pearl onions accompany the meat and decorate the platter. They are prepared separately to ensure even cooking.

Since all of these vegetables are readily available, this dish can be offered year-round and can be prepared for small groups or large.

This dish is always a very popular item due to its delicious flavor and relatively low price.

Braised Beef " Bourgeoise "

Procedure Diagram

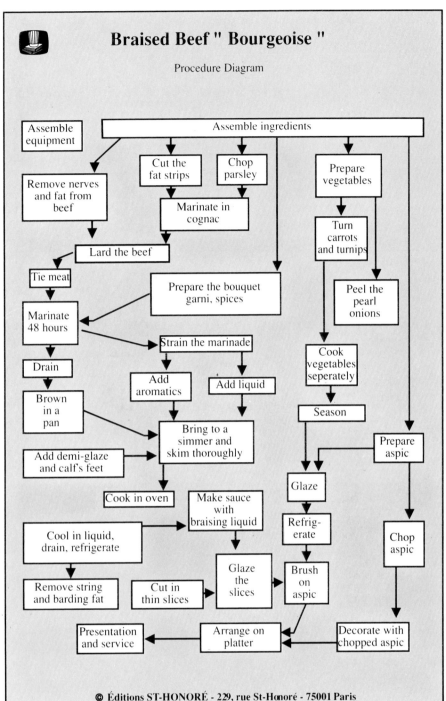

Prime Rib with Young Vegetables

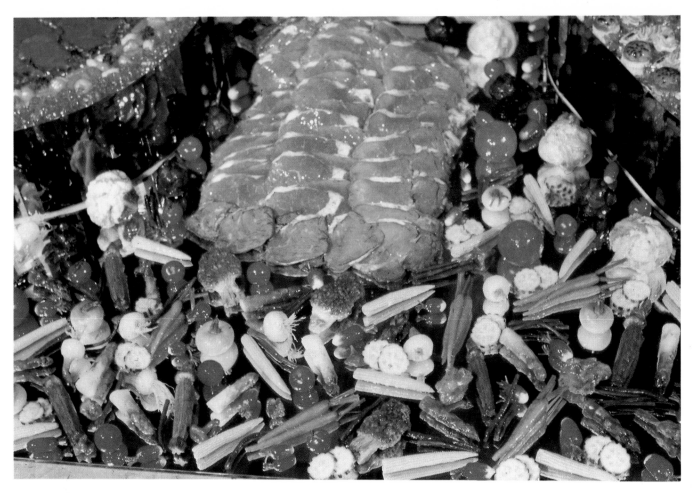

Introduction

The prime rib is a real showpiece for an elegant buffet.

The succulent, rosy meat is always appreciated and the form of this cut makes an impressive display.

The size of the prime rib is ideal for a medium-sized buffet.

A piece containing 4-5 ribs provides 40-45 servings.

For this presentation, order a prime rib weighing about 5 kg (10 1/2 lbs) untrimmed.

Counting about 30-35% loss from trimming, the trimmed prime rib will weigh 3.5 kg (8 lbs)

The price of this dish is quite high but is certainly justified by the delicious taste of the meat and the impressive presentation.

The preparation is very straight forward and does not require much time.

The classic cooking method presents no particular difficulties.

For the best results, the meat should be cooked in advance and refrigerated for 2-3 days to ensure easy slicing.

The arrangement of ingredients on the platter in not more difficult than the other elaborate meat dishes described in this chapter.

The sliced meat is glazed with a delicious aspic that makes the final presentation shine and keeps the meat from drying out. The meat should be arranged on the platter and glazed at the last moment to ensure freshness.

To enhance the dish, serve with a mayonnaise-based sauce, served on the side in a sauceboat. An assortment of mustards and a bowl of crisp " cornichons " (small sour gherkins) would also be appropriate.

Equipment

Cutting board, boning knife, paring knife, slicing knife, vegetable peeler, kitchen twine, aluminum foil, roasting pan, skimmer, spouted spoon, stainless steel baking sheets, cooling racks, large pot, large bowls, colander, pastry brush, measuring cup.

Ingredients

Main Ingredients
prime rib (5 ribs) about 5 kg (11 lbs)
50g (1 1/2 oz) clarified butter
6 cl (1/4 cup) oil
Salt and pepper

For glazing: 2.5 L (10 cups) meat aspic flavored with sherry

Garnish Ingredients
Watercress
Miniature cucumbers
Cherry tomatoes
Radishes
Miniature zucchini
Miniature cauliflower
Miniature corn
Small turnips
Spring onions
Green beans
Asparagus
Small artichokes
Girolles
Morilles

Decoration
1.5 L (5 cups) firm aspic, chopped

Procedure

Preparing the Prime Rib

Place the meat on a cutting board to facilitate the work.
Cut around the top of each rib with a boning knife and scrape to expose the bones (about 3.5 cm (1 1/2 ")).

Trim away excess fat, giving the meat a neat smooth form. A very thin layer of fat should remain, which will melt when the meat is browned and will serve to protect the meat while it is roasting.

Tie kitchen twine between each rib, pulling tightly when the string is knotted to make sure it is secure.
Wrap aluminum foil over the end of each rib so that they do not brown to much in the oven.

Cooking

Heat the clarified butter and oil in a roasting pan.
Sear the meat over high heat, turning the meat to brown the ends as well as the sides.

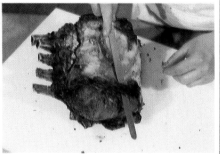
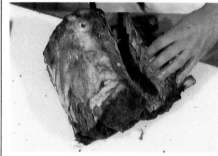

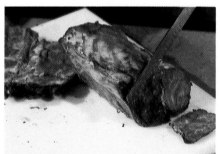

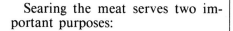

Searing the meat serves two important purposes:

• to give the meat an attractive golden brown color;

• to seal in the meat juices so that the meat will not dry out during cooking.

It is important to remember that the surface of the meat should not be pierced while being turned or transferred which would release juices and cause the meat to dry out.

Roast the prime rib for 30 minutes at 230 °C (450 F), turning and basting the meat several times.

Lower the heat to 210 °C (400 F) and continue to roast for 1 hour. Turn and baste the meat every 10 minutes.

Check the cooking by testing the texture with your fingers.

Cooling

Transfer the cooked prime rib to a cooling rack so that the melted fat will drain thoroughly and the meat will cool quickly.

Set the meat on the rack with the ribs down so that the rack does not mark the meat.

When the meat is drained and no longer hot, refrigerate uncovered.

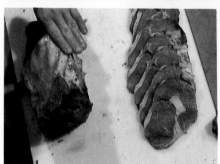

When the meat has cooled throughout, cover with plastic wrap and chill for 2-3 days. During this time the meat fibers completely " relax " and the juices are thoroughly absorbed into the meat.

This makes the meat more moist and succulent and therefore easier to cut.

Final Preparation of the Meat

Carefully remove the string from around the meat. Trim away any fat with a paring knife, giving the meat an even form and a smooth surface.

Place the prime rib on a cutting board.

Using a thin-bladed knife, cut along the ribs to free the ribs as shown.

Make sure that the blade of the knife is angled toward the bones so that it does not cut into the meat.

Take the roast-shaped piece of boned meat and trim if necessary.

Cut very thin slices with a well-sharpened slicing knife (3 mm (1/8 ")).

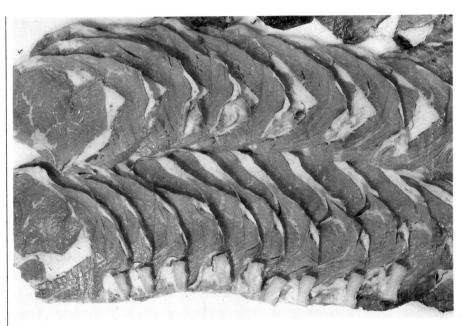

Keep the slices in order so that when the dish is assembled the slices can be arranged in an even pattern.

Cook each vegetable in the boiling water until tender but still slightly firm.

Drain them thoroughly in a colander then spread them out on paper towels to dry. Cover and refrigerate until ready to assemble the dish.

• Cooked in the oven. The mushrooms are washed, drained then sautéed in clarified butter.

They are finished in the oven in a covered pan and cooked until tender but a little firm. Drain and refrigerate.

Preparing the Garnishes

The large number of garnishes for this presentation requires lengthy preparation.

To facilitate the work, many of the garnishes can be prepared one day in advance and refrigerated.

The garnishes can be organized into three groups:

• No cooking required. The watercress, cherry tomatoes, cucumbers and radishes can be rinsed and drained the day before then trimmed and cut the day of the event.

• Cooked in salted water. (Zucchini, cauliflower, corn, turnips, carrots, onions, green beans, asparagus, artichokes).

The tender miniature vegetables do not need to be peeled, preserving their bright colors and natural appearance.

One day in advance, wash and cut (if necessary) the vegetables.

Cook them separately in lightly salted boiling water.

A copper recipient is used here which imparts a chemical that keeps the colors a little brighter.

A heavy pot that conducts heat well can also be used.

The garnishes can be adapted to take advantage of seasonal availablity. Here, delicate spring vegetables provide a colorful touch.

The tender young vegetables can be prepared whole and unpeeled then arranged in " bouquets " on the platter.

The preparation of the vegetables is quite lengthy and should be done in advance so that they can drain thoroughly on paper towels and are chilled.

Presentation

Pat the vegetables with a paper towel to dry them completely then spread them out on a rack.

Stir liquid aspic over ice to thicken slightly.

Brush on a coat of aspic to make the vegetables shine.

Chill to set. A second coat is not necessary.

Place the prime rib on the platter and fan out the slices in an attractive pattern.

Coat the meat with aspic using a soft-bristled pastry brush.

Arrange the vegetables around the meat, taking full advantage of the variety of shapes and colors to create a stunning display.

Often the ingredients are transported separately and the final assembly is done at the location of the event.

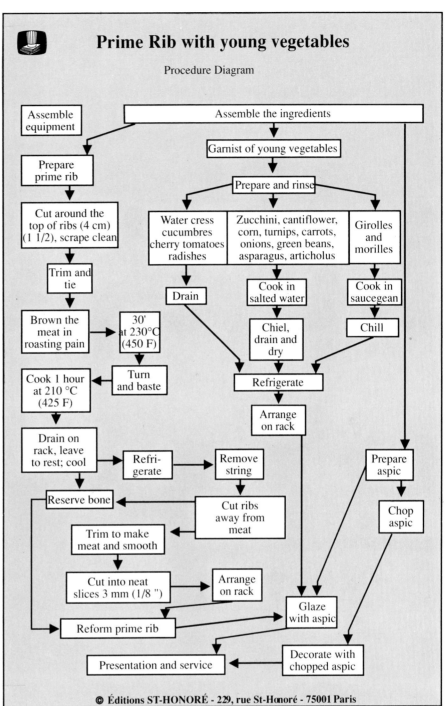

Prime Rib with young vegetables

Procedure Diagram

Assemble equipment

Assemble the ingredients

Garnist of young vegetables

Prepare and rinse

Prepare prime rib

Cut around the top of ribs (4 cm) (1 1/2), scrape clean

Water cress cucumbres cherry tomatoes radishes

Zucchini, cantiflower, corn, turnips, carrots, onions, green beans, asparagus, articholus

Girolles and morilles

Trim and tie

Brown the meat in roasting pain

30' at 230°C (450 F)

Drain

Cook in salted water

Cook in saucegean

Cook 1 hour at 210 °C (425 F)

Turn and baste

Chiel, drain and dry

Chill

Refrigerate

Drain on rack, leave to rest; cool

Refrigerate

Remove string

Arrange on rack

Prepare aspic

Reserve bone

Cut ribs away from meat

Chop aspic

Trim to make meat and smooth

Cut into neat slices 3 mm (1/8 ")

Arrange on rack

Reform prime rib

Glaze with aspic

Presentation and service

Decorate with chopped aspic

© Éditions ST-HONORÉ - 229, rue St-Honoré - 75001 Paris

Breast of Veal with Dried Fruits

Introduction

Veal is not often used for cold meat dishes because the meat has a tendency to be dry and tough when chilled.

The breast of veal however is less dry than other cuts of veal and when boned, the large flat piece can be filled and rolled around a moist forcemeat stuffing.

In addition, the breast of veal is less expensive than other cuts.

This dish will provide a large number of servings so it is ideal for large receptions with a moderate budget.

The presentation can be modest or more elaborate, depending on the occasion and budget.

The lovely slices are particularly attractive when arranged on a mirror. The imagination and talent of the chef can take full advantage of the colorful garnishes and spiraled slices to create a lovely display.

Equipment

Cutting board, boning knife, thin-bladed knife, paring knife, chef's knife, vegetable peeler, kitchen twine, large bowls, spatula, meat grinder (optional), food processor (optional), roasting pan, measuring cup, stainless steel sheet pans, cooling racks, pastry brush, barquette or tartelette molds, pastry bag and star tip, plastic scraper, platter or mirror for presentation

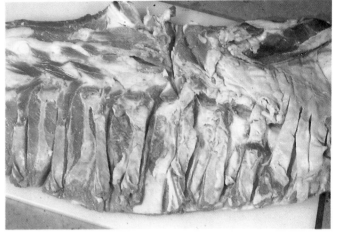

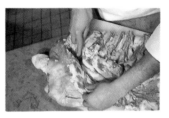 

 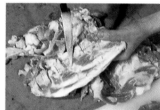

Ingredients

Main Ingredients
Breast of veal 6.6-7 kg (15 lbs) (about 75 portions)
100 g (3 1/2 oz) clarified butter
5 cl (1/4 cup) peanut oil

Forcemeat Ingredients
2 kg (4 lbs) pork (1/2 lean-1/2 fat)
1 kg (2 lbs) ground veal (shoulder)
100 g (3 1/2 oz) chopped pistachios
100 g (3 1/2 oz) chopped parsley
200 g (7 oz) chopped onions
Salt, pepper

Aromatics and Seasonings
300 g (10 oz) carrots
200 g (7 oz) onions
200 g (7 oz)) leeks
80 g (2 1/2 oz) celery
250 g (8 oz) tomatoes
Bouquet garni (1 bay leaf, 2 sprigs thyme, 8 parsley stems)

Liquid Ingredients
1/2 L (2 cups) dry white wine
1 1/4 L (5 cups) reduced veal stock
Salt and pepper

Garnish Ingredients
750 g (1.5 lbs) basic pie pastry
300 g (10 oz) purée of foie gras
25 prunes
25 dates
25 dried apricots
15 lychees
15 kumquats
15 cashews
15 almonds
15 hazelnuts
15 walnuts

For glazing:
2 L (8 cups) aspic flavored with sherry

Decoration
2 L (8 cups) firm aspic, chopped

Procedure

Preparing the Breast of Veal

Flatten out the meat on a cutting board, as shown and trim away all excess fat.

Turn the meat over, and trim away the small bits of cartilage, excess fat and tough skin that held the ribs in place.
The breast meat is very thin, so careful attention must be paid to not pierce through the meat.

The lean trimmings and cartilage can be reserved for making stock. Discard the fat.

Preparing the Forcemeat

Pass the meats through the fine disk of the meat grinder.

79

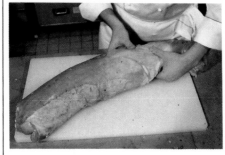

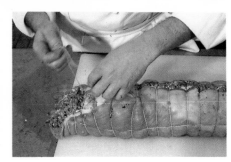

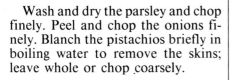

Wash and dry the parsley and chop finely. Peel and chop the onions finely. Blanch the pistachios briefly in boiling water to remove the skins; leave whole or chop coarsely.

Season with salt and pepper and mix all the ingredients thoroughly.

Poach or pan-fry a spoonful of forcemeat, taste and correct seasoning if necessary.

The choice of forcemeat ingredients is very important as it makes up a large portion of each slice. It should be flavorful, moist and colorful so that each slice is attractive.

In this presentation, pistachios add a colorful note and a combination of ground pork and veal makes the forcemeat rich and succulent.

The method of cooking is also very important. Braising the meat with aromatics and a full-flavored veal stock ensures that the meat will be moist and delicious.

Stuffing and Rolling the Meat

Lay the trimmed breast of veal flat on the work surface with the skin side down.

Spread an even layer of the forcemeat over the surface of the meat leaving a small margin around the edges.

With the aid of a second person, roll the meat around the stuffing. It is helpful for the assistant to hold the rolled meat in place while the meat is tied in an even form by the chef.

Tie the meat tightly so that it holds its shape during the remainder of the procedure.

Cooking

Melt the clarified butter and oil in a roasting pan over high heat.

Brown the veal evenly on all sides.

Add the aromatic vegetables to the pan around the meat. (Carrots, peeled and cut in large dice; onions, peeled and chopped coarsely; leeks, washed and sliced; celery, rinsed and cut in dice; tomatoes, rinsed and cut in quarters; bouquet tied in kitchen twine.)

Cook in a hot oven (230 °C (450 F)) for about 20 minutes to brown the vegetables.

Pour in the dry white wine and veal stock and continue to cook at 210 °C (400) for 1 1/4-1 1/2 hours.

Baste frequently and turn the meat over from time to time.

Check the doneness with a skewer inserted into the center which should be warm to the touch and the juices should be clear.

Cooling

Transfer the cooked meat to a cooling rack to drain thoroughly and cool quickly.

Refrigerate, unwrapped, until cold in the center.

Cover the chilled meat with plastic wrap and refrigerate 3-4 days.

The flavors will develop and thorough chilling facilitates slicing. Preparing the meat in advance allows more time on the day of the event for more detailed work.

Final Preparation

Depending on the work schedule, the chilled breast of veal can be sliced and glazed one day in advance or the day of the event.

Remove the strings carefully without tearing the meat which sometimes sticks to the string.

Using a well-sharpened slicing knife, cut the rolled veal into even slices no more than 1 cm (3/8") thick.

Place the slices on a rack and refrigerate before glazing.

Stir the sherry-flavored aspic over ice until it thickens slightly.

Use a soft-bristled pastry brush to apply the aspic. Chill to set.

Shortly before assembling the dish, brush on a second coat of aspic to ensure a smooth finish.

Brush the foie gras tartelettes with aspic.

Assortment	Apricots	Lychees
Prunes	Pistachios	Walnuts
Kumquats	Pistachios (shelled)	Dates
Cashews	Almonds	Hazelnuts

Preparing the Garnishes

Since many flavors go well with veal, the garnish can be chosen especially with the tastes of the client in mind.

The garnish also can be adapted to take advantage of seasonal fruits.

Dried fruits are a good choice because a wide variety is available at all times and the subtle taste and colors marry well with the mild-flavored veal.

Bake the pastry barquette or tartelette shells one or two days in advance.

Poach the dried fruits one day in advance. Remove pits and trim other fruits if necessary.

The day of the event, pipe the purée of foie gras into the pastry shells and place a small piece of dried fruit on top. Chill to set.

The dried fruits may be brushed with a little aspic (but is not necessary) but the nuts should not be glazed.

Presentation

Arrange the slices of meat on a large platter or a presentation mirror.

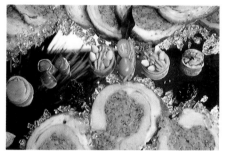

Decorate with the assortment of fruits and nuts and the foie gras tartelettes.

Complete the decoration with firm aspic cut in small dice.

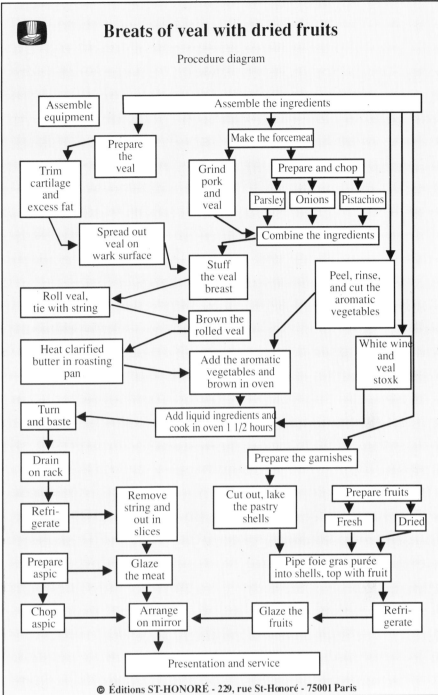

Breats of veal with dried fruits

Procedure diagram

```
Assemble        ┌──────── Assemble the ingredients ────────┐
equipment                            │
                Prepare          Make the forcemeat
                  the
                 veal        Grind      Prepare and chop
   Trim                      pork
 cartilage                   and     Parsley  Onions  Pistachios
   and                       veal
 excess fat                          Combine the ingredients
              Spread out
              veal on                              Peel, rinse,
              wark surface    Stuff               and cut the
                              the veal             aromatic
  Roll veal,                  breast               vegetables
  tie with string
                           Brown the
  Heat clarified           rolled veal              White wine
  butter in roasting                                and
  pan                    Add the aromatic           veal
                         vegetables and             stoxk
  Turn                   brown in oven
  and baste
              Add liquid ingredients and
  Drain       cook in oven 1 1/2 hours
  on rack
                         Prepare the garnishes
  Refri-
  gerate   Remove      Cut out, lake      Prepare fruits
           string and  the pastry
           out in      shells          Fresh      Dried
           slices
  Prepare                        Pipe foie gras purée
  aspic     Glaze                into shells, top with fruit
            the meat
  Chop      Arrange    Glaze the        Refri-
  aspic     on mirror  fruits           gerate

              Presentation and service
```

© Éditions ST-HONORÉ - 229, rue St-Honoré - 75001 Paris

Leg of Lamb with Mint

Introduction

Young lamb is a delicious, mild-flavored meat. The caterer should avoid using stronger tasting mutton for this dish.

In France, the most prized lamb comes from the marshes around Paulliac where the animals eat the salty grasses which gives their flesh a unique flavor.

Although the leg of lamb is not a large cut, it is very meaty.

The price is quite high but once it is prepared and boned it yields a large number of very neat slices. In France, the legs are often sold attached in pairs called a " culotte " then separated and prepared by the chef.

The rosy color of the meat when cooked medium rare is very pretty when presented cold and glazed.

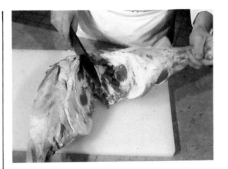

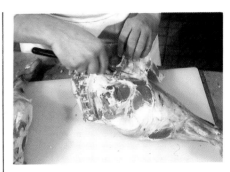

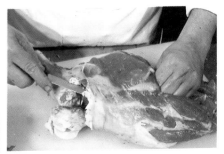

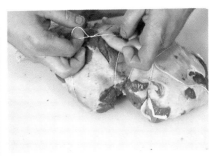

Ingredients

Main Ingredient

4 legs of lamb, total untrimmed
    weight: 14 kg (30 lbs)
150 g (5 oz) clarified butter
1 dl (1/3 cup) peanut oil
Salt and pepper

For assembly:

150 g (5 oz) liver purée

Sauce Ingredients

1.5 L (6 cups) lamb stock
8-10 fresh mint leaves
Cooked roux (optional)
15-20 g (1/2 oz) gelatin (leaves or
    powder)
Salt and pepper

Garnish Ingredients

Red and Green Pepper Bavarians

40 g (1 1/2 oz) clarified butter
300 g (10 oz) red peppers
300 g (10 oz) green peppers
8 g (1/4 oz) gelatin
150 g (5 oz) meat aspic
125 g (4 oz) heavy cream
Salt   Rounds of bread, toasted

Cold Ratatouille Tartlettes

1 dl (1/3 cup) olive oil
1/2 green pepper 4 tomatoes
3 garlic cloves
2 zucchini
2 eggplant
Bouquet garni (leek, 6 parsley
    stems, 2 sprigs thyme, 1/2 bay leaf)
Salt and pepper

Cold Zucchini Mousse

30 g (1 oz) clarified butter
40 g (1 1/2 oz) butter
100 g (3 1/2 oz) onions
30 g (1 oz) garlic
450 g (scant 1 lb) zucchini
150 g (5 oz) fresh spinach
40 g (1 1/2 oz) flour
5 dl (2 cups) white veal stock
10-15 g (1/2 oz) gelatin per liter (qt)
2 dl (3/4 cup) heavy cream
Bouquet garni (4 parsley stems, leek
    green, 1 sprig thyme, 1/2 bay leaf)
Salt and pepper

Tri-color Pepper Tartelettes

5 cl (1/4 cup) olive oil
125 g (1/4 lb) red pepper
125 g (1/4 lb) green pepper
125 g (1/4 lb) yellow pepper
30 g (1 oz) garlic
Salt

Decorations

Miniature pattypan squash
Miniature zucchini
Cherry tomatoes
1.5 L (1.5 qts) firm aspic, chopped

For glazing:
1.5 L (1.5 qt) meat aspic

Equipment

Cutting board, chef's knife, boning knife, paring knife, slicing knife, cleaver, vegetable peeler, palette knife, hotel pan, measuring cup, kitchen twine, large bowls, two small pots with covers, stainless steel baking sheets, cooling racks, roasting pan, heavy baking sheet, drum sieve, plastic scraper, spatula, pastry brush, frying pan, colander, skimmer, pastry bag and tip, barquette and round tartelette molds and cutters, food processor (optional), platter or presentation mirror

Procedure

Preparing the Garnishes

The four garnishes that accompany the lamb can be partially prepared one day in advance then assembled the day of the event.

Cold Ratatouille Tartelettes
Peel the eggplants, cut them in two, cut out the seeds and cut into small dice. Put the dice in a small stainless steel hotel pan and sprinkle lightly with salt.

The salt will draw out moisture and prevent the eggplant from absorbing too much oil when cooked.
Peel the onions and cut in small dice.
Remove the stem from the peppers, cut in half and trim the white membranes and seeds.

Peel the tomatoes by dipping them in boiling water to loosen the skins. Cut in half, squeeze out the seeds and cut in small dice.

Peel the garlic, cut in half to remove the green sprout then chop finely.

Rinse the zucchini and cut off the ends. Cut into small dice, eliminating the seeds in the center.

The cooking is done in two stages:

• In a small pot, cook the onions and peppers in the olive oil over low heat until soft but not brown.

Add the tomatoes, garlic and bouquet garni and and continue to cook over low heat.

• In a frying pan, sauté the zucchini in olive oil over high heat just

88

enough to soften. Drain in a strainer.

Repeat the same operation with the eggplant that has been drained of all liquid from the degorging process.

Mix all the vegetables together and cook in a moderate oven for about 10 minutes. The vegetables should be soft but not falling apart.

Remove the bouquet garni and refrigerate.

Cold Zucchini Mousse

The zucchini mousse is described on page 200 of Volume 2 of this series. This presentation requires additional gelatin so that the mousse is firm enough to be piped into the tartelettes.

Pepper Bavarian

Peel the peppers, remove the stem and seeds and cut into small dice.

Cook the peppers in clarified butter over medium heat until very soft.

Purée in the food processor then pass the mixture through a sieve to make it perfectly smooth.

Heat the aspic and soften the gelatin in cold water. Stir the gelatin into the hot aspic until it is completely melted. Combine with the pepper purée and chill to thicken over ice or in the refrigerator.

Beat the heavy cream until soft peaks are formed, season with a little salt and fold gently into the purée.

Fill the small molds (plastic molds are very easy to unmold) and refrigerate to set before unmolding onto the toasted rounds of bread. (The bread can be cut out in advance then toasted the day of the event.)

Tri-color Pepper Tartelettes

Peel the peppers, remove the stems, cut in half and remove the white membranes and seeds. Cut into small dice.

Peel the garlic, remove the green sprout, and chop very finely or pound in a mortar.

Combine the peppers, garlic and olive oil in a small pot. Season with salt and cook over medium heat until tender. Refrigerate.

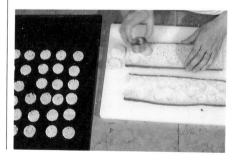

The glaze is made with lamb stock infused with fresh mint. (This stock is generally made with the bones and trimmings from the leg.) It is strained and degreased, then gelatin is added so that it will set when brushed on the meat. Mint and lamb is a classic taste combination that is always enjoyed by guests.

The leg of lamb can be served in thin slices or cut in cubes and reformed like the ham cut in cubes described in this chapter.

It can be cooked and presented on the bone, but the slices are not as uniform.

Even though the leg of lamb is not as large and impressive as other cuts of meat in this chapter, a stunning display is possible with the right choice of platter or presentation mirror.

For a large event several legs of lamb can be presented together; some in slices and others in cubes for example.

When preparing a large elaborate display, one leg of lamb can be left uncut with the others arranged around it. In general for large receptions, if four legs of lamb are being presented, prepare six.

The presentation decribed here includes several elegant garnishes. The subtle tastes and colors marry extremely well with the lamb.

The garnishes can be prepared in advance for the most part and assembled and glazed the day of the event.

Preparing the Leg of Lamb

If the legs are attached in pairs, seperate them with a cleaver.

On a cutting board, trim and bone each leg. Begin by removing the thin skin that covers the leg.

If the lamb is to be cooked with the bone, simply trim nerves and fat then tie up the leg to maintain a perfect shape during cooking.

The leg has three bones. The hindshank, which protrudes from the pointed end and forms a convenient handle for carving, is usually not removed. The end may need to be sawed off if the torsal bone is still attached.

The pelvic bone, which is exposed on the rounded side of the leg, is easily removed by cutting around the edges and following the contour of the bone with the knife until it is loosened from the flesh. This bone is attached to the leg bone by a ball and socket joint. Cut through the ligaments around this joint and remove the pelvic bone.

Follow the contour of the leg bone and cut through the ligaments that join it to the hindshank and remove. Be careful to not cut through the meat.

Remove the cartilage that attaches the bones to the flesh and trim excess fat.

Cut away the fat from the trimmings and reserve the lean portion for the stock.

Tie each leg of lamb with kitchen twine to give it a uniform shape. The string should be tight enough so that the lamb will hold its shape during the cooking process.

Cooking

In a roasting pan, melt the claified butter and oil. Over high heat, sear each leg of lamb, turning it over to brown it evenly on all sides.

The " crust " that forms on the outside of the meat holds the juices in during cooking. It is therefore important not to pierce the meat which would release juices and cause the meat to dry out.

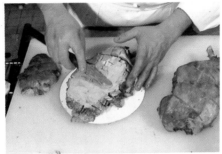

Roast the meat in a 220 °C (425 F) oven for 30-35 minutes for medium rare meat, basting and turning the meat from time to time.

A meat thermometer inserted into the meaty part of the leg will read 60 °C (140 F) for rare and 65 °C (150 F) for medium rare. The meat can also be tested by inserting a finger into the the hole left by the pelvic bone; the meat should feel evenly warm to the touch.

Cooling

Transfer the cooked legs of lamb to a rack to drain and cool quickly.

When they have cooled to room temperature, wipe off melted fat and juices that drained from the meat. Cover with plastic wrap or foil and refrigerate for 2-3 days.

Preparing the Pastry Shells

Press the basic pie pastry into the barquette and tartelette molds, chill then blind bake. This can be done one day in advance.

Fill the baked shells the day of the event.

Decoration

The platter is decorated with delicate miniature pattypan squash and zucchini which are cooked one day in advance in salted boiling water, refreshed and refrigerated. The red and yellow cherry tomatoes can be rinsed and dried the day before assembly.

Final Preparation of the Lamb

Carefully remove the strings from around the lamb.

There are two possibilities for serving the leg of lamb:
- The lamb can be cut in bite-size cubes and reassembled in its original form like the ham described at the beginning of this chapter.

The liver purée is used to hold the rows of cubes together and the assembled lamb is chilled to set before glazing.
- Cut the lamb in thin slices, which are arranged on the platter around whole cooked legs of lamb or ones that have been cut in cubes.

As with the other elaborate meat dishes, the slices are chilled before being glazed.

Making the Sauce

Bring the lamb stock to a boil. Off the heat, add the fresh mint leaves

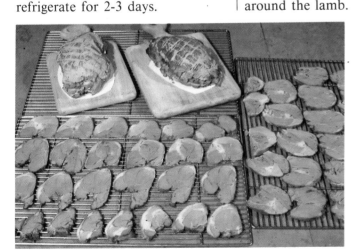

and set aside to infuse. When the stock has cooled, remove the leaves.

Bring the stock back to a boil and whisk in a little cooked roux to achieve a light coating consistency.

Soften the gelatin in cold water then stir it into the warm sauce until it is completely melted.

Stir the sauce over ice until it thickens slightly. Brush a coat of glaze on the slices of chilled lamb, the zucchini mousse, and the pepper bavarian.

Presentation

Glaze the meat a second time just before assembling the dish.

Arrange the slices or reassembled legs of lamb on platters or presenta-

tion mirrors in an attrative pattern that will make serving as easy as possible. Place the elegant garnishes around the platter to "frame" the meat. Decorate the platter with the miniature vegetables and the glistening chopped aspic.

This impressive display can be further embellished with a decorative base created especially for the occa-

Leg of lamb with mint

Procedure diagram

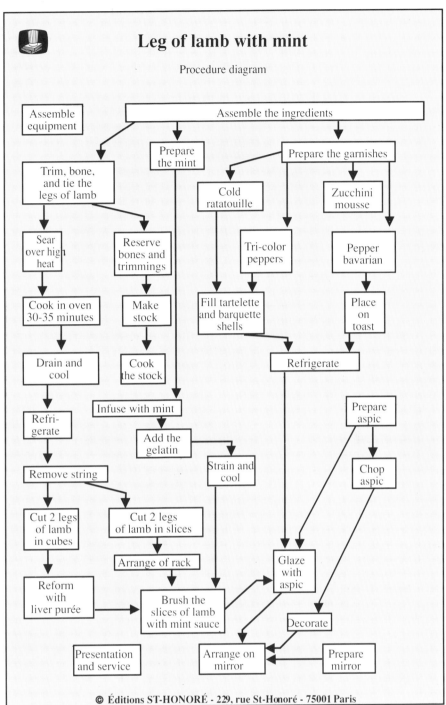

```
Assemble                    Assemble the ingredients
equipment

              Prepare                      Prepare the garnishes
              the mint
Trim, bone,                   Cold            Zucchini
and tie the                   ratatouille     mousse
legs of lamb

Sear          Reserve         Tri-color       Pepper
over high     bones and       peppers         bavarian
heat          trimmings

Cook in oven  Make            Fill tartelette  Place
30-35 minutes stock           and barquette    on
                              shells           toast

Drain and     Cook                            Refrigerate
cool          the stock
                                                         Prepare
Refri-        Infuse with mint                           aspic
gerate
              Add the                                    Chop
              gelatin         Strain and                 aspic
Remove string                 cool

Cut 2 legs    Cut 2 legs                       Glaze
of lamb       of lamb in slices                with
in cubes                                       aspic
              Arrange of rack
Reform                        Brush the                Decorate
with          Presentation    slices of lamb
liver purée   and service     with mint sauce  Arrange on   Prepare
                                               mirror       mirror
```

© **Éditions ST-HONORÉ - 229, rue St-Honoré - 75001 Paris**

sion. A fanciful touch is the addition of fruits and vegetables cut in various shapes (broccoli " tree ", pineapple " palm tree ").

These extremely elaborate displays are usually assembled at the location of the event.

Noisettes of Venison

Introduction

Among the elaborate meat dishes featuring game, the noisettes of venison is certainly the most refined. The meat is very tender and the taste is delicate.

These dishes can only be offered during the relatively short hunting season and are appreciated by clients who like game.

Equipment

Cutting board, slicing knife, paring knife, chef's knife, vegetable peeler, cleaver, measuring cup, kitchen twine, stainless steel baking sheets, cooling racks, conical sieve, tongs, roasting pan, large pot, large bowl, ladle, spatula, whisk, pastry brush, 2 saucepans, tartelette molds and cutters, barquette molds and cutters, pastry bag and star tip, plastic scraper, platter

Ingredients

Main Ingredient
4 venison filets
35 g (1 oz) clarified butter
3 cl (2 tbls)) peanut oil

Since the season is short, it is often necessary to order game meat well in advance so that the purveyor reserves a certain quantity for you.

Sauce Ingredients
35 g (1 oz) clarified butter
Marinade ingredients
1.5 L (1.5 qts) reduced game stock
Cooked roux 10-12 g (scant 1/2 oz)
Gelatin (leaves or powder)
For glazing: 1.5 L (1.5 qts) meat aspic

Marinade Ingredients
200 g (7 oz) carrots
125 g (1/4 lb) onions
40 g (1 1/2 oz) garlic
40 g (1 1/2 oz) celery
Bouquet garni (1 leek green, 8 parsley
    stems, 2 sprigs thyme, 1/2 bay
    leaf
Salt
15 peppercorns
15 coriander seeds
10 juniper berries
1 L (1 qt) full-bodied red wine
1/4 L (1 cup) dry white wine
3 cl (2 tbls) cognac
2 cl (4 tsps) olive oil

Garnish Ingredients
600 g (1 lb 3 oz) basic pie pastry
150 g (5 oz) foie gras purée
400 g (14 oz) whole chestnuts
1 L (1 qt) consomée
Salt, pepper
300 g (10 oz) cranberries
1/2 L (2 cups) port
3 strips of orange zest
80 g (1 1/2 oz) sugar

The noisettes are cut from the tender filet of venison which are smaller than beef filets. They are found along either side of the backbone of the animal.

The filets are then trimmed of all nerves and tendons.

The trimmed filets are then tied securely to maintain an even form during cooking.

The meat is then marinated in wine with aromatic vegetables which adds flavor and further tenderizes the meat.

Since the filet is already quite tender and not very large the marinating time is short (12-24 hours).

The marinade is later used to make the sauce that is brushed on the noisettes.

The small, tender filet cooks quickly. The meat is best when cooked medium rare.

The cooked filet is chilled then cut into neat noisettes, which are arranged on a rack, chilled then glazed.

The noisettes are set on toasted rounds of brioche which makes them easier to handle and delicious to eat.

Since the venison filet is quite small, the dish can easily be made for a small group. Several filets can be prepared for a larger event.

Several game presentations can be arranged on a buffet table with decorations reflecting the season. They can also be used in combination with milder meat dishes to offer an assortment.

The garnishes for this presentation are perfect accompaniments for game: cranberry-orange barquettes and tartelettes filled with foie gras and chestnuts.

Procedure

If the venison is procured on the bone, carefully bone out the filets without damaging the flesh.

The noisettes will not be uniform if the meat is not handled correctly at this stage.

Trim away the silver skin and nerves.

Tie the filets with kitchen twine so that the meat will maintain its shape during cooking, ensuring even slices.

Preparing the Marinade

Peel and rinse the vegetables then cut into small dice. Tie kitchen twine around the bouquet garni.

Tie up the spices in cheesecloth so they do not get skimmed away when the sauce is made.

Place these ingredients in a non-reactive hotel pan.

Pour in the liquid ingredients (red and white wine, olive oil and cognac).

Marinating the Meat

Arrange the trimmed filets in the marinade.

Small, tender cuts of meat need to marinate a shorter time (12-24 hours maximum) than tougher cuts.

Turn the filets over from time to time so that the marinade flavors the meat evenly.

Transfer the marinated filets to a rack to drain thoroughly.

Drain the vegetables in a sieve, reserve the wine. Set aside these ingredients for the sauce.

Cooking the Meat

Pat the meat dry with a clean handtowel.

Melt the butter and oil in a roasting pan over high heat.

Sear the meat on all sides without piercing it, turning it over until it is evenly browned.

Cook in a hot oven (230 (450 F) for 10-12 minutes. Press on the meat to verify the doneness.

Drain the cooked meat on a rack and cool completely. Refrigerate until the final assembly.

Making the Sauce

Cook the strained vegetables from the marinade in butter until soft and light brown.

Deglaze with the reserved wine and reduce by half. Skim the foam that rises to the surface.

Add the game stock and reduce by half. Skim the impurities from the surface.

Whisk in a little roux to thicken the sauce to a light coating consistency and make it velvety.

Soften the gelatin in cold water. Off the heat, stir the softened gelatin into the hot sauce until it is completely melted.

Pass the sauce through a conical strainer to make it perfectly smooth and set aside. (Refrigerate if not glazing the meat right away.)

Note: The sauce can be thickened with a little blood from the deer which adds a deep, rich flavor. Whisk a little warm sauce into the blood then stir it back into the pot. Stir constantly, without letting the sauce boil, until the sauce thickens.

Making the Game Stock

Game stock, which is reduced and used to make the sauce, is fully explained in chapter 2 of this volume.

Reminder: Chop the bones and brown them along with the meat trimmings.

Add the aromatics and brown. Deglaze with wine.

Add the brown veal stock and simmer gently. Skim the impurities, wash down the sides.

Strain, skim the fat that rises to the surface. Refrigerate.

Preparing the Garnishes

Bake the pastry shells one day in advance, set aside in a dry place.

Poach the cranberries with the sugar and orange zest without boiling which would cause the cranberries to burst.

Refrigerate.

The day of the event, pipe foie gras purée into the barquettes, decorate with cranberries and blanched orange zest. Chill.

Poach the chestnuts in a little consommé or clear stock. (Cooked chestnuts in a jar can be used.) Refrigerate.

Pipe foie gras purée into the tartelette molds and top with with chestnut. Chill.

Final Preparation of the Meat

Carefully remove the string without damaging the meat.

Slice each filet in neat, even medallions 15 mm (3/5 in) thick and arrange on a rack.

Refrigerate.

Stir the glaze over ice until it thickens slightly. Brush on a thin coat of glaze and chill to set.

Brush on a second coat of glaze to make a smooth finish. Chill to set.

Stir the aspic over ice to thicken slightly and brush the glazed slices of meat to make them shine and protect the sauce.

Presentation

Cut out rounds of brioche the same size as the noisettes and toast them in the oven.

Spread a little foie gras purée on the toasts to adhere them to the meat. Set a noisette on each toast round.

Arrange the noisettes of venison on the platter in an attractive pattern and set the garnishes around the meat to make a lovely presentation.

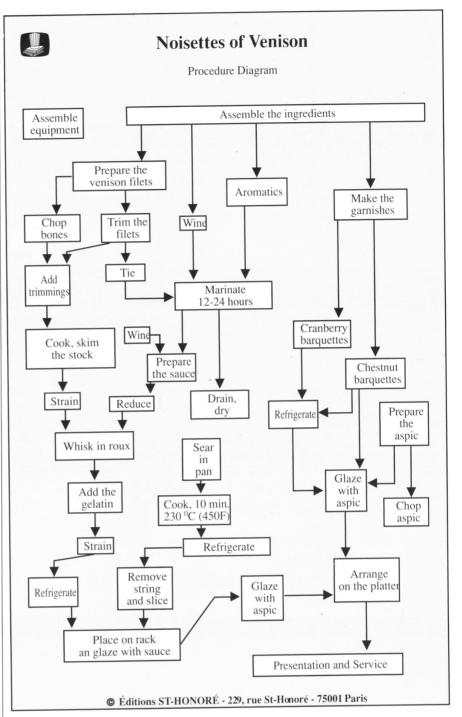

Noisettes of Venison

Procedure Diagram

Assemble equipment

Assemble the ingredients

Prepare the venison filets

Aromatics

Make the garnishes

Chop bones — Trim the filets — Wine

Add trimmings — Tie

Marinate 12-24 hours

Cranberry barquettes

Cook, skim the stock — Wine

Chestnut barquettes

Prepare the sauce

Strain — Reduce — Drain, dry

Refrigerate

Prepare the aspic

Whisk in roux

Sear in pan

Add the gelatin

Cook, 10 min. 230 °C (450F)

Glaze with aspic

Chop aspic

Strain — Refrigerate

Refrigerate — Remove string and slice

Glaze with aspic

Arrange on the platter

Place on rack an glaze with sauce

Presentation and Service

"Dodines" of Wild Boar

Introduction

The meat used for this dish is "marcassin" (young boar) whose meat tastes like venison but slightly more pronounced.

It is milder than the meat of full grown wild boar.

In France, this meat is very popular with customers who enjoy eating game.

It can be hung until the flavor develops according to the request of the client.

"Dodine" refers to the "plump" round shape of these individual portions.

Ingredients

Forcemeat Ingredients
1.75 kg (1.5 lb) wild boar jowl, with
    bones (about 1.5 kg (5 lb 5 oz))
250 g (8 oz) fatback
500 g (1 lb) pork liver
30 g (1 oz) pork jowl
30 g (1 oz) butter
500 g (1 lb) spinach
2 sprigs tarragon
Small bunch of chives
Salt and pepper
1 large piece caul fat

Garnish Ingredients
1 large head curly endive
350 g (10 1/2 oz) bread crumbs
1dl (1/2 cup) peanut oil
For the sauce:
Garlic
Salt and pepper
Wine vinegar
Corn or peanut oil

For glazing:
1.5 L (6 cups) meat aspic

For cooking:
50 g (1 1/2 oz) clarified butter
5 cl (1/4 cup) peanut oil

Equipment

Cutting board, boning knife, paring knife, chef's knife, meat grinder, hotel pans, large bowls, strainer, pastry scraper, spatula, roasting pan, stainless steel baking sheets, cooling racks, pastry brush, tongs, clean dishtowels, salad spinner, salad bowl, skillet, measuring cups, whisk, presentation platters

Procedure

Making the Forcemeat

Bone the jowl of young boar with a small boning knife. Remove the skin and rub off any fur that remains.

Do not trim the small amounts of fat which will contribute to the texture of the mixture.

Cut the meat into cubes before grinding.

Remove the skin of the pork jowl and cut into cubes.

Trim the blood vessels from the pork liver and cut into pieces.

Pass the three meats through the meat grinder fitted with a medium or fine disk. Season with salt and pepper.

Combine the meats with the other forcemeat ingredients:

• The spinach is trimmed, washed and steamed. They are pressed to extract the maximum amount of moisture then chopped.

• The chives are trimmed and cut into very small pieces starting from one end of the bunch. (Chopping them results in unattractive pieces.)

• The tarragon leaves are removed from the stem, rinsed and chopped finely.

Stir to mix all the ingredients completely. Poach or pan-fry a spoonful of forcemeat, taste and correct seasoning if necessary.

Divide the forcemeat into individual portions: each dodine should weigh about 80-100 g (2 1/2-3 1/2 oz).

This can be quickly done by weighing out 400 g (14 oz) at a time and dividing in 4-5 equal parts.

It is important that each one weighs the same since they are usually sold by the piece.

The presentation is better when all the portions are the same.

Roll each portion into a round shape.

The caul fat is spread out on the work surface and cut into small pieces large enough to cover one dodine. (The caul fat shrinks a little during cooking.)

There needs to be enough caul fat to amply cover, but too much makes the dodines greasy and difficult to glaze.

They can be refrigerated before cooking.

Cooking

Brown the dodines in a roasting pan with clarified butter and oil.

Finish the cooking in the oven (220 °C (375 F) for about 25 minutes.

Baste and turn the dodines as they cook.

Drain them on a rack, then refrigerate.

When they are thoroughly chilled, wipe them off with paper towels or a clean handtowel to remove fat and cooking liquids that are attached that would ruin the appearance.

The cooked dodines can then be covered with plastic wrap and refrigerated for up to 5 days.

This recipe combines the meat of the young boar with pork for several reasons.

• The pork adds moisture to the mixture.

• The pork tones down the strong taste of the boar resulting in an interesting dish to everyone's liking.

• The pork is less expensive, thus lowering the food cost of the dish.

The forcemeat includes other savory ingredients that contribute to the flavor and texture.

The correct seasoning is also important.

The dodines can be prepared several days in advance and the simple last minute details make serving this dish relatively quick and easy.

Traditionally the dodines are served with a salad and croutons.

Presentation

The final preparation should be done the day of the event.

The dodines of wild boar are so flavorful that they need only a simple glaze of plain meat aspic.

They are easy to handle and are usually set on small rounds of toasted bread to facilitate the service.

This delicious, simple dish is often served with a zesty salad and garlic flavored croutons.

They can also be sliced and served on rounds of French bread that have been toasted and rubbed with garlic.

« Dodines » of Wild Boar

Procedure Diagram

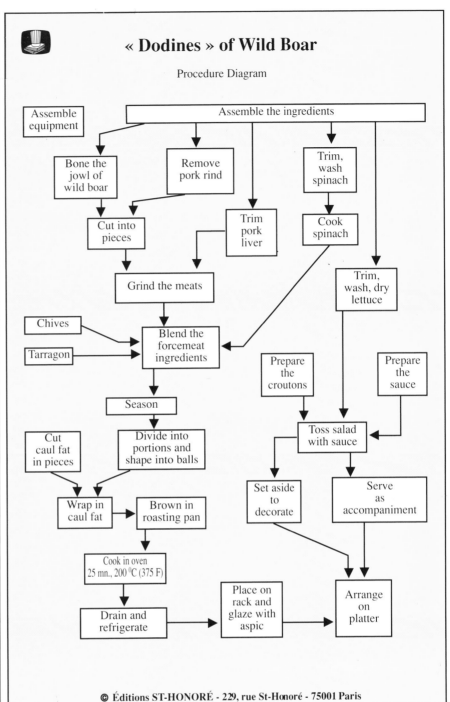

```
Assemble equipment        Assemble the ingredients

Bone the jowl of wild boar    Remove pork rind    Trim, wash spinach

Cut into pieces    Trim pork liver    Cook spinach

Grind the meats                    Trim, wash, dry lettuce

Chives
Tarragon → Blend the forcemeat ingredients

                    Prepare the croutons    Prepare the sauce

Season

Cut caul fat in pieces    Divide into portions and shape into balls    Toss salad with sauce

Wrap in caul fat    Brown in roasting pan    Set aside to decorate    Serve as accompaniment

Cook in oven 25 mn., 200 °C (375 F)

Drain and refrigerate → Place on rack and glaze with aspic → Arrange on platter
```

© Éditions ST-HONORÉ - 229, rue St-Honoré - 75001 Paris

Saddle Of Hare " Royale "

Introduction

This dish has traditionally graced the finest tables and is still an impressive choice for elegant dinners.

It is best to use a good-sized, meaty hare that is not too " high " (the strong gamey taste that results from long hanging).

The hare must not have been damaged by the hunt.

After being skinned and gutted, the hare is carefully boned then reshaped and stuffed with a delicious mixture containing fattened goose liver and truffles.

The hare is then wrapped in caul fat, which helps prevent the stuffing from leaking out.

In addition to the caul fat, the hare is wrapped in a thin sheet of barding fat also, which keeps the hare moist during cooking.

The hare is trussed with kitchen twine, which helps to keep its shape and makes slicing easier.

The hare is cooked by braising it in a combination of red and white wines, with aromatics and seasonings that highlight its distinctive flavor.

A stock made from the hare carcass is used as part of the braising liquid, which balances the acidity of the wine.

As with all elaborate centerpieces, it is best to begin preparation at least one day in advance. In some cases,

four to five days are necessary to allow the flavors of the meat and other ingredients to mellow and marry.

After the hare is cooked, the braising liquid is reduced slightly and thoroughly degreased. If necessary,

110

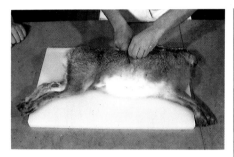

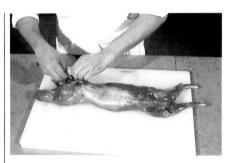

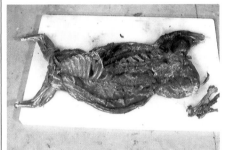

gelatin is added to give it enough body to set.

The cooled hare is cut into slices.

When completely cold, the slices are glazed with the sauce which is lightly set.

The final step is a glazing with a thin coat of aspic, which gives the piece a beautiful shine and also prevents the sauce and meat from drying out.

The saddle of hare " royale " should be accompanied by a simple garnish of three vegetable mousses-sweet potato, celeriac and chestnut. This trio of mousses adds interest to the visual aspect, and their fine light textures and flavors complement the saddle of hare.

The mousses are presented on crisp toast rounds.

A large attractive serving platter would be appropriate for the final presentation.

As the name of this dish indicates, it is a " royal " preparation, whose ingredients are relatively expensive, and therefore it is generally served for many special occasions.

Equipment

Cutting board, paring knife, slicing knife, boning knife, chef's knife, vegetable peeler, scissors, kitchen twine, cleaver, large bowls, spatulas, meat grinder (optional), fish poaching pan or other long braising pan, measuring cup, 2 sauté pans, 2 large saucepans, conical sieve, baking sheet, plain round 5 cm (2 in) pastry cutter, food processor (optional), drum sieve, plastic scraper, racks, sheet pans, pastry brush, small ladle, pastry bag and plain tip, presentation platter.

Ingredients

Main Ingredients

1 hare, undressed weight 3.75 kg (8 1/4 lbs)
(dressed weight 2.75 kg (6 lbs))

Forcemeat Ingredients

The hare liver
400 g (13 oz) lean pork
200 g (7 oz) pork jowl
250 g (1 lb) veal cushion
30 g (1 oz) clarified butter
75 g (2 1/2 oz) onions
60 g (2 oz) shallots
10 g (1/3 oz) garlic
Small bouquet garni
Salt, pepper
1 bunch parsley
8 cl (1/3 cup) dry white wine
3 cl (2 tbsp) cognac

Assembly Ingredients

400 g (13 oz) fresh fattened goose liver
75 g (2 1/2 oz) truffles
1 large piece caul fat
1 large piece barding fat

Cooking Ingredients

Braising Liquid

200 g (7 oz) carrots
150 g (5 oz) onions
20 g (2/3 oz) garlic
75 g (2 1/2 oz) leek, white part only
75 g (2 1/2 oz) celery
1 bouquet garni (1 leek green, 8 parsley stems, 1 sprig thyme, 1/2 bay leaf)

Liquid Ingredients

5 dl (2 cups) full-bodied red wine
2.5 dl (1 cup) dry white wine
1.5 dl (2/3 cup) light hare stock

Sauce Ingredients

Roux
8-10 g (about 1/3 oz) gelatin per liter (quart) sauce
Hare blood

Glazing Ingredients

1.5 l (3 cups) aspic

Garnish Ingredients

a) Sweet Potato Mousse
500 g (1 lb) sweet potatoes
45 g (1 1/2 oz) sugar
2 pinches cinnamon
2 strips pared orange zest
Water
Salt, pepper
45 g (1 1/2 oz) butter

b) Celeriac Mousse
500 g (1 lb) celeriac
Water
Salt, pepper
75 g (2 1/2 oz) apple purée
45 g (1 1/2 oz) butter

c) Chestnut Mousse
250 g (1/2 lb) unsweetened chestnut purée
45 g (1 1/2 oz) butter
5 cl (1/4 cup) cream
Salt, pepper, celery salt

Toasts

Decorative Ingredients

1 l (1 qt) chopped aspic

Procedure

Preparing the Hare

The saddle of hare " royale " may be made from either a dressed or undressed hare. The hare must be skinned and gutted, if this has not already been done.

Cut the skin down the middle of the back after loosening the flesh from the skin.

Pull the skin towards the head and tail.

Continue to pull the skin toward the tail, turning it inside out. It may be necessary for a second person to hold the front end of the hare during this step.

Repeat the operation to pull the skin off the front end of the hare.

Gut the hare delicately through the stomach. Reserve the liver to use in the forcemeat.

Bone the hare, leaving the bones in the front and rear paws, beginning at the belly opening and the ribs and moving up the back bone.

This is an important step requiring careful attention because the flesh must not be pierced or damaged in order to have even slices.

Reserve the bones.

Keep the meat refrigerated until ready to use.

Making the Stock

Refer to the explanation for rabbit stock in Chapter 2 of this volume.

Preparing the Fattened Goose Liver and Truffles

Cut the goose liver into strips and cut the truffles into julienne.

Preparing the Aromatic Garnish

Wash, peel and cut the vegetables into large dice. Sweat them lightly in butter until soft but not browned.

These ingredients will be used for braising the hare.

Making the Forcemeat

Assemble the pork (of which the fresh ham is lean and the jowl is fatty), the cushion of veal and the reserved hare liver.

Chop the meats with the meat grinder fitted with a fine disk.

Sweat the onions and shallots in butter until soft but not colored, then deglaze the pan with the white wine and cognac. Combine this with the chopped meats, the garlic and the chopped parsley.

Season with salt and pepper.

Mix the ingredients well. Fry a spoonful of the forcemeat and taste; correct seasoning if necessary.

Reshaping and Assembling the Hare

Spread out the boned hare.

Spread the forcemeat on the hare in an even layer. Add the strips of goose liver and truffles.

Close up the hare, shaping it to give it its original form.

Wrap the hare carefully in the caul fat, which will help it keep its shape, help keep the forcemeat from leaking out and moisten the meat.

After cooking, the caul fat will be barely visible and is completely edible.

Wrap the hare again in a sheet of barding fat. This must be removed after cooking.

Tie the hare neatly but not so tightly that the twine leaves marks in the meat.

Cooking the Hare

Brown the hare in the pan with the diced vegetables. The hare should cook a little but does not need to be browned.

Add the red wine (which contributes color and flavor), the white wine (which adds acidity) and the hare stock, which should be light and not too reduced.

Cook the hare in the oven at 200 °C (375 F) for 1 1/4 - 1 1/2 hours.

The braising should be slow and gentle.

Degreasing the Braising Liquid

Strain the braising liquid through a conical sieve.

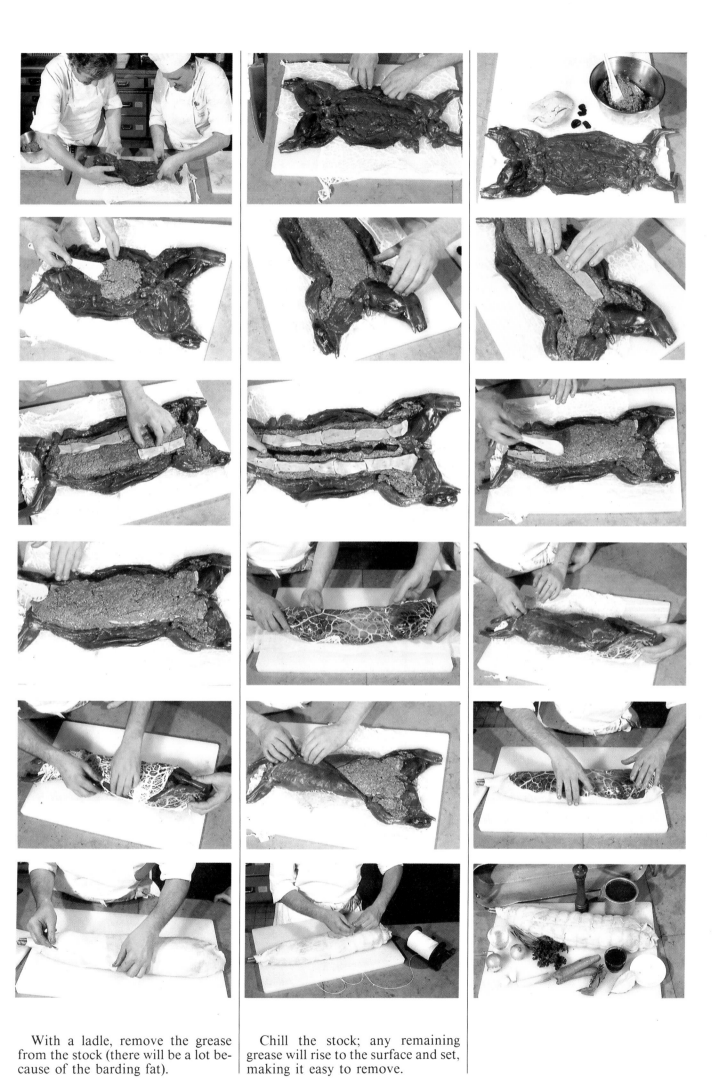

With a ladle, remove the grease from the stock (there will be a lot because of the barding fat).

Chill the stock; any remaining grease will rise to the surface and set, making it easy to remove.

113

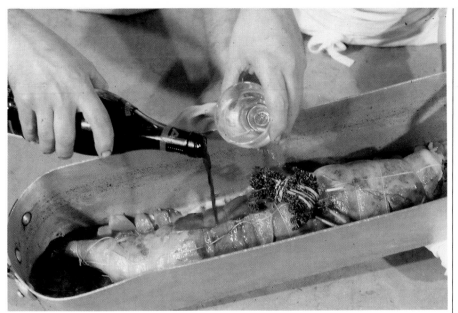

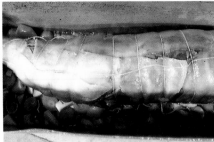

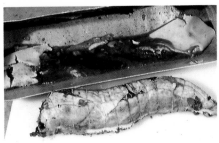

Cooling

Leave the hare to cool in the poaching liquid to keep it moist.

When it is completely cool, remove it from the liquid and place it on a rack to drain.

Dry the hare thoroughly with a kitchen towel or absorbent paper.

Store the hare in the refrigerator at 5 °C (40 F).

The hare may be stored 4-5 days at this temperature if carefully wrapped in plastic film or aluminum foil.

Making the Mousse Accompaniments

The Sweet Potato Mousse

In a sauté pan or large saucepan, cook the sugar, orange zests and cinnamon to a caramel. Deglaze with a little water.

Meanwhile, peel the sweet potatoes and cut them into large chunks.

Cook the sweet potato in the caramel, with the pan covered.

Season with salt and pepper.

When the sweet potatoes are tender, drain them, put them in a shallow pan and leave them in a warm oven for a while to dry out.

Remove the zests and purée in a food processor or with a drum sieve.

Add the butter and cream.

Add a little of the cooking liquid to loosen the mixture if it is too stiff.

Taste and correct seasoning.

The Celeriac Mousse

Peel and chop the celeriac and cook it in boiling salted water.

Drain it and dry it in the oven.

Purée it with the food processor or a drum sieve.

If the purée is too soft, dry it out a little by stirring it over the stove.

Add the apple purée (made by sautéing some apple and puréeing it in the food processor or with a drum sieve). The apple purée will sweeten the flavor of the celeriac mousse.

Add the butter; season with salt and pepper. Taste and correct seasoning.

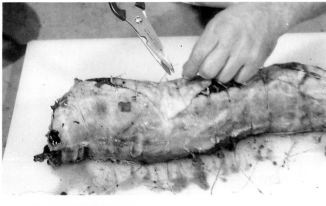

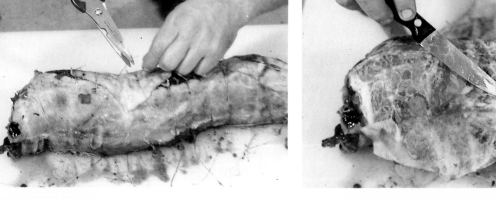

The Chestnut Mousse

The purée may be made with fresh chestnuts that are shelled, blanched and cooked in a little consommé before puréeing.

A quick and successful alternative is to use canned unsweetened chestnut purée. This should be dried out slightly over the stove. Add butter, mix the purée in a food processor to lighten the texture, add the cream and season with salt, pepper and celery salt. Taste and correct seasoning.

Finishing the Garnishes

Stamp out rounds of bread with the pastry cutter and toast them.

Using the pastry bag and plain tip, pipe mounds of the mousses on the toasts.

Chill to set the mousses and make it easier to glaze with aspic.

When set, glaze the mousse canapés with aspic.

Finishing the Sauce

Finish degreasing the chilled braising liquid. Strain it through a conical sieve.

Reduce the stock slightly if necessary to give it full flavor.

If the stock needs more body, thicken it with a cooked roux.

Add the gelatin which will make the sauce set well.

Strain the sauce through a conical sieve.

Chill the sauce over an ice bath.

Final Preparation of the Hare

Remove the kitchen twine from the cooled hare.

Peel off the barding fat, taking care not to disturb the caul fat.

Wipe the hare carefully with a towel to remove any grease.

Slicing the Hare

Cut off the two ends of the hare.

Cut into slices of about 6 mm (1/4 in) and lay the slices on a rack.

Chill for a few minutes to make glazing easier.

Presentation

Using the pastry brush, coat the slices with a thin layer of the sauce, which has been chilled so it is slightly set.

Chill the slices.

Coat the slices with a thin layer of aspic to make them shine and help prevent them from drying out.

To serve, arrange the slices and the canapés of mousse attractively on the serving platter.

Hare « à la Royale »

Procedure Diagram

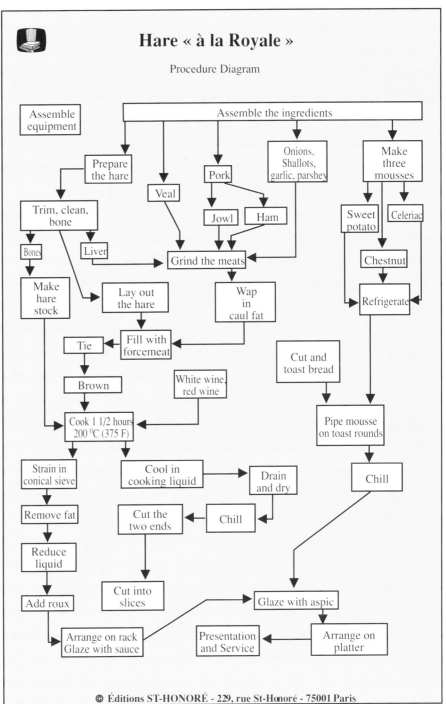

- Assemble equipment
- Assemble the ingredients
- Prepare the hare
- Veal
- Pork
- Onions, Shallots, garlic, parsley
- Make three mousses
- Trim, clean, bone
- Jowl
- Ham
- Sweet potato
- Celeriac
- Bones
- Liver
- Grind the meats
- Chestnut
- Make hare stock
- Lay out the hare
- Wap in caul fat
- Refrigerate
- Tie
- Fill with forcemeat
- Cut and toast bread
- Brown
- White wine, red wine
- Pipe mousse on toast rounds
- Cook 1 1/2 hours 200 °C (375 F)
- Strain in conical sieve
- Cool in cooking liquid
- Drain and dry
- Chill
- Remove fat
- Cut the two ends
- Chill
- Reduce liquid
- Cut into slices
- Glaze with aspic
- Add roux
- Arrange on rack Glaze with sauce
- Presentation and Service
- Arrange on platter

© Éditions ST-HONORÉ - 229, rue St-Honoré - 75001 Paris

Ballotine of Pheasant " en Volière "

Introduction

Pheasant is the most beautiful of the game birds. The colorful feathers have been used to decorate dishes down through the ages, and are used to embellish this ballotine " en volière " (" in flight ").

Equipment

Cutting board, paring knife, boning knife, chef's knife, cleaver, vegetable peeler, slicing knife, roasting pan, small pot, small bowls, large bowls, measuring cup, meat grinder, plastic wrap, spatula, cheesecloth, galantine bandages, string, fish poacher, thermometer, cooling racks, stainless steel baking sheets, pastry brush, presentation platters, barquette molds and cutters, piping bag and star tip, pastry scraper, whisk, wire.

Ingredients

2 male pheasants
1 free-range chicken

Garnish Ingredients

1 kg (2 lb) pheasant and chicken breast meat
Salt and pepper, saltpeter, ground allspice, bay leaf, thyme
4 cl (8 tsp) dry white wine, 2 cl (4 tsp) Cognac

300 g (10 oz) tongue
60 g (2 oz) pistachios

Decoration Ingredients

Basic pie pastry
Puréed liver
Truffles
1 L (4 cups) firm aspic, chopped

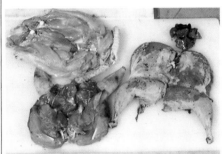

For the Pheasant Stock: See Game Stock

Forcemeat

1 kg (2 lbs) pheasant and chicken meat (not the breast meat)
700 g (1 1/2 lbs) pork jowl
100 g (3 1/2 oz) poultry livers (pheasant and chicken)
30 g (1 oz) shallots
15 g (1/2 oz) garlic
Salt and pepper, saltpeter, ground allspice
1 dl (1/2 cup) dry white wine
4 cl (8 tsps) Cognac
400 g (14 oz) puréed liver
2 eggs

For glazing: 1.5 L (6 cups) aspic

Procedure

For this dish, the pheasants are usually purchased with the plumage attached.

Removing the feathers is a lengthy procedure, and requires close attention so the skin of the bird is not damaged.

Pass the bird over a flame to burn off the small downy feathers. Wipe the skin with a dry hand towel to make it clean and smooth. This is important because the skin forms the outside of the ballotine.

Boning the Pheasant

This is a delicate operation because the flesh of the pheasant is very fragile.

Cut the neck off close to the body, pull off the skin and trim as much meat from the bones as possible. Reserve the meat for the forcemeat and the bones for stock.

With a small sharp boning knife, cut along each of the breast bone. Cut around the wishbone with the tip of the knife, scrape away the flesh and remove it. This facilitates the boning of the rib cage.

Follow the contour of the carcass and pass the knife around the wings and legs, cutting through the tendons to detach them from the carcass.

Remove the carcass, trim any bits of meat attached and set aside for the

forcemeat and reserve bones for stock.

Remove the breast meat, wings and legs, working carefully with the sharp knife.

Trim the nerves found below the surface of the breast meat using the tip of the knife.

Bone the wings and legs. Make an incision along the bones to expose them, cut through the tendons. Lift out the bones then trim all nerves and bits of cartilage and tendons.

This is an important operation because carefully trimmed meat will make a better forcemeat.

Reserve the trimmings for the stock and set aside the small pieces of meat for the forcemeat.

Reserve the skin in one neat piece to assemble the ballotine.

Preparing the Forcemeat

Trim the pork jowl then cut all the meats for the stuffing into small pieces.

Cut the breast meat into long strips.

Pour the cognac and wine along with the spices over these meats (placed separately in a non-reactive hotel pan), cover with plastic wrap and marinate in the refrigerator for 12-24 hours.

Drain the forcemeat ingredients and pass through the fine disk of the meat grinder. Combine with the foie gras and eggs and mix well. Reserve the marinated strips for the assembly.

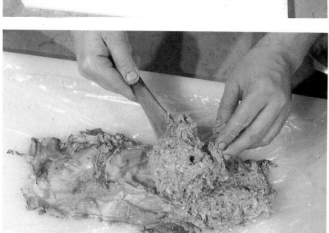

120

Assembling the Ballotine

Cut the tongue into long thin strips. Remove the skins from the pistachios.

Spread a sheet of plastic wrap on the work surface. Lay the skin out flat.

Spread a thin layer of the force-meat (about 1/3 of the total amount) over the skin.

Arrange the strips of pheasant and tongue in even rows. Sprinkle the pistachios evenly over the surface.

Repeat the procedure so that there are two layers of strips and three layers of forcemeat.

Rolling the Ballotine

Use the edge of the plastic wrap to roll the skin securely around the forcemeat. (Be careful to not roll the plastic inside the ballotine.)

Wrap the ballotine in cheesecloth, twist the ends tightly and tie with string.

The ballotine can be wrapped in strips of cloth (galantine "bandages") which makes the shape evenly rounded and compacts the forcemeat.

Wrap them around the ballotine twice.

Tie the ballotine like a roast, as shown.

Making the Pheasant Stock

Chop the bones then brown them in the oven along with the aromatic vegetables.

Deglaze the pan, place bones and vegetables in a small stockpot, add about 5 L (5 qts) water and bring to boil. Skim, lower the heat and simmer.

The stock should not be too strong.

Cooking the Ballotine

Poach the ballotine in the light pheasant stock for about 1 1/2 hours. Place the ballotine in cooled stock and bring the temperature to 75 °C (80 F) and maintain this temperature throughout poaching.

Let the ballotine cool in the liquid. Refrigerate for up to 5-6 days in the liquid.

Preparing the Aspic Glaze

One day in advance of serving, clarify the cooking liquid or another light stock (which can be flavored with sherry).

Final Preparation of the Ballotine

Drain the ballotine on a rack. Remove the strings, bandages, cheese-cloth and plastic.

Dry the surface completely with a clean handtowel and cut into even slices 1 cm (3/8 "). Arrange these slices on a rack and chill before glazing.

Stir the aspic over ice to thicken slightly then brush a thin coat on the chilled slices. Chill to set.

Shortly before serving, brush on a second coat of aspic to make them shine.

Its delicate, flavorful meat makes pheasant a favorite choice on buffet menus.

Pheasant appears in both hot and cold dishes. Chilled, it is usually made into terrines, gallantines or ballotines.

In these cases, the pheasant is most often blended with other meats, which makes the dishes more moist without masking the taste of the pheasant.

Another poultry meat can be used, such as chicken or turkey, which lowers the overall food cost.

For this ballotine, pork is used, which makes it moist and delicious.

The forcemeat is also enriched with the pheasant livers, foie gras and eggs.

Strips of tongue, pheasant and pistachios add a colorful decorative touch to each slice.

The seasonings should be measured with care to ensure that the taste of the foremeat is well balanced.

The garnishes can be simple or elaborate depending on the event.

For this presentation, the sliced ballotine is surrounded by barquettes of foie gras and glistening chopped aspic.

The stunning plumage of the pheasant adds a final dramatic touch.

During hunting season, this dish is always a favorite among clients.

124

Presentation

Arrange the slices and the barquettes with foie gras in an attractive pattern on the platter.

Decorate with chopped aspic.

The dramatic " pheasant in flight " is mounted on a loaf of firm bread, using wire to attach the wings, neck and head.

The hunting theme can be carried out with a decoration of autumn leaves and tree branches, and hunting paraphenalia.

This exciting display is always greatly admired by guests.

Pheasant Ballotine « en volière »

Procedure Diagram

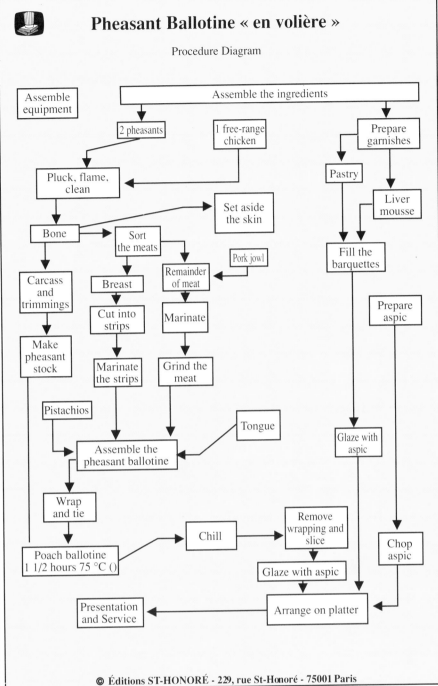

Chapter 2
Stocks, Glazes and Aspics

The Foundation of French Cuisine

When making sauces and other preparations with stocks, the quality of the stock plays an important role in the taste of the final dish.

Stocks come in a wide variety of flavors (meat, poultry, fish, vegetable) and can be reduced to concentrate the color and the taste. Many cooking procedures require stock (poaching, braising for example) and it is the main ingredient in many sauces and glazes.

Making good tasting stocks demand careful cooking (skimming often, even temperature) and proper storage (quick cooling, clean containers).
Stocks wih a well-balanced flavor can be made in sizeable quantities and used in many different dishes.

Stocks can also be made from a single ingredient to reinforce the flavors of a particular dish.

General Advice

Introduction

Many years ago stocks were made with great quantities of meat. It is no longer feasible to make such luxurious stocks because the price of ingredients and labor is prohibitive.

It is, however, as important as ever to choose top-quality ingredients to make stocks.

Stocks made with only bones and vegetable scraps will never have the deep flavor of ones that are carefully made using a percentage of meat or fish flesh and fresh vegetables.

The meat that contributes so much flavor can often be used in another dish (cold meat salads, stuffings) or served in a sauce to the personnel.

It goes without saying that the quality of the stock will be reflected in the taste of the final dish. The chef should always strive for perfection in the making of stocks.

Reduction

During the cooking process, stocks reduce and become concentrated.

The strained stock can be further reduced to make demi-glaze and meat glaze which have a thicker consistency.

The consistency of these reduced stocks depends on the amount of natural gelatin in the stock. Veal knuckles and feet, pork rind and the bones of flat fish are especially high in gelatin.

The light coating consistency of a carefully reduced stock has replaced the need, in many cases, for heavier thickeners like roux and cream in the modern kitchen.

The flavors will concentrate as well. It is therefore important to season the stock enough but not too much.

Stocks can be reduced to achieve just the right balance of taste and texture required for a particular dish.

Making Stocks

To make stocks that are consistently of high quality it is important to follow precise recipes that outline the quantity and preparation of the various ingredients.

Each ingredient contributes an important quality. The chef should respect the proportions and procedure.

Each step is important: browning the bones, degreasing the pan, frequent skimming of impurities.

The cooking must be carefully monitored. Each stock requires a different amount of cooking depending on the ingredients.

Making Large Quantities of Stock for Future Use

Since most stocks involve lengthy cooking, they are usually made in a large quantity and used for many dishes.

Proper storage of the stock is important for taste and hygiene and also for the organization of the kitchen.

Caterers do not use stocks on a daily basis in the quantities that a restaurant does. It is usually made in large quanitities, divided into small containers and frozen for future use. It is recommended to choose containers that are microwavable so that the amount of stock needed for a particular dish can be quickly thawed.

Cooling the Stock

It is imperative that stocks are cooled as quickly as possible. This is important for two reasons:

• Flavor is lost with the steam that rises as the stock cools. Quick cooling ensures a better tasting stock.

• Microbes multiply fastest at lukewarm temperatures. Quick cooling of the stock rapidly drops the temperature of the hot stock, not giving microbes a chance to develop.

In France, health regulations require that stocks are cooled either in an ice bath with cold running water to keep the temperature constant or in a special convection refrigerated unit called a " cellule froide " which circulates cold air around the hot item to cool it as quickly as possible.

While the stock is cooling, skim fat that rises to the top that would otherwise form a layer on top and trap heat inside.

Storing the Stock

If the stock will be used within 24 hours it can be stored, once properly cooled, in the refrigerator.

To store quantities of stock for future use, divide into smaller containers that have been cleaned and sterilized.

Containers are available in graduated sizes which allow the caterer to store portions ready for particular recipes. Freeze for up to 4 weeks.

It is important to mark each container with indelible ink with the kind of stock and date it was made. Each container should then be marked on an inventory that is kept up to date, allowing the chef to keep the freezer stocked with enough of each kind of stock.

Using containers that will go in the microwave speeds up the thawing process and therefore helps to avoid spoilage. Use as soon as possible after thawing.

Stocks are classified in " families " according to their ingredients and uses.

Nine families of stocks are described in this chapter:

Photo n°

A. **White Stocks** (veal, poultry) 1, 2
B. **Brown Stocks** (veal, " estouffade ") 3, 4
C. **Demi-glaze, Glazes and Essences** 5
D. **Secondary Sauces** (rabbit, duck, game, sweetbreads) ... 6, 7, 8, 9
E. **" Minute " Stocks** (pigeon, lamb, pheasant) 10, 11, 12
F. **Meat Juices and Deglazing Juices** 13
G. **Braising Juices** 14, 18
H. **Fish Stocks** 15
I. **Aspics and Consommés** (meat, poultry, fish) 16
J. **Court Bouillons and " Nages "** 17

White Veal Stock

Introduction

White veal stock should be light, clear and free of fat.

The flavor of this stock is very refined, due to the mild flavor of the veal and the choice of aromatic vegetables.

The clarity is due primarily to the lean meat which releases less fat to cloud the stock, and to the procedure which involves blanching the bones to draw out blood, fat and impurities which rise to the surface to be skimmed away. The stock is skimmed often during the long cooking process to eliminate any remaining impurities.

Uses

The stock is used in making all light veal-based sauces (" bouchées à la reine ", " blanquette ", " ivoire "). It is also used for poaching certain light meats (veal blanquette, quenelles).

Ingredients

Main Ingredients

7 kg (15.5 lbs) veal bones, preferably
  knuckles
2 kg (4.5 lbs) veal trimmings
2 calves' feet
2 kg (4.5 lbs) poultry trimmings
  (wings, necks, etc of chicken or
  turkey)
1.5 kg (3 lbs) veal shank

Aromatics and Seasonings

750 g (1.5 lbs) carrots
500 g (1 lb) onions
50 g (1.5 oz) garlic cloves
100 g (3.5 oz) shallots
400 g (14 oz) leeks
200 g (7 oz) celery
Bouquet garni (2 bay leaves, 3 sprigs
  thyme, 20 parsley stems)
2 cloves
Tied in cheesecloth: 1 tsp black peppercorns, 1 tsp coriander seed
3 g (1/2 tsp) salt per liter (quart)
  of liquid
35 L (about 38 qts) water

These quantities yield approximately
25 L (about 27 qts) finished stock,
depending on the degree of reduction.

Equipment

Large stock pot, paring knife; kitchen
twine, skimmer, cutting board, ladle,
2 large stainless steel bowls, pastry
brush, large colander, vegetable
peeler, conical sieve, measuring
cup

Procedure

Put the veal bones, veal trimmings, poultry trimmings and calves'
feet in the stock pot.
    Add cold water to cover, bring to a
boil and boil for 5 minutes. Skim off
any foam as it appears (the foam con-
tains fat and blood from the
bones).
    Put the pot under cold running
water and rinse the contents until
they are cold and free of any bits of
blood or impurity.
    Drain the contents well.

Preparing the Veal Shins

Tie the shin securely so the meat
will stay on the bone during cooking.
Leave a length of twine to tie onto
the pot handle; this will make retrieval of the shin easier.

Preparing the Vegetables

Peel and wash all the vegetables.

Tie the leeks and celery together in
a bundle. Stud the onions with the
cloves. Tie up the peppercorns and
coriander seeds in the cheesecloth so
they do not get skimmed away with
the foam.

Cooking the Stock

Place the veal bones and trimmings in the bottom of the stock pot, arranging them so the meat and gelatinous parts do not touch the bottom where they might stick and burn.

Add the poultry trimmings, then the calves' feet.

Add the vegetables: carrots, studded onions, garlic (unpeeled), shallots, leeks, celery and the bouquet garni.

Bring to a boil.

Skim thoroughly.

Simmer over a low heat for about 2 hours, then add the tied veal shin and attach the extra twine to the handle of the stockpot.

Add the cheesecloth bag of spices. Add salt in the proportion of 3 g (1/2 tsp) per liter (quart) of water.

Continue to cook the stock at a very low simmer, skimming thoroughly and frequently, which will help make the stock clear, light and flavorful.

The stock should cook for 6-8 hours.

Important note: The concentrated stock that adheres to the inside of the stockpot as the stock cooks must be dissolved with a pastry brush dipped in water. Any impurities combined with this concentrated stock will rise to the surface and be skimmed away.

Straining the Stock

With a large ladle, transfer the stock from the stockpot to a large bowl or recipient, taking care not to stir up the contents as this could cloud the stock. When most of the stock has been transferred with the ladle, pour out the contents of the stockpot into a large conical sieve and let them drain into another bowl. Do not squeeze or press on the solid material, which would alter the taste of the stock and could cloud it.

If necessary, the strained stock may be made more flavorful by cooking it longer, which reduces it and concentrates the flavor.

Cooling the Stock

Correct cooling of the stock is imperative, as it ensures good flavor and hygiene. The stock must be cooled as rapidly as possible, either in an ice bath with running water, or preferably in a " cold-chamber " which is a convection refrigerator especially made for this purpose.

Storing the Stock

Put the stock into containers that have been sanitized by treatment with an antiseptic and which can be sealed tightly, then quick-freeze the containers and store in the freezer.

Important note: once the stock is thawed, it should not be left at room temperature for very long.

The individual containers may be removed from the freezer as needed.

To hasten thawing, use a microwave oven or place in a warm water bath.

White Poultry Stock

Introduction

White poultry stock is similar in character to white veal stock, but the flavor of the poultry is slightly more pronounced. The procedure is the same as for the veal stock. The important qualities of this stock are its flavor, light color and clarity.

Uses

White poultry stock is used for poaching poultry and in making certain sauces: "suprême", "ivoire" and poultry "velouté", for example.

Ingredients

Main Ingredients

7 kg (15.5 lbs) veal bones, preferably knuckles
4 kg (9 lbs) poultry carcasses (chicken or turkey)
4 kg (9 lbs) poultry trimmings (wings, necks, meat trimmings of chicken or turkey) 2 calves' feet

These quantities yield approximately 25 L (about 27 qts) of stock depending on the degree of reduction.

Aromatics and Seasonings

750 g (1.5 lbs) carrots
500 g (1 lb) onions
50 g (1.5 oz) garlic cloves
100 g (3.5 oz) shallots
400 g (14 oz) leeks
200 g (7 oz) celery
Bouquet garni (2 bay leaves, 3 thyme sprigs, 20 parsley stems)
Tied in cheesecloth: 1 tsp black peppercorns, 1 tsp coriander seed
3 g (1/2 tsp) salt per liter (quart) water
35 L (about 38 qts) water

Equipment

Large stockpot, paring knife, kitchen twine, vegetable peeler, skimmer, cutting board, ladle, 2 large stainless steel bowls, large colander, conical sieve, pastry brush, measuring cup

Procedure

Blanching the Bones

Place the veal bones, the poultry carcasses, the poultry trimmings and the calves' feet in the stockpot.

Add cold water to cover, and continue with the procedure described in the section on white veal stock.

Preparing the Vegetables

Peel and wash all the vegetables. Tie the leeks and celery together in a bundle. Stud the onions with the cloves.

Make the bouquet garni. Tie up the peppercorns and coriander seed in the cheesecloth so they do not get skimmed away with the foam.

Cooking the Stock

Place the blanched bones, poultry carcasses, poultry trimmings and calves' feet in the stockpot.

Add the vegetables and the bouquet garni and add cold water (35 L (38 qts)).

Bring to a boil over high heat. Skim off any foam, lower the heat and simmer for about 2 hours.

Add the spice bag and the salt and continue to cook at a very low simmer for about 6 hours.

It is important to frequently and carefully skim off any foam or fat that accumulates during cooking.

Straining the Stock

Strain the stock through a conical sieve to separate the liquid from the solids. As with the white veal stock, do not press on the solids.

Cooling the Stock

The precautions for cooling white veal stock also apply to cooling white poultry stock: rapid cooling, sanitary conditions and complete removal of any fat, which could form a hard film on the surface of the stock and prevent it from " breathing " and cooling properly.

Storing the Stock

Using sanitary procedures and equipment, divide the cooled stock into quantities that are appropriate for future use.

Quick freeze the filled containers, then store them in the freezer, to be removed and thawed as needed.

135

Brown Veal Stock

Introduction

The deep golden color and pronounced flavor of brown veal stock is achieved by browning the bones and meat and deglazing the meat juices that " caramelize " in the roasting pan.

Aromatic vegetables, with an addition of tomato paste, intensify the color and flavor of this stock.

Although the color is darker than white veal stock, this stock should also be clear, free of impurities and fat. Careful degreasing, slow cooking at an even temperature and cleaning the sides of the pot during cooking will ensure a clear stock.

Brown veal stock is used to make brown sauces such as " espagnol ", and is a valuable ingredient when reduced to a demi-glaze, concentrating its color and flavor.

Ingredients

Main Ingedients
6 kg (13 lbs) veal bones
2 kg (4.5 lbs) veal trimmings
2 kg (4.5 lbs) poultry trimmings
1 kg (2 lbs) pork rind – 1 calf's foot
2 kg (4.5 lbs) veal shin

Aromatics and Seasonings
750 (1.5 lbs) carrots

500 g (1 lb) onions
50 g (1.5 oz) garlic cloves
100 g (3.5 oz) shallots
300 g (10 oz) tomato paste
400 g (14 oz) leeks – 200 g (7 oz) celery
Bouquet garni (2 bay leaves, 3 sprigs thyme, 20 parsley stems)
2 cloves – Grated nutmeg
Tied in cheesecloth: 1 tsp black peppercorns and 1 tsp coriander seed
3 g (scant 1/2 tsp) salt per liter (quart) liquid

Equipment
Large stockpot, paring knife, kitchen twine, skimmer, cutting board, ladle, pastry brush, 2 large stainless

steel bowls, large sieve, conical strainer, two-tined fork, measuring cup, roasting pan, frying pan

Procedure

Browning the Bones

In a large roasting pan spread out the bones in a single layer. Roast them in a hot oven (230 °C/475 F) until well browned and the fat has melted off. While the bones are browning, tie up the meats in kitchen twine and brown them in clarified butter and oil over high heat.

Using a two-tined fork, turn the meats to brown them evenly on all sides. Lift the meats by the strings to avoid pricking them with the fork which would release juices and cause the meat to dry out. Strain off as much fat as possible from the browned bones and meat. Tip the roasting pan so the fat drains to one corner and can be easily removed. Deglaze the two pans with water.

Preparing the Vegetables

Peel and wash the vegetables.

Secure the leeks and celery together with kitchen twine, and tie up the bouquet garni as well. Make a cheesecloth bundle with the peppercorns and coriander seeds. Stud the onions with the cloves.

Cooking the Stock

Place the bones in a large stockpot along with the veal and poultry trimmings, the calf's foot and pork rind. The veal shin will be added after the stock has cooked for two hours.

Add the vegetables and bouquet garni, then add cold water. Bring the stock to a boil, skim the impurities that rise to the surface. Lower the temperature and simmer the stock for two hours.

Add the veal shin and seasonings (salt and bundle of spices). Continue to simmer for 8-10 hours.

Skim the impurities from the surface at frequent intervals to ensure a clear, good tasting stock.

Cooking the Veal Shin

Check the veal shin after about

one hour. When it is done, remove it and reserve for another dish such as cold meat salad or stuffing.

Straining the Stock

Strain the stock through a conical sieve. Follow the previously explained guidelines to avoid clouding the stock at this stage.

Be sure to drain the bones and vegetables completely.

Cooling and Storing the Stock

Place the stock in an ice bath with running water or in a " cold chamber " to cool it quickly. Rapid cooling is imperative for good flavor as well as safety.

Divide the cooled stock into quantities appropriate for future use. Quick freeze the containers, then store in the freezer to be removed as needed.

Brown Stock " Estouffade "

Introduction

This delicious brown stock combines beef, veal and poultry along with flavorful vegetables and herbs for a well-balanced taste.

Uses

This stock can be used to make numerous sauces. It can be reduced to make demi-glaze and is often used to make rich stocks from rabbit, duck and guinea hen.

Ingredients

Main Ingredients

3.5 kg (8 lbs) veal bones
3.5 kg (8 lbs) beef bones
1 kg (2 lbs) beef trimmings
2 kg (4.5 lbs) poultry trimmings
1 kg (2 lbs) beef shank
1.5 kg (3 lbs) oxtail
1 calf's foot
1 kg (2 lbs) pork rind

Aromatics and Seasonings

750 g (1.5 lbs) carrots
500 g (1 lb) onions
50 g (1.5 oz) garlic cloves
400 g (14 oz) leeks
200 g (7 oz) celery
300 g (10 oz) tomato paste
Bouquet garni (2 bay leaves, 3 sprigs
    thyme, 20 parsley stems)
2 cloves
Tied in cheesecloth: 1 tsp black pep-
    percorns and 1 tsp coriander
    seeds
3 g (1/2 tsp) salt per liter (per quart)
    liquid
Grated nutmeg
35 L (about 38 qts) water

These quantities yield approximately 25 L (about 27 qts) stock, depending on the degree of reduction.

Equipment

Large stockpot, paring knife, kitchen twine, skimmer, cutting board, ladle, 2 large stainless steel bowls, large colander, pastry brush, conical sieve, two-tined fork, measuring cup, roasting pan, frying pan

Procedure

Browning the Bones

In a large roasting pan, spread out the bones in a single layer. Roast them in a hot oven (230 °C (475 F)) until well-browned and the fat has melted off.

While the bones are browning, tie up the meats in kitchen twine and brown them in clarified butter and oil.

Strain off as much fat as possible from the browned bones and meat. Tip the pans so the fat drains to one corner and can be easily removed. Deglaze the pans with water.

Reserve the oxtail for another use.

Thoroughly blanch the calves' feet and pork rind.

Place the meats in cold water, bring to boil and boil 5 minutes, then refresh in cold water and drain.

Cooking the Stock

Place the bones in a large stockpot along with the poultry and beef trimmings, the calves' feet and the pork rind.

Add the vegetables and bouquet garni.

Cover with cold water (about 35 L (about 38 qts)). Bring the stock to a boil, skim the impurities that rise to the surface. Lower the temperature and simmer the stock for two hours.

Add the shank and oxtail, which have been tied in kitchen twine; tie the end of the twine to the handle of the stockpot for easy retrieval of the meats. Add the tomato paste and nutmeg.

Add salt in the proportion of 3 g (1/2 tsp) per litre (quart). Add the cheesecloth bag of spices.

Continue to simmer for 8-10 hours, skimming frequently, which will ensure a clear, flavorful stock.

Important note: The concentrated stock that adheres to the inside of the stockpot as the stock reduces must be dissolved with a pastry brush dipped in water.

Straining the Stock

Strain the stock through a conical sieve. Thoroughly drain the bones and vegetables, without pressing on them.

Cooling the Stock

Cool the stock quickly in an ice bath with running water or in a "cold chamber" to maintain hygenic conditions and give the best flavor.

Storing the Stock

Divide the cooled stock into quantities appropriate for future use.

Quick freeze the containers, then store in the freezer to be removed as needed.

Demi-glaze and Meat Glaze

Introduction

Demi-glaze or " demi-glace " is a stock that has been reduced to concentrate its flavor and color. Estouffade stock is a good choice due to its well balanced flavor. White wine adds a touch of acidity and red wine contributes flavor and a deep color.

The stock can be reduced a little or a lot depending on how the demi-glaze will be used. If, for example, the demi-glaze is used to make a full-flavored stock (such as rabbit or duck) or is added to a braised dish, it will reduce further during cooking and therefore should not be too concentrated to start with. In these cases, a strong demi-glaze would cover up the flavor of the other ingredients.

If the demi-glaze is added toward the end of cooking, to make a sauce or deglaze a roasting pan to make " au jus ", for example, the demi-glaze should be more concentrated.

Procedure for Demi-glaze

For 12 L (about 13 qts) of Estouffade Stock

Bring the stock to a boil and skim the foam that rises to the surface, lower the heat and simmer to reduce a little.

Add 1/2 L (2 cups) dry white wine and 75 cl (3 cups) full-bodied red wine.

Continue to simmer and reduce by half. Skim away the impurities on the surface at regular intervals and dissolve the stock that accumulates on the sides with a pastry brush dipped in water.

General Advice for Reducing Stock

Choose a heavy stockpot that distributes the heat evenly so the stock can reduce steadily over low heat which is essential for achieving a clear liquid. The pot should have straight sides and not be too wide, so the stock reduces slowly. The size of the pot should be just large enough to hold the stock as it will reduce by quite a bit.

The same guidelines outlined for skimming the foam from stocks apply to making demi-glaze. Eliminate these impurites that rise to the surface at regular intervals.

Concentrated stock will adhere to the sides of the pot as the stock reduces and evaporates. It is important to periodically dissolve this rich accumulation of stock with a pastry brush dipped in water.

Maintaining a steady temperature and skimming thoroughly are important for the clarity and taste of the demi-glaze.

Uses

Demi-glaze is used to make several classic brown sauces-" Madère ", " Bordelaise ", and " Perigeux " for example. It is also added as the liquid for braising meats and for making hearty stocks from rabbit, duck and game.

Storing

The precautions outlined for storing Estouffade stock apply to the proper cooling and storage of demi-glaze.

Procedure for Making Meat Glaze

To make meat glaze or " glace de viande ", reduce demi-glaze until it is syrupy and very dark brown: i.e. to about 1/10 its original volume.

It is important to skim the foam away as it rises to the surface and to

dissolve the concentrated stock that adheres to the sides of the pot as it evaporates.

To facilitate skimming, you may want to transfer the glaze to a smaller pot as the quantity diminishes. The flavorful demi-glaze that is left in the larger pot should be dissolved with a little water and reserved for making stock.

Uses

This intensely flavored glaze is not used " straight ". Its concentrated flavor and color are used to reinforce stocks and sauces.

Storing

Meat glaze keeps very well due to its thick consistency. Store meat glaze for 2-3 weeks in the refrigerator or freeze.

Brown Stock made with Rabbit

Introduction

As with all brown stocks, the color and flavor depends on thoroughly browning the bones and meat trimmings then deglazing the flavorful juices that adhere to the pan.

This preparation is grouped with " secondary brown stocks ".

This stock is used to make sauces to accompany rabbit dishes. When reduced to a glaze, it adds flavor and moistness to rabbit-based forcemeats as described in volume 2 of this series.

Ingredients

Main Ingredient

4 rabbit carcasses plus trimmings (1.5 kilos (about 3 lbs))

Aromatics and Seasonings

50 g (1.5 oz) clarified butter or oil
150 g (5 oz) carrots
100 g (3.5 oz) onions
60 g (2 oz) shallots
60 g (2 oz) garlic
150 g (5 oz) leek
100 g (3.5 oz) celery
Bouquet garni (6 parsley stems, 1/2 bay leaf, 12 branches thyme)
150 g (5 oz) tomatoes

3 grams (1/2 tsp) salt per liter (quart) of liquid

Tied in cheesecloth: 10 black peppercorns, 10 coriander seeds

4 dl (1 2/3 cups) dry white wine

1 L (1 qt) demi-glaze, not too reduced

Equipment

Cutting board, cleaver, paring knife, skimmer, kitchen twine, pastry brush, measuring cup, roasting pan, stockpot, ladle, colander, large bowl, conical strainer

Procedure

Chop the carcasses and meat trimmings into small pieces with a cleaver and place them in a single layer in a roasting pan brushed with oil or clarified butter.

Brown the bones in a hot oven.

Peel and cut the onions, shallots and carrots into small dice. When the bones and trimmings are light brown, add these vegetables and the garlic in its skin and return the pan to the oven. Continue to cook until the vegetables and bones are golden brown.

Drain the browned bones and vegetables in a large colander to eliminate all the fat. Pour off all the fat from the roasting pan then deglaze with a little white wine. Scrape the pan with a wooden spoon to release and dissolve the meat juices that adhere to the pan.

Place the drained bones and vegetables into a small stockpot. Add the deglazing liquid and the remainder of the white wine and bring to a boil to eliminate the acidity of the wine.

Tie the leek and celery together with kitchen twine and add this to the stockpot along with the bouquet garni.

Add the tomato and coarse salt which draws flavor out of the ingredients.

Next add the peppercorns and coriander which are tied in cheesecloth so they will not be skimmed away during cooking.

Add the demi-glaze, bring to a boil and skim away the foam that rises to the surface.

Lower the heat and simmer the stock for 1-2 hours, skimming frequently.

When the stock has a pronounced rabbit flavor, drain the stock through a large conical sieve into a large bowl. Press on the bones to extract as much flavor as possible.

Skim all fat that rises to the surface.

Cool the drained stock quickly, following the guidelines previously described.

Brown Duck Stock

Introduction

This brown stock is used to make sauces to accompany dishes featuring duck. Duck glaze, used to flavor sauces and forcemeats, is made with this stock.

Ingredients

Main Ingredient

4 duck carcasses, raw or cooked.

Aromatics and Seasonings

50 g (1.5 oz) oil or clarified butter
60 g (2 oz) garlic
150 g (5 oz) leek
80 g (2.5 oz) celery
Bouquet garni (10 parsley stems, 1/2 bay leaf, 2 sprigs thyme)
150 g (5 oz) tomatoes
1/2 L (2 cups) dry white wine
3 L (about 3 qts) demi-glaze
3 g (1/2 tsp) coarse salt per liter (qt) liquid

Tied in cheesecloth: 10 black peppercorns, 10 coriander seeds

Equipment

Cutting board, cleaver, paring knife, skimmer, kitchen twine, pastry brush, ladle, measuring cup, roasting pan, stockpot, vegetable peeler, colander, large bowl, conical sieve

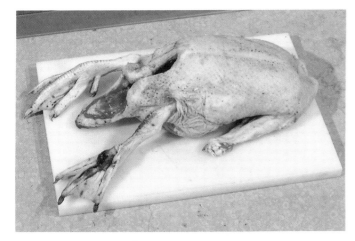

Procedure

Browning the Bones

This stock can be made with raw or cooked carcasses of duck. In either case the bones should be trimmed of as much fat as possible.

Chop the bones into small pieces with a cleaver.

Place the bones in a single layer in a roasting pan with oil or butter and brown in a hot oven. If combining cooked and raw bones, brown the raw ones a little first then add the bones from the cooked duck. Add the garlic in its skin.

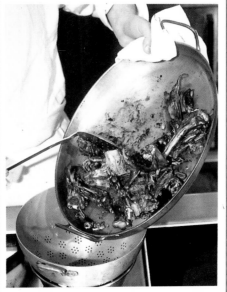

Drain the browned bones in a colander and pour off all the fat from the roasting pan.

Drain the stock into a large bowl. Remove as much fat from the surface as possible.

Cool the stock quickly, following the guidelines described in previous sections.

Deglaze the pan with white wine, scraping the pan with a wooden spoon to release and dissolve all the meat juices.

Cooking the Stock

Place the bones and vegetables in a stockpot and add the deglazing liquid and the remainder of the white wine. Bring to a boil to eliminate the acidity of the wine.

Add the demi-glaze and seasonings and return to boil. Skim away the impurities that rise to the surface.

Lower the heat and simmer for 1-2 hours until the stock has a pronounced flavor of duck. The length of cooking, and therefore strength of the stock, will depend on the final use of the stock.

Skim the foam from the surface at regular intervals.

Brown Stock made with Game

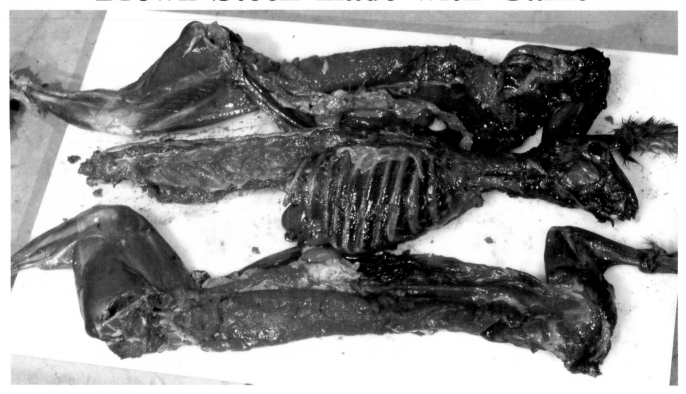

Introduction

Sauces made with these full-flavored stocks are ideal for highlighting the assertive taste of game. Wild rabbit and pheasant stocks are described here. These stocks are grouped with the "secondary brown stocks".

Ingredients

Wild Rabbit Stock

Main Ingredient

1.5 kilos (3 lbs) rabbit carcasses and trimmings

Aromatics and Seasonings

50 g (1.5 oz) oil or butter
150 g (5 oz) carrots
100 g (3.5 oz) onions
50 g (1.5 oz) garlic
150 g (5 oz) leek
Bouquet garni (10 parsley stems, 1/2 bay leaf, 2 sprigs thyme)
Tied in cheesecloth: 10 peppercorns, 10 coriander seeds
3 g (1/2 tsp) coarse salt per liter (qt) of liquid
1 dl (1/2 cup) dry white wine
1/2 L (2 cups) full-bodied red wine
3 L (about 3 qts) demi-glaze

Pheasant Stock

Main Ingredient

50 g (1.5 oz) oil or clarified butter
120 g (4 oz) carrots
80 g (2.5 oz) onions
30 g (1 oz) garlic
100 g (3.5 oz) leek
Bouquet garni (10 parsley stems, 1/2 bay leaf, 2 thyme sprigs)
Tied in cheeseclth: 10 black peppercorns, 10 coriander seeds
3g (1/2 tsp) coarse salt per liter (qt) of liquid 4 dl (1 2/3 cups) dry white wine
3 L (about 3 qts) demi-glaze

Procedure

Peel the vegetables and cut into small dice. Chop the carcasses into small pieces with a cleaver.

Place the bones in a single layer in a roasting pan with oil or butter. Brown the bones in a hot oven, stirring them around so they brown evenly.

When the bones are light brown, add the diced vegetables and continue browning them together.

Drain the browned bones and vegetables and pour off the fat from the roasting pan.

Depending on the stock, deglaze with red or white wine. Bring to a boil to eliminate the acidity of the wine and reduce a little.

Add the demi-glaze and the seasonings.

Skim the foam from the surface, lower the heat and simmer for about 1 1/2 hours, frequently skimming away the impurities.

Pass the stock and press on the bones to extract flavor.

Cool the stock quickly, following the same guidelines for storage as the other stocks in this chapter.

Stock made with Sweetbreads

Introduction

This stock is rarely made. Its refined flavor augments the flavor of braised sweetbreads and also imparts a delicious taste to sauces that accompany sweetbread dishes.

The rich texture of the sweetbreads releases a lot of fat during cooking which must be skimmed away.

Ingredients

Main Ingredient

2 kg (about 4 lbs) sweetbread trimmings

Aromatics and Seasonings

15 g (1/2 oz) garlic
70 g (2.5 oz) shallots
100 g (3.5 oz) leek
30 g (1 oz) celery
Bouquet garni: 10 stems parsley, 1/2
  bay leaf, 2 thyme sprigs
Tied in cheesecloth: 10 peppercorns,
  10 coriander seeds
3 g (1/2 tsp) coarse salt per liter
  (quart) liquid

1 dl (1/2 cup) dry white wine
1 dl (1/2 cup) madeira, port or
  sherry (optional)
1.5 L (3 cups) demi-glaze

Equipment

Cutting board, small stockpot, colander, large bowl, roasting pan, pastry brush, paring knife, ladle, skimmer, vegetable peeler, kitchen twine

Procedure

Degorge the sweetbread trimmings under cold running water to draw out blood and impurities.

Place them in a roasting pan and sauté briefly over high heat then finish browning in the oven.

Drain the browned trimmings and pour off the fat from the roasting pan.

Deglaze the pan with dry white wine, dissolving the delicious meat juices that adhere to the pan.

Add the port, madeira or sherry depending on the dish the stock will be used for. Bring to a boil to eliminate the acidity of the wine.

Put the meat trimmings in a small stockpot, pour in the deglazing juices and add the aromatic vegetables.

Add the demi-glaze, bring to a boil, skim the surface, lower the heat

and simmer for 1 1/2 hours. Continue to skim the fat and impurities that rise to the surface during cooking.

This step is essential as the sweetbreads are very fatty.

Dissolve the concentrated stock that adheres to the sides of the pot with a pastry brush dipped in water.

Strain the stock through a conical sieve.

Cool the stock quickly. Remove the layer of fat that rises to the top.

Follow the previously described guidelines for storing and freezing stock.

Pigeon Stock

Introduction

This delicious stock is quick to make as it is usually made in small quantities and does not require long cooking.

This stock is in the category of " minute stocks ".

Uses

This stock makes a delicious " au jus " when used to deglaze the pan from roasted pigeons and served as a simple accompaniment.

Ingredients

Main Ingredients
4 pigeons (carcasses, thighs, wings, gizzards, necks, livers)

Aromatics and Seasonings
3 garlic cloves, unpeeled
Bouquet garni (1 sprig thyme, 1/2 bay leaf, 6 parsley stems, 1 stalk celery leaves, 1 leek green)

Liquid Ingredients
Cognac
1dl (1/2 cup) dry white wine
1l (1qt) lightly reduced demi-glaze
3 g (1/2 tsp) salt per liter (quart) liquid

Equipment
Roasting pan, paring knife, cutting board, ladle, skimmer, pastry brush, large bowl, conical sieve, kitchen twine, strainer.

Procedure

Chop up the bones with a cleaver, or break them into little pieces by first placing them in a heavy pot and pounding with the end of a French rolling pin.

Brown the bones in a frying pan, or the roasting pan in which the pigeons have been cooked. Add the garlic cloves in their skins.

Drain the browned bones to remove the fat and pour off the fat from the pan. Return the bones to the pan and flame with cognac.

Deglaze the pan with the white wine and bring to a boil to eliminate the acidity of the wine.

Pour in the demi-glaze and add the bouquet garni.

Bring to a boil and skim the foam that rises to the surface. Lower the heat and simmer 1/2 hour.

Cook for 15 minutes and add the salt.

Skim the surface frequently and dissolve the stock that adheres to the sides with a pastry brush dipped in water.

Pass the stock through a conical sieve. (Press on the bones to extract maximum flavor.)

Cool quickly and follow the guidelines for storage previously described.

Lamb Stock

Introduction

Lamb stock is cooked for a relatively short period of time using lamb bones and lamb trimmings with all the fat removed.

Uses

Generally the lamb stock is used shortly after it is made, to deglaze the pan in which the meat is roasted (for example a rack of lamb or lamb noisettes).

Ingredients

Main Ingredients

1 kg (2 lbs) lamb bones
300 g (10 oz) lamb trimmings, excess fat removed
3 cl (2 tbsp) olive oil

Aromatics and Seasonings

50 g (1 1/2 oz) carrots
100 g (3 1/2 oz) onions
20 g (2/3 oz) garlic
50 g (1 1/2 oz) leek
40 g (1 1/3 oz) celery
50 g (1 1/2 oz) shallots
100 g (3 1/2 oz) tomatoes
Bouquet garni (1 sprig thyme, 1/2 bay leaf, 10 parsley stems, 1 sprig rosemary)

Tied in cheesecloth: 5g (1tsp) black peppercorns, 5 g (1 tsp) coriander seed

3 g (1/2 tsp) salt per liter (quart) liquid

Liquid Ingredients

1 dl (1/2 cup) dry white wine
1 l (1 qt) demi-glaze
1/2 l (2 cups) water

Equipment

Cutting board, cleaver, boning knife, paring knife, vegetable peeler, frying pan, large saucepan, skimmer, colander, stainless steel bowl, pastry brush, pastry scraper, measuring cup, conical sieve

Procedure

With a cleaver, chop up the bones and trimmings.

Brown the bones in the pan over high heat.

When the bones are almost completely browned, add the diced carrots, sliced onions, and unpeeled garlic cloves and continue to cook for a few minutes to brown.

Strain the ingredients from the pan and pour off the fat. Deglaze the pan with the white wine, making sure to dissolve all the caramelized meat and vegetable juices. Cook for a few seconds to eliminate the acidity of the wine.

Replace the bones and vegetables and return the pan to the heat. Add

the demi-glaze and the water.

Add the leek, celery, tomatoes, bouquet garni and spices.

Simmer gently over medium heat for about one hour.

Season with salt halfway through the cooking time.

Skim the grease from the surface during cooking.

Strain the stock through a conical sieve.

The stock may be used for deglazing the lamb roasting pan.

Guinea Hen Stock

Introduction

The carcasses of cooked guinea hens are most often used to make this quick-cooking stock.

The stock is light, delicate and flavorful and may be made using either white or red wine.

Uses

The stock is used to deglaze the roasting pan in which the guinea hens are roasted and for sauces such as " salmi " sauce served with roasted or braised guinea hen.

Ingredients

Main Ingredients

2 guinea hens (carcasses, trimmings, thighs and wing tips)
Clarified oil or butter

Aromatics and Seasonings

50 g (1 1/2 oz) carrots
40 g (1 1/3 oz) onions
30 g (1 oz) garlic
10 g (1/3 oz) celery
30 g (1 oz) tomato
Bouquet garni (1 sprig thyme, 1/2 bay leaf, 4 parsley stems)
Tied in cheesecloth: 5 g (1 tsp) black peppercorns, 5 g (1 tsp) coriander seed
3 g (1/2 tsp) salt per liter (quart) liquid

Liquid Ingredients

Cognac
7.5 cl (3 cups) dry white wine
7.5 cl (3 cups) demi-glaze

Equipment

Frying or roasting pan, cleaver, cutting board, ladle, skimmer, stainless steel bowls, vegetable peeler, paring knife, colander, conical sieve, pastry brush

Procedure

Remove the skin from the carcasses and trimmings and chop them with a cleaver.

Brown the pieces in the roasting pan in which the hens were first roasted or in a frying pan.

Add the carrots and onions cut in fine dice, the unpeeled garlic, and brown lightly.

Strain the ingredients from the pan, and discard the fat, return the pan to the heat and flame with a splash of cognac.

Deglaze the pan with the white wine, making sure to dissolve any caramelized meat and vegetable juices and boil for a few seconds to eliminate the acidity of the wine.

Add the demi-glaze and the bouquet garni and spices.

Simmer for about 45 minutes.

Skim frequently during cooking and wash down the inside of the pot with a pastry brush.

Strain the stock through a conical sieve and use as needed.

161

Meat Juices

Introduction

These preparations are made specifically to accompany the roast meat from which they are made, in contrast to a stock, demi-glaze or meat glaze, which may be made independently to use in many different preparations.

In English they are sometimes referred to as " au jus ".

The technique of making a meat juice is designed to dissolve all the caramelized meat juices that accumulate on the bottom of the pan and which are very intensely flavored.

Meat juices are made very quickly and only in small quantities. They need to be carefully degreased before serving.

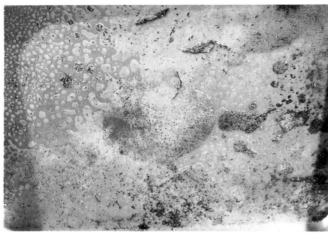

Uses

They are served with roast meats, usually in a sauce boat or poured over the meat.

Procedure

Meat juices are made from the cooking juices accumulated in the roasting pan or casserole.

Pour off most or all of the fat from the pan.

Heat the pan so the meat juices caramelize on the bottom.

Deglaze with dry white wine to completely dissolve the juices. If possible use a pastry brush to help dissolve the juices adhered to the sides of the pan.

Add the stock and bring to a boil to thoroughly dissolve the juices and to eliminate the acidity in the wine.

Continue cooking to reduce the volume a bit, then strain the liquid through cheesecloth.

Taste and correct the seasoning and serve with roast meats.

Braising Liquids

Introduction

As with the meat juices, braising liquids are made to accompany the meat from which they are made.

In contrast to the meat juices, which are served only with roast meats, braising liquids are used to flavor the braised meats during cooking, adding moisture and mingling flavors of the meat and the aromatic garnish.

The braising liquid is used to moisten and flavor braised or roast meats during cooking.

Uses

These preparations are used in braising meat (bœuf à la mode), or roasting meat (veal and pork roasts).

Ingredients

Main Ingredients

3 kg (6 1/2 lb) pork sirloin

Aromatics and Seasonings

125 g (4 oz) carrots
100 g (3 1/2 oz) onions
20 g (2/3 oz) garlic
50 g (1 1/2 oz) shallots
25 g (3/4 oz) celery
50 g (1 1/2 oz) tomato
Bouquet garni (1 sprig thyme, 1 bay leaf, 10 parsley stems, 1 sprig rosemary)
3 g (1/2 tsp) salt per liter (quart) liquid
Pepper

Liquid Ingredients

1.5 dl (2/3 cup) dry white wine
4 dl (1 2/3 cup) demi-glaze

Equipment

Roasting pan, cutting board, 2-tined fork, paring knife, vegetable peeler, measuring cup, conical sieve, pastry brush

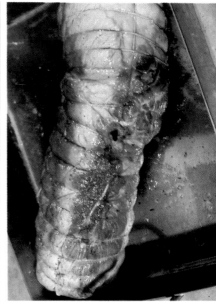

Procedure

Prepare the vegetables by cutting the carrots, onions, celery and shallots into dice and separating the garlic cloves.

Brown the pork roast in a roasting pan over high heat, turning frequently, but taking care not to pierce it. Cook until it is an even golden brown.

Off the heat, add the vegetables to the roasting pan and put into a hot oven (230 °C/450 °F) to brown the vegetables.

Remove the pan from the oven. Add the white wine, tomatoes, bouquet garni and season with salt and pepper.

Return to the oven for about 30 minutes at 230 °C (450 °F).

Remove from the oven and add the demi-glaze.

Lower the heat to 200 °C (375 F). Cover the roast with aluminum foil and continue cooking for 45-50 minutes.

Check to see that the meat is cooked and remove it from the liquid.

Strain the braising liquid through a conical sieve.

Reduce the liquid a little if necessary and thicken it slightly with a cooked roux if desired.

Serve separately in a sauceboat or nap the slices of pork roast with the sauce.

Fish Stock

Uses

Fish stock is the base for all fish-based sauces. It may also be used as a poaching liquid.

When clarified, it may be used in aspics to glaze foods or in chaud-froid preparations.

Ingredients

The quantities of ingredients will be different depending on whether only bones or bones and fish flesh are used, as the flesh adds much more flavor.

For the following recipe, substitute 5 kg (11 lbs) of mixed fish for the 10 kg (22 lbs) fish bones.

Main Ingredients

10 kg (22 lbs) fish bones, heads and trimmings (turbot, sole, and preferably some salt-water crayfish and crab carcasses)
100 g (3.5 oz) clarified butter

Liquid Ingredients

2 L (2 qts) dry white wine
15 L (about 16 qts) water

Aromatics and Seasonings

400 g (14 oz) onions
400 g (14 oz) shallots
600 g (1 1/4 lbs) leeks
500 g (1 lb) mushrooms
300 g (10 oz) fennel
Bouquet garni (2 bay leaves, 3 sprigs thyme, 30 parsley stems)
Chervil
3 g (1/2 tsp) salt per litre (quart) liquid
1 tsp black peppercorns

These quantities will yield approximately 12 L (13 qts) fish stock.

Equipment

Large stockpot, cutting board, spatula, measuring cup, paring knife, fish filet knife, ladle, large bowls, skimmer, large colander, conical sieve

Procedure

Preparing the Fish

Gut the fish, chop it into pieces and wash it carefully then drain it. Do not leave the fish to soak in water, as this will draw out flavor.

Preparing the Vegetables

Wash and peel all the vegetables, then slice the onions, shallots, leeks, mushrooms and fennel.

Tie up the bouquet garni and the chervil.

Add 2 liters (2 quarts) of white wine and simmer about 5 minutes to eliminate the acidity in the wine. Add water, season with salt and add the bouquet garni and the chervil.

Bring to a boil and simmer 30-40 minutes.

Add the pepper about 5 minutes before the end of the cooking time.

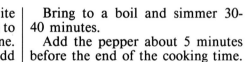

Cooking the Stock

Cook the vegetables over low heat until soft but not colored.

Add the pieces of fish.

Cover and cook about 10 minutes.

Be sure to skim the stock thoroughly and frequently during cooking, and brush the inside rim of the stockpot.

Pass the fumet through the colander and then through a fine conical sieve.

Cooling the Stock

Like all stocks, the fish stock must be cooled rapidly for the best flavor and to avoid bacteria growth.

Fish stock should be cooled in the same manner as other stocks: in an ice bath with cold running water or in a " cold chamber ". It is important to thoroughly degrease the surface of the stock to prevent the formation of a film which could inhibit effective cooling.

Storing the Stock

Fish stock is very delicate and has a short shelf-life (2-3 days maximum at 4 °C (40 F)).

It is best to divide the fish stock into smaller containers which can be sealed tightly and frozen until needed.

Aspic

Introduction

Aspic has numerous functions in restaurant and catering operations. It may be based on various ingredients, which will be reflected in the name (chicken aspic, fish aspic).

All aspics are made in two steps:
  a) making the stock
  b) clarifying the stock

Making the Stock

The stock for an aspic is usually made in the ordinary way with the addition of more gelatinous ingredients: knuckle bones, pork rind, pork tails, poultry feet.

For fish aspic, a regular fish stock is made with a high proportion of bones from flatfish (turbot, sole, brill) which are higher in gelatin.

Clarifying the Aspic

It is crucial that the stock be completely degreased before clarifying it. The purpose of clarifying the stock is to remove all sediment or impurities which cloud the liquid, leaving a crystal clear, beautifully colored aspic.

Several ingredients are used in clarifying, each one with a specific function: leek greens have chlorophyll; chopped meat (for meat and poultry aspics) has blood; and fish flesh (for fish stock) has fish protein-all of which help remove impurities.

The albumin in egg whites coagulates during cooking, which also absorbs and traps the impurities.

Aromatic vegetables bring flavor and color to all aspics.

After cooking, the aspic is passed through a fine-meshed conical sieve or a drum sieve lined with cheese-

cloth or clean kitchen towel to strain out any remaining impurities.

After straining the clarified stock, rectify the seasoning.

Check the firmness of the aspic with the following test. Chill a small amount of aspic and see how firmly it sets.

It is possible to increase the amount of gelatin by adding more gelatin in powdered or leaf form.

The seasoning must be correct as well.

The aspic may be flavored with port, madeira, sherry or another wine. Fish aspics could be flavored with an anise liqueur.

The addition of tarragon and chervil to the stock will give flavor to the natural aspic also.

The aspic is used for chaud-froid dishes, molded aspics, eggs in aspic, glazing, decorating pâtés and chopped aspic for decorating serving platters.

Equipment

Stockpot, large bowls, large conical sieve or drum sieve, clean cheesecloth or kitchen towel, ladle, measuring cup, meat grinder, spatula

Straining the Aspic

The raft, or crust, of coagulated ingredients on top of the stock must be completely set before beginning to strain out the liquid.

With a ladle, break a hole in the surface of the raft and carefully ladle out the clarified stock bit by bit.

Strain the clarified stock through a fine-meshed conical sieve or a drum sieve lined with clean cheesecloth or kitchen towel. The technique filters out any remaining particles in the clarified stock.

Storing the Aspic

Aspics have a short storage time (as do most stocks). They will quickly become cloudy and spoil. It is there- fore best to divide the aspic into small containers and freeze them until needed. The setting power of the gelatin may be diminished slightly by freezing, but that may be rectified at the time of use.

Meat Aspic

Ingredients

Main Ingredients
2 kg (4 1/2 lbs) veal bones
2 kg (4 1/2 lbs) beef bones
1 kg (2 lbs) poultry trimmings
1.5 kg (3 lbs 5oz) veal shank
1.5 kg (3 lbs 5oz) beef shank
1.5 kg (3 lbs 5oz) pigs' tails
1.5 kg (3 lbs 5oz) pork rind

Aromatics and Seasonings
750 g (1 1/2 lbs) carrots
500 g (1 lb) onions
50 g (1 1/2 oz) garlic cloves
100 g (3 1/2 oz) shallots
500 g (1 lb) tomatoes

150 g (5 oz) tomato paste (optional)
400 g (13 oz) leeks
200 g (7 oz) celery
Bouquet garni (2 bay leaves, 3 sprigs thyme, 20 parsley stems)
2 cloves.
Tied in cheesecloth: 5 g (1 tsp) black peppercorns, 5 g (1 tsp) coriander seed
Grated nutmeg
Salt

Equipment
Large stockpot, frying pan (optional), paring knife, cutting board, ladle, skimmer, vegetable peeler, 2-tined fork, string, stainless steel bowls, conical sieve, large colander.

Procedure

Place the veal and beef bones, the poultry trimmings, the pork rind and the pig tails in the stock pot.

Blanch them by covering with cold water, bringing to a boil and boiling for about 5 minutes. Skim the foam from the surface.

Refresh with cold running water to cool and rinse off the ingredients in the stockpot. Drain thoroughly.

Making the Aspic

In the stockpot, combine the veal and beef bones, the poultry trimmings, the pig tails, the pork rind, and the aromatics and seasonings (carrots, onions studded with cloves, unpeeled garlic cloves, shallots, tomatoes, leeks, celery, bouquet garni.

Cover generously with cold water (about 35 L; about 38 qts).

Bring to a boil, skim the surface and leave to simmer about 2 hours. Add the shanks and continue to simmer for 5-6 hours.

Remove the stock from the heat. Degrease it carefully with a ladle and strain through a colander.

Strain the liquid through a conical sieve to remove any remaining impurities.

Cool quickly by placing the stock-pot in ice to facilitate complete degreasing.

Clarifying the Aspic

Clarifying Ingredients (for 30 L; about 32 qts stock)

1.5 kg (3 lbs) lean beef
200 g (7 oz) carrots
150 g (5 oz) onions
130 g (4 1/2 oz) shallots
30 g (1 oz) garlic
200 g (7 oz) mushrooms
40 g (1 1/3 oz) tomatoes
Bouquet garni (1 sprig thyme, 1 bay leaf, 10 parsley stems)
1 bunch chervil
Tied in cheesecloth: 1 tsp (5 g) crushed black peppercorns
500 g (1 lb) leek greens
2 L (2 qts) egg whites

Clarifying Procedure

The Meat

Trim away all fat on the meat, which could make the aspic greasy.

Meat serves two functions in clarifying the aspic: first it adds flavor; second, the blood combines with the egg whites to coagulate and remove impurities.

Chop the meat in a meat grinder fitted with a medium disk.

The Vegetables

Wash and peel the vegetables. Cut into a very fine dice (brunoise).

The vegetables also serve two functions in the clarification: They enhance the flavor, and the chlorophyll in the leeks combines with the egg whites to clarify the aspic.

The bouquet garni adds an herbal flavor to the aspic.

The egg white is the essential ingredient that serves to link all the others and make the clarification process work. When it coagulates, it traps and retains all the impurities in the stock.

In a large bowl, mix all the ingredients with a spatula: vegetables, meat, egg whites, and a little bit of stock to dilute.

Add this mixture to the liquid in the pot.

Return to the heat and bring to a gentle boil, stirring constantly and slowly to avoid clouding. Be sure to scrape the bottom to prevent the egg whites from sticking.

As soon as the liquid boils, stop stirring to allow the egg whites to solidify and draw out the impurities.

The egg whites will form a crust, or " raft ", which floats on the surface of the aspic.
Strain the aspic.

Poultry Aspic

Introduction

Poultry aspic is made using the same technique as meat aspic but with slightly different ingredients in the basic stock recipe (chicken carcasses, trimmings and feet).

To clarify the poultry aspic, use the recipe and techniques described in the section on meat aspic.

Uses

Poultry aspic can be used in any poultry based dish such as molded aspics with poultry or poultry glazed with chaud-froid.

Ingredients

Main Ingredients
2 kg (4.5 lbs) veal bones 2 kg (4.5 lbs) poultry carcasses 1 kg (2 lbs) poultry trimmings 1.5 kg (3 lbs) chicken feet 1 kg (2 lbs) veal shank 1.5 kg (3 lbs)pig's tails 1 kg (2 lbs) pork rind

Aromatics and Seasonings
750 g (1.5l bs) carrots 500 g (1lb) onions 50 g (1 1/2 oz) garlic 100 g (3 1/2 oz) shallots 500 g (1 lb) to-matoes 400 (14 oz) leeks 200 g (7 oz) celery

Bouquet garni (2 bay leaves, 3 sprigs thyme, 20 parsley stems)

2 cloves

Tied in cheesecloth: 1tsp pepper-corns,

1 tsp coriander seeds Salt

Fish Aspic

Introduction

Fish aspic is made from a rich fish stock made preferably with the bones of turbot, brill or sole along with fish trimmings and small whole fish so that the stock is very flavorful.

The fish stock must be thoroughly degreased.

The clarifying technique is similar to that used for meat and/or poultry aspics. The goal of clarifying is to obtain a crystal clear aspic. The clarifying ingredients include leek greens, and egg whites, with the meat replaced by lean fish flesh (whiting is a good choice). The aromatics and flavorings may be adapted so the flavors correspond with the final dish.

After clarifying the fish stock, pass it through a fine conical sieve. Check the consistency (pour a little aspic on a plate to see how well it sets). Taste and add seasoning if necessary.

Uses

The fish aspic may be used for glazing cold seafood dishes, decorated fish in aspic and chaud-froid preparations.

Ingredients

Main Ingredients

5 kg (11 lbs) fish (trimmings, bones and heads, preferably flat fish) 50 g (1 1/2 oz) clarified butter

Aromatics and Seasonings

200 g (7 oz) onions 200 g (7 oz) shallots 300 g (10 oz) leeks 250 g (8 oz) mushrooms 150 (5 oz) fennel

Bouquet garni (1 bay leaf, 3 sprigs thyme, 20 parsley stems) 1 small bunch chervil

6 g (1 tsp) coarse salt per liter(qt) liquid Black pepper

Liquid Ingredients

1 L (1 qt) dry white wine 10 L (about 11 qts) light fish stock

Procedure

Making the Stock

The first step is to make a full-flavored fish stock. Rinse the bones in cold water. Peel and wash the vegetables and cut in small dice.

Melt the clarified butter over medium heat, add the vegetables and cook without browning.

Add the fish, cover and cook over low heat about 10 minutes. Pour in the wine and bring to a simmer to eliminate the acidity of the wine.

Pour in the fish stock, add the bouquet garni, chervil and salt, bring to a simmer. Skim all impurities that come to the surface.

Continue to simmer 30-40 minutes, skimming frequently.

Pass the stock through a large colander.

Clarifying the Stock

Clarifying Ingredients: for 20 liters (about 21 qts) stock

1 kg (2 lbs) whiting flesh 300 g (10 oz) leek greens 100 g (3 1/2 oz) shallots 30 g (1 oz) celery 100 g (3 1/2 oz) mushrooms 100 g (3 1/2 oz) carrots Bouquet garni 1 bunch chervil 1 L (1 qt) egg whites

Mix these ingredients with the egg whites, adding a little stock if necessary to loosen the mixture. Pour this mixture into the stock. Add the bouquet garni.

Bring slowly to a simmer, stirring gently to prevent the egg whites from settling to the bottom of the stockpot.

When the stock comes to a simmer, stop stirring to allow the egg whites to coagulate and bring the impurities to the surface.

Strain the aspic through cheesecloth or a fine conical strainer.

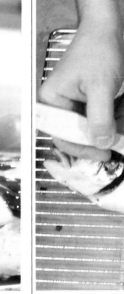

Court Bouillons

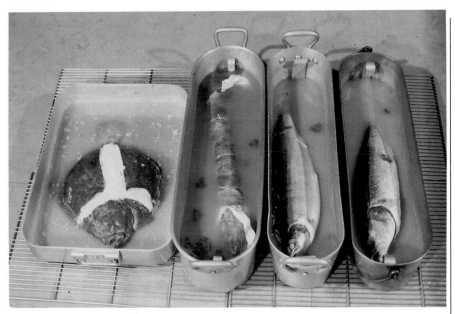

Ingredients

Court Bouillon with Vinager

10 L(about 11 qts) water
2.5 dl (1 cup) white wine vinegar
150 g (5 oz) salt
Bouquet garni (10 parsley stems,
    2 bay leaves, 3 thyme sprigs)
400 g (14oz) onions
400 g (14 oz) carrots
200 g (7oz) celery
1 Tbl black peppercorns

Court Bouillon with White Wine

10 L (about 11 qts) water
120 g (scant 4oz) salt
Bouquet garni (10 parsley stems,
    2 bay leaves, 3 sprigs thyme)
200 g (7 oz) onions
300 g (10 oz) carrots
100 g (3 1/2 oz) celery
200g (7oz) tomatoes
150 g (5 oz) leek
5 unpeeled garlic cloves
1 Tbl black peppercorns
1/2 lemon

Introduction

The term " court bouillon " or
" quick stock " denotes a cooking liquid made with water to which is
added of an acidic liquid (dry white
wine, vinegar, lemon juice) which is
flavored with aromatic vegetables.

Uses

Courts bouillons are used to poach
fish and to cook shellfish.

The type and quantity of vegetable
may vary depending on the type of
fish to be poached.

The choice of wine, vinager or
lemon juice also affects the flavor.

When poaching fish, the court
bouillon should be cold at the beginning and brought gradually to a simmer, whereas when cooking shellfish,
the court bouillon is brought to a boil
before the shellfish are added.

Poaching or cooking time depends
on the size and texture of the fish or
shellfish.

Procedure

Making a court bouillon is very
easy.

Cut the vegetables into small
pieces and combine with the liquid
ingredients. Add the salt and pepper
and bouquet garni.

Bring to a boil, then lower the heat
and simmer gently so that the vegetables release their flavor and the liquid does not reduce too much.

Cover and leave to simmer for
about one hour.

Strain and cool.

Court Bouillon with White Wine

10 L (about 11 qts) water
1 L (1 qt) dry white wine
150 g (5 oz) salt
Bouquet garni
(10 parsley stems, 2 bay leaves,
3 sprigs thyme)
400 g (14 oz) onion
400 g (14 oz) carrots
200 g (7 oz) celery
1 Tbl black peppercorns
1/2 lemon

Court Bouillon for Shellfish

10 L (about 11 qts) water
120 g (scant 4 oz) salt
Bouquet garni
(10 parsley stems, 2 bay leaves,
3 sprigs thyme)
200 g (7 oz) onions
300 g (10 oz) carrots
100 g (3 1/2 oz) celery
200 g (7 oz) tomatoes
150 g (5 oz) leeks
5 unpeeled garlic cloves
1 tbl black peppercorns
1 lemon cut in slices

" Nages "

This preparation is generally used to poach small pieces of fish, fish filets, scallops or crayfish.

The name comes from the French " nager " (to swim) because the cooked seafood is sometimes served " swimming " in this clear, light liquid. In other cases the liquid is thickened with roux or cream to make a sauce (sauce Normande, for example).

For certain dishes, featuring smoked fish for example, fish filets can be poached in milk with salt and pepper added.

Ingredients

20 g (2/3 oz) clarified butter
30 g (1oz) shallots
30 g (1 oz) mushrooms
Bouquet garni (3 parsley stems,
    1 sprig thyme,
1/4 bay leaf
5 cl (1/4 cup) dry white wine
5 cl (1/4 cup) dry white vermouth
1/4 L (1 cup) fish stock

Procedure

Cut the shallots and mushrooms into small dice.
Combine all the ingredients and bring to a boil.
Cover and simmer about 15 minutes.
Cool before poaching fish in the " nage ".

Consommés

Consommés may be made with meat or poultry stocks as well as fish or shellfish stocks.

Consommés are usually served as a soup and can be served hot or cold.

They can be garnished with many different ingredients which show through the crystal clear liquid. In classic French cooking the name of each consommé indicates what the garnish is.

Occasionally, a consommé will be used as a cooking liquid. In this case it should not be too strong. It can also be used to thin out a sauce and contribute a wonderful flavor.

Since consommés are expensive and lengthy to prepare, they are not as popular as they once were. This is unfortunate, because a properly prepared consommé is delicious.

Introduction

Consommés are made from rich, full-flavored stocks which are clarified resulting in a clear broth with a refined taste.

They are clarified using the same techniques as aspics but the ingredients usually include an even higher percentage of meats which contribute a deep, rich flavor.

Chapter 3

Sauces

There are many different sauces, each with a distinct taste and texture.

The great number of sauces in French cuisine can be grouped into "families"-basic sauces and their derivatives.

Whether hot or cold, the principle role of the sauce is to accompany and augment another food (fish, meat, poultry, eggs, vegetables, salad). They can also serve as an enrichment and binder in some preparations, such as a meat glaze blended into a forcemeat.

The sauces can be thick or thin, depending on the final use. To hold the elements of a dish, as in a "bouchée", the sauce must be thick enough to not spill out of the pastry shell. Sauces used to nap a plain piece of meat should be a light coating consistency.

Sauces can be thickened in different ways. Very refined sauces can be made by simply reducing a gelatin-rich stock or rich cream and concentrating the texture and flavor.

Many different methods are available to the chef for achieving just the thickness and texture needed for a particular dish. Often the final result is a combination of one or more techniques (as in a reduced sauce ""mounted" with butter or a roux-based sauce enriched with cream).

The 144 Basic Sauces

Classic French cuisine centers around a very strong tradition of sauces. There are basic sauces and countless variations.

Denis Ruffel presents the basic sauces grouped in families with derivatives personalized for his original dishes.

Liasons

Reductions

Roux: white, blond and brown

Beurre Manié, Cornstarch, Cream

Arrowroot, Blood, Butter

White Sauce, Parmesan Sauce, Cream Sauce

Bechamel, Soubise, Mornay, Parmesan, Sabayon à la crème, Cream Sauce with Truffles

Fish Sauces

Américaine, Normande, Beurre Blanc, Nantua, Mussels with Curry, Chervil Cream, Lime Cream, Chive Cream, Sauce for Seafood and Sole Bouchées, Safran Cream with Chives, Dugléré, Fish velouté, Bretonne and derivatives (Shrimp Sauce, Orange and Safran, Bâtarde, Joinville)

Sauces for Meat and Poultry

Sauce for Bouchées with Mushrooms and "à la Reine", Raspberry Vinegar, Sherry, Poivrade, Seasoned cream, Suprême, Périgueux, Financière, Basic Brown Sauce, Aurore, Ivoire, Poulette, Bordelaise, Bercy, Madeira, Port, Piquante, Sweet and Sour, Pineapple gastrique, Chasseur, Diable, Bigarrade, Charcutière, Grand Veneur, Matelote, Marrow

Cold Emulsified Sauces

Basic Mayonnaise, Mayonnaise with: Herbs, Safran, Tarragon, Tomato, Curry, Cocktail, Andalouse, Curry and Anchovy, Chantilly, Green Sauce, Italienne, Tartar, Aïoli, Rouille, Zucchini Mousse

Presented by Denis Ruffel

Hot Emulsified Sauces

Hollandaise, Bearnaise, Chantilly, Maltaise, Mikado, Mustard, Paloise, Tyrolienne, Choron, Foyot

Quiche Custards

Roquefort, Seafood with Saffron, Lorraine, Julieene of Vegetables, Endive, " Trianon ", Leek Flamiche, Asparagus and Frogs' Legs, Mussel and Pesto, Mushroom, Cheese

Chaud-froid Sauces

Poultry Chaud-froid, Fish, Herb, Curry, Paprika, Périgueux, Ketchup, Duck à l'orange

Vinaigrettes

Dressing with Soy Sauce and Ginger, Dressings for Mixed Salads: Meli-Melo, Cinderella, Exotic, Brazilian, Taboulé, Shellfish, Haddock, Pasta with Seafood, Chicken and Sweetbreads, Gourmande, Landaise, Country Beef Salad, Chive vinaigrette, Ravigote

Compound Butters, Mousses, Cream-based Spreads and Sauces

Maître d'hôtel, Shallot, Tarragon, Horseradish, Bercy, Marchand de Vin, Seasoned Butter, 21 Seasoned Butters and Mousses for Coating Canapés

Other Sauces

Tomato, Pizza, Cumberland

Marinades

Reductions and "Liaison" Sauces

Introduction

Stocks are a basic ingredient for many sauces-therefore a specific stock, such as those made with rabbit, pheasant, fish, or sweetbreads, can be used to personalize the sauce. These stocks should always be made following the classic guidelines to ensure a good taste.

Wine is often added as a stock reduces to add a rich flavor and color.

The aromatic seasonings can be varied to achieve the desired taste and should be added in precise amounts.

The ingredients-meats, vegetables, cream, eggs, wines, etc. should always be of the best quality to ensure a good tasting sauce.

The " new style " of cooking in recent years has inspired chefs to create light, quickly-made sauces that are often a simple reduction of cooking juices mounted with butter. For restaurant dishes, these delicate sauces are very successful.

For the caterer, however, dishes are usually made in advance and reheated and such fragile sauces would not hold up.

The sauce chef holds a very important position in the French kitchen, as the making of sauces takes skill and careful attention to detail.

" Liaison " Sauces

Sauces that are served hot can be grouped into two categories according to thickness:

" *Napping* " *sauces;* sauces with a light coating consistency, used to accompany foods.

" *Liason* " *sauces;* thicker sauces used to hold the elements of a dish together.

These " liason " sauces are usually thickened with a flour based roux or other starch because the dishes they are used in are very often reheated just before serving (" bouchées à la reine " and other dishes served in a pastry casing).

Not only can flour be used in varying amounts to give the sauce a thin, medium or thick consistency, but the sauce is very stable when reheated.

On the other end of the scale, are sauces made by reduction.

The consistency of these sauces depends on the amount of natural gelatin (from bones) in the stock that is reduced.

These " napping " sauces thicken slightly as the moisture is eliminated through evaporation over a low steady heat. The sauce is constantly skimmed of impurities to ensure a good taste. The reduction can be served " nature " or enriched with cream, butter or egg yolks or thickened with a little roux.

Arrowroot

Arrowroot is a powdery starch wich comes from a tuber grown in tropical regions (Madagscar, Antilles).

It is very easy to use. First dissolve in a cold liquid (stock or water) then whisk into a boiling liquid (stock, milk etc.) which thickens immediately.

Arrowroot is very digestible and the taste is neutral.

Use about 10 g (1/2 oz) per liter (quart) of stock.

Blood

A few sauces are thickened with blood (pork or hare).

Blood adds color, texture as well as a rich flavor.

It must be used only in very hygenic conditions.

Blood is a fragile liason. It should be warmed with a little hot sauce then whisked in over a gentle heat. The sauce should be stirred while the blood cooks and thickens but the suace must never boil which would cause the blood to separate.

Mounting with Butter

" Fresh " butter (not melted or clarified) can be added to a sauce in small pieces just before the sauce is serve.

The butter is absorbed into the sauce, giving it a richer, velvety texture. The fat as well as the milk solids play a role in adding texture.

The cold butter is added in small pieces and is gently incorporated by moving the pot back and forth over moderate heat.

The sauce must not boil after the butter is added.

Reductions

In the chapter on stocks, we discussed the role of reduction in developing the taste, texture and color. This process is of prime importance in the making of sauces.

A good tasting sauce is the combination of carefully controlled reduction with just the right amount of flavoring and liason.

Among the most refined sauces are reductions of a gelatin rich cooking liquid or stock with no addition of starch (roux, beurre manié, cornstarch) to thicken.

The texture in these full-flavored sauces comes from the concentration of the natural gelatin imparted from the bones when the stock was made. Veal knuckles and pork rind are rich in gelatin as are the bones of flat fish (turbot, sole, brill).

A reduction sauce does not reheat as successfully as thicker sauces and is impractical to make in on-site kitchens so are rarely used by caterers.

Roux

There are three kinds of roux:
- Brown roux
- Blond roux
- White roux

They are very different in taste and color but they are used in a similar way to thicken sauces.

It is very practical to prepare roux in a large quantity and have it on hand to make sauces. Brown roux, which cooks for a long time, must be made in advance whereas blond and white roux can be made quickly to order.

Roux is made from equal parts butter and flour. 500 g (1 lb) of each ingredient is a manageable amount. A more compact roux can be made with a little extra flour.

Brown Roux

500 g (1 lb) clarified butter
500 g (1 lb) flour

As its name indicates, brown roux is cooked to a dark brown. The butter is clarified so that it doesn't burn.

The color comes from the flour which darkens during the long cooking process.

The roux is cooked over medium heat until it takes on a chocolate color. The heat expands the particles of flour so that they are ready to absorb the liquid when added to the suace.

Brown roux has a stong taste and is only used in brown suases such as Espagnole. It is rarely used in today's cooking.

Blond Roux

500 g (1 lb) butter
500 g (1 lb) flour

The method for making blond roux is the same but the cooking time is shorter.

The butter does not have to be clarified because this roux cooks at a lower temperature.

Blend the butter and flour together over low heat and cook intil it becomes golden blond. This roux is used more than the others for thickening sauces. It can be made in sizeable batches and kept on hand (refrigerated) as part of the kitchen's "mise en place". This is the roux referred to in the recipes in this series.

White Roux

500 g (1 lb) butter
500 g (1 lb) flour

This roux is cooked only long enough to eliminate the taste of raw flour and should remain white for thickening cream and milk-based white sauces.

Beurre Manié

500 g (1 lb) butter
500 g (1 lb) flour

Beurre manié, which means "kneaded butter" is an uncooked roux.

Although it is quickly prepared and easy to use, it is not recommended for most sauces because the final product lacks shine and often has a taste of raw flour.

Blend softened butter with flour to a smooth paste and store for short periods of time in the refrigerator.

Starch

Cornstarch and potato starch are rarely used in French sauces because the sauces are a dull color and lack shine and taste.

They can be used in conjunction with other liasons to make a flavorful sauce (Parmesan sauce for example). The amount of starch used should be carefully measured.

Cream

Heavy cream and "crème fraîche" can be used to give texture to sauces.

Heavy cream, similar to the French "crème fleurette" is more liquid and has a lighter flavor than crème fraîche. It can be reduced to concentrate its unctuous qualities or used "straight" to add a little richness to a sauce.

Crème fraîche, which is not a common ingredient outside of France, is a thicker cream with a slight acidic taste that is not appropriate for all sauces. Due to a lower water content, it thickens quickly when reduced.

Heavy cream performs well in most recipes that call for crème fraîche.

Bechamel, Parmesan Sauce, Cream Sauce

These three sauces are grouped together because of their white color.

Milk or cream is the basic ingredient for these sauces.

Bechamel is a classic sauce made with milk and thickened with roux. It is the base for many derivative sauces.

Mornay sauce, for example, is bechamel with a liaison of egg yolks and cream, and flavored with grated cheese.

Soubise sauce is another derivative of bechamel with a puree of onions that cooks with the sauce and the milk is perfumed with a bouquet garni. The soubise can be cooked in the oven, much like bechamel was many years ago.

This is most often used to lightly coat a dish as in Veal Orloff.

Parmesan sauce is very useful in the caterer's kitchen. It is made like a pastry cream, i.e. a mixture of eggs with starch is whisked into hot milk and grated cheese and cream are added to the sauce at the end.

This thick preparation is often used as a " liason " sauce to hold together a mixture of ingredients in a pastry shell or is used " as is " to fill " gougères ", puff pastry " roulades " and small pastry hors d'œuvres. Since it holds up well when reheated, it is ideal for these dishes.

Cream sauce, is as its name implies a sauce based on a reduction of heavy cream or crème fraîche and is often enriched with butter at the end of cooking.

The cream can be reduced with a reduced stock or demi-glaze that will give it a flavor to go with a specific dish (fish demi-glaze to with fish dishes etc.). This works well for dishes that will be browned under the broiler.

This is a versatile group of sauces that are used to accompany a variety of dishes.

Recipes: Bechamel Sauce, Parmesan Sauce, Cream Sauce

Bechamel Sauce

Roux (60 g (2 oz) butter + 60 g (2 oz) flour)
3/4 L (3 cups) milk
Liaison (3 egg yolks + 8 cl (1/3 cup) cream)
Salt, pepper, nutmeg

Procedure: Volume 2, page 97.

Mornay Sauce

125 g (4 oz) butter
125 g (4 oz) flour
1.5 L (1.5 qt) milk
Salt, pepper, nutmeg
250 g (1/2 lb) grated cheese
Procedure: Volume 3, page 130.

Soubise Sauce

This sauce is a derivative of becha-mel, used primarily to lightly coat or glaze (Veal Orloff for example). It is the consistency of slightly thick " coulis " (purée).

750 g (1.5 lbs) onions
100 g (3 1/2oz) clarified butter
50 g (1 1/2 oz) butter
50 g (1 1/2 oz) flour
1 L (1 qt) milk
Salt, pepper, nutmeg
6 egg yolks
4 tbls cream

Peel the onions, cut into small dice and blanch in boiling water.
Drain, cool and press on the on-ions to extract the maximum amount of water.
Make the roux; stir in the milk, then the onions.
Stir the sauce carefully so it does not scorch and stick to the bottom.
Pass the sauce through a conical sieve.
Whisk the egg yolks over a low heat in a heavy-bottomed saucepan or over a water bath until they are thick and foamy.
Incorporate the mounted yolks into the sauce. Do not allow the sauce to boil after the eggs are added.

Parmesan Sauce

1 L (1 qt) milk
130 g (4 oz) butter
100 g (3.5 oz) cornstarch
4 eggs
250 g (1/2 lb) grated cheese
Salt, pepper

Procedure: Volume 3, p. 133

Cream Sauce with Truffles

3 dl (1 1/3 cups) heavy cream
30 g (1 oz) butter
20 g (3/4 oz) truffles
Salt, pepper, nutmeg

Procedure: Volume 3, p. 159

Sabayon Cream Sauce

4 dl (1 1/4 cups) fish stock
4 dl (1 1/4 cups) heavy cream
Roux
5 egg yolks + water (sabayon)
Salt, pepper
25 g (scant 1 oz) truffles (optional)

Procedure: Volume 3, p. 42

Fish Sauces

Fish sauces are specifically made to accompany fish and shellfish dishes. They can be made with different consistencies to go with poached or baked fish, or to hold together a seafood filling in a pastry shell.

Fish sauces are as varied as the fish they are served with. For example, personalized fish stocks can be made with a single fish or shellfish to give a specific flavor to the sauce for a special dish. The aromatics and seasonings can also vary (curry or saffron for example) to make a stock with a distinct flavor.

The seasonings however, should not be too strong, because fish sauces have a delicate taste.

Dry white wines as well as sherry and madeira can be added during the cooking process to add a delicious flavor.

Fish sauces are often light in texture, thickened with egg yolks and cream that enrich the sauce and gives it a thin coating consistency.

These fragile thickeners create sauces that must be reheated carefully over low heat. They must not boil once the egg yolks are added, as

the egg would curdle and the sauce would be ruined.

It is recommended to make these egg yolk enriched sauces at the last minute if possible. It is possible to make them in advance and keep them warm in a thermos bottle.

A simple and less fragile sauce can be made from a reduced fish stock with an addition of cream and butter.

There are two principle families of fish sauces -sauce Américaine and its derivatives, and sauce Normande and its derivatives. Fish stock is the main ingredient for both of these basic sauces.

Américaine Sauce

Américaine sauce is a very important basic sauce, made from shellfish. It may be used in an " Américaine " dish, e.g. lobster à l'Américaine, or as a flavoring element in complex preparations. When the sauce is to be used in this case, the carcasses from various shellfish can be used: lobsters, spiny lobsters, crayfish, crabs-either alone or mixed together.

Main Ingredients

6 kg (13 lbs) shellfish carcasses
2 dl (3/4 cup) olive oil

Aromatics and Seasonings

60 g (2 oz) clarified butter
250 g (1/2 lb) carrots
100 g (3 1/2 oz) shallots
100 g (3 1/2 oz) fennel
60 g (2 oz) garlic
200 g (7 oz) tomatoes
1 bouquet garni (10 parsley stems,
   1 sprig thyme, 1 bay leaf, 1 leek
   green)
1 small bunch chervil
1 small bunch tarragon
1 dl (1/2 cup) cognac
1.5 L (1 1/2 qts) dry white wine
6 L (6 qts) light fish stock
Salt, cayenne pepper
Tomato paste
Roux (optional)

Procedure

Roughly chop the shellfish carcasses.

Peel the carrots, onions, shallots and fennel and cut them into small dice.

Assemble the other seasonings and the liquid ingredients (garlic, tomatoes, bouquet garni, chervil, tarragon, cognac, white wine, fish stock).

Brown the chopped carcasses in olive oil, then drain.

Cook the diced vegetables in oil until soft but not brown.

Combine the browned carcasses and the vegetables.

Flame with the cognac.

Add the tomatoes, garlic, bouquet garni, chervil and tarragon.

Add the white wine and bring to a boil. Add the fish stock.

Season with salt and pepper, then add the tomato paste.

Bring to a boil.

Simmer the sauce for 1 - 1 1/2 hours, skimming carefully throughout the cooking.

Strain through a conical sieve.

The consistency of the sauce will vary depending on the use. If the sauce needs to be thick, bind it with some cooked roux.

The sauce may be enriched with cream or bound with a liaison of egg yolks and shellfish roe. These fragile liaisons should be added at the last minute.

Normande Sauce

45 g (1 1/2 oz) butter
45 g (1 1/2 oz) flour
1/2 L (2 cups) fish stock
1/4 L (1 cup) scallop stock
5 cl (1/4 cup) mushroom cooking liquid
3 egg yolks
1.5 L (1 1/2 qts) heavy cream
Salt, pepper
45 g (1 1/2 oz) butter

Procedure: Volume 3, pages 164-165.

" Beurre Blanc " (White Butter Sauce)

20 g (2/3 oz) clarified butter
80 g (2 1/2 oz) shallots (2)
5 cl (1/4 cup) dry white wine
5 cl (1/4 cup) wine vinegar
3 cl (2 tbsp) heavy cream
200 g (7 oz) cold butter

Procedure: Volume 1, page 135.

Curried Mussels Sauce

1/2 L (2 cups) unreduced mussel cooking liquid
Roux
2 dl (3/4 cup) heavy cream
30 g (1 oz) butter
Salt, curry powder

Procedure: Volume 1, page 143.

Nantua Sauce

2 dl (3/4 cup) " Américaine " sauce
4 dl (1 2/3 cups) fish stock
Roux (optional)
1.5 dl (2/3 cup) heavy cream
30 g (1 oz) crayfish butter
Salt, cayenne pepper
2 cl (4 tsp) cognac
20 crayfish

Procedure: Volume 3, page 53.

Chervil Sauce

20 g (2/3 oz) clarified butter
2 shallots
45 g (1 1/2 oz) mushrooms (stems
  and peelings)
10 sprigs chervil
7 cl (1/3 cup) dry white wine
7 cl (1/3 cup) dry vermouth
1/4 L (1 cup) fish stock
1/2 L (2 cups) heavy cream
Salt, pepper
60 g (2 oz) butter

Procedure: Volume 1, page 147.

Lime Cream Sauce

5 cl (1/4 cup), reduced to a glaze

1/4 L (1 cup) heavy cream
100 g (3 1/2 oz) butter
Salt, pepper

Procedure: Volume 1, page 151.

Chive Cream Sauce

20 g (2/3 oz) clarified butter
20 g (2/3 oz) shallots
30 g (1 oz) mushroom trimmings
10 chervil stems
8 cl (1/3 cup) dry white wine
8 cl (1/3 cup) dry vermounth
3 dl (1 1/4 cup) fish stock
5 dl (2 cups) heavy cream
Roux (optional)
45 g (1 1/2 oz) butter
Salt, pepper
10 sprigs chives, chopped

Procedure: Volume 3, page 52.

Saffron and Chive Cream Sauce

1/4 L (1 cup) mussel cooking
  liquid
2 dl (3/4 cup) heavy cream
45 g (1 1/2 oz) roux
8 sprigs chives
Salt, pepper, saffron

Procedure: Volume 3, pages 152-153.

Seafood Bouchée Sauce

1/2 L (2 cups) fish stock
2 dl (3/4 cup) scallop and monkfish
  poaching liquid
2 dl (3/4 cup) mussel cooking
  liquid
1 dl (1/2 cup) mushroom cooking
  liquid
Roux made from 100 g (3 1/2 oz)
  butter and 100 g (3 1/2 oz) flour
Liaison (4 egg yolks + 2 dl (3/4
  cups) heavy cream)
Salt and pepper

Procedure: Volume 3, page 147.

Filet of Sole Bouchée Sauce

1.5 dl (2/3 cup) fish stock
1.5 dl (2/3 cup) mushroom cooking
  liquid
1 dl (1/2 cup) reduced "Américaine" sauce
8 cl (1/3 cup) heavy cream
Roux made from 45 g (1 1/2 oz)
  butter + 45 g (1 1/2 oz) flour
1 cl (2 tsp) cognac
15 g (1/2 oz) shellfish butter
Salt, cayenne pepper

Procedure: Volume 3, page 149.

Dugléré Sauce

650 g (1 lb 5 oz) tomatoes
5 cl (1/4 cup) olive oil
45 g (1 1/2 oz) onions
45 g (1 1/2 oz) shallots
30 g (1 oz) garlic
1 bouquet garni (thyme, bay leaf,
  parsley stems, leek green)
1 dl (1/2 cup) fish stock
2 dl (3/4 cup) heavy cream
Salt, pepper

Procedure: Volume 3, pages 167-168.

Fish Velouté

This sauce is the basis for many
other fish sauces, notably Normande
sauce.

It is made by thickening a fish stock with a roux; the quantity of roux will vary depending on the desired thickness of the sauce.

Ingredients
1 L (1 qt) fish stock
Roux made with 45 g (1 1/2 oz) butter and 45 g (1 1/2 oz) flour

Procedure
Make a blond roux.

Add the fish stock to the roux over the heat.

Bring the sauce to a simmer and cook for 15-20 minutes, skimming frequently during cooking. Be sure to stir carefully so the sauce does not stick to the pan and scorch.

Strain the sauce through a conical sieve.

Cool the sauce quickly by stirring it with a spatula so the heat dissipates rapidly.

Bretonne Sauce

This sauce is most often served with poached fish.

45 g (1 1/2 oz) clarified butter
30 g (1 oz) leek (white part only)
30 g (1 oz) celery
30 g (1 oz) shallots
30 g (1 oz) mushrooms
5 cl (1/4 cup) dry white wine
3/4 L (3 cups) fish velouté sauce
1.5 dl (2/3 cup) cream
45 g (1 1/2 oz) butter

Procedure
Cut the vegetables into fine dice, then cook them in the clarified butter until soft but not brown.

Deglaze the pan with white wine.

Add the fish velouté.

Simmer for a few minutes, then add the cream.

Strain the sauce through a conical sieve, then mount it with the cold butter.

Shrimp Sauce

1 L (1 qt) fish stock
2 dl (3/4 cup) heavy cream
100 g (3 1/2 oz) shrimp butter

45 g (1 1/2 oz) tomato butter
Cayenne pepper

Add the cream to the fish velouté. Simmer for a few minutes. Strain the sauce through a conical sieve. Mount with the shrimp butter and the tomato butter. Taste and correct the seasoning; the sauce should be slightly spicy from the cayenne pepper.

Orange Saffron Sauce

1 L (1 qt) fresh orange juice
1.5 dl (2/3 cup) "Américaine" sauce
5 dl (2 cups) fish stock
1.5 dl (2/3 cup) heavy cream
30 g (1oz) butter
Salt, pepper, saffron

Reduce the orange juice to a glaze, then deglaze the reduction with the "Américaine" sauce. Reduce this mixture by half. Add the fish stock and reduce by one-third.

Bind with the roux, if a thicker sauce is desired. Add the cream and reduce slightly. Add a pinch of saffron, then taste and correct seasoning. Strain the sauce through a conical sieve, then mount with the butter.

"Bâtarde" Sauce
1 L (1 qt) fish velouté
6 egg yolks
2 dl (3/4 cup) heavy cream
45 g (1 1/2 oz) butter
1 teaspoon mustard
Few drops lemon juice
Salt, pepper
Chopped fresh herbs (flat parsley, chervil, chives, tarragon)

Bring the velouté to a boil. Whisk in a liaison of egg yolks and cream, taking care not to curdle the yolks. Strain through a conical sieve.

Mount the sauce with the butter and the mustard. Add the lemon juice and the chopped herbs. Taste and correct seasoning.

Joinville Sauce

1 L (1 qt) basic Normande sauce
45 g (1 1/2 oz) crayfish butter
45 g (1 1/2 oz) shrimp butter
Truffles (optional)

Make a classic Normande sauce (described in this chapter), but instead of mounting it with plain butter, mount it with the crayfish and shrimp butters.

Depending on its use, a julienne of truffles may be added to the sauce.

Sauces for Meat and Poultry

Here we discuss two families of sauces:

Sauces that accompany meat dishes (lamb, veal, beef, pork)

Sauces that accompany poultry (chicken, duck, pheasant)

The principle role of this diverse group of sauces is to highlight the taste of the meat or poultry with which it is served. This is best achieved by making the sauce with a stock that has a specific taste. For example the delicate taste of sweetbreads is reinforced by a sauce made with a reduction of sweetbread stock.

Wine is often added to these sauces. Since wine influences the taste, it must be chosen with the final dish in mind. Meat dishes may need the strong taste and dark color of a full-bodied red wine while a dry white wine adds a touch of acidity to a sauce for chicken.

The making of sauces involves several steps. The chef must pay close attention during each step, from the purchase of high quality ingredients to the final passing of the sauce. Among the procedures the sauce chef must master are the following:

- Combining the right amounts of various ingredients for a balanced taste.
- Reducing stocks
- Deglazing pan juices
- Making caramel

Note : The caramel used in making meat-based sauces can be made with sugar (as in duck à l'orange) or by reducing fruit syrup (as in ham with pineapple). The caramel is dissolved with vinegar which gives a nice touch of acidity to the sauce.

The techniques involved demand the skill of a trained chef. In France, the position of " saucier " in the great restaurants is always held by a chef with a great deal of experience.

This grouping of meat and poultry sauces is too vast to be classified here. A simple distinction is often made between white and brown sauces:

White sauces made from white veal or poultry stock, usually enriched with cream and butter.

Brown sauces made from brown veal stock or demi-glaze, examples include Périgueux, Madère and Chasseur.

" Bouchées à la Reine " Sauce

3/4 L (3 cups) light stock
1 dl (1/2 cup) reduced mushroom cooking liquid
1.5 dl (2/3 cup) reduced sweetbread braising liquid
Roux made with 75 g (2 1/2 oz) butter and 75 g (2 1/2 oz) flour

Procedure: Volume 3, page 137.

Raspberry Vinegar Sauce

6 cl (1/4 cup) raspberry vinegar
1/2 L (2 cups) demi-glaze
Roux (optional)
30 g (1 oz) butter

Procedure: Volume 1, page 155.

Sherry Sauce

4 dl (1 2/3 cup) sweetbreads braising liquid
Roux
2 dl (3/4 cup) cream
45 g (1 1/2 oz) butter
Salt, pepper
Few drops sherry

Procedure: Volume 1, page 157.

Poivrade Sauce

30 g (1oz) clarified butter
150 g (5 oz) carrots
120 g (4 oz) onions
1.5 dl (2/3 cup) wine vinegar
3 dl (1 1/4 cups) full-bodied red wine
8 parsley stems
1 branch thyme
1/2 bay leaf
Salt Demi-glaze
2 crushed black peppercorns
Roux (optional)
45 g (1 1/2 oz) butter

Procedure: Volume 2, pages 73-74.

Seasoned Whipped Cream

1 L (1 qt) heavy cream
Salt, pepper, paprika

Procedure: Volume 2, page 214.

Suprême Sauce

8 dl (3 1/3 cups) chicken stock
2.5 dl (1 cup) heavy cream
Roux (optional)
30 g (1 oz) butter
Salt, pepper

Procedure: Volume 3, page 53.

" Périgueux " Sauce

4 dl (1 2/3 cup) madeira
5 dl (2 cups) demi-glaze
15 g (1/2 oz) roux
5 cl (1/4 cup) truffle juice
20 g (2/3 oz) butter
Salt, pepper
30 g (1 oz) truffles

Procedure: Volume 3, page 53.

" Financière " Sauce

1 L (1 qt) demi-glaze
1.5 dl (2/3 cup) reduced mushroom cooking liquid
1.5 dl (2/3 cup) reduced sweetbread braising liquid
Roux made with 100 g (3 1/2 oz) butter and 100 g (3 1/2 oz) flour
5 cl (1/4 cup) truffle juice
15 g (1/2 oz) butter
Salt, pepper

Procedure: Volume 3, page 142.

Mushroom Bouchée Sauce

Roux made with 45 g (1 1/2 oz) butter and 45 g (1 1/2 oz) flour
4 dl (1 2/3 cup) mushroom cooking liquid
2 dl (3/4 light stock)
1 dl (1/2 cup) port
3 egg yolks
2 dl (3/4 cup) heavy cream
30 g (1 oz) parsley
Salt, pepper

Procedure: Volume 3, pages 144-145.

Brown Sauce

2 cl (4 tsp) white wine
5 cl (1/4 cup) madeira
4 dl (1 2/3 cup) demi-glaze
30 g (1 oz) butter
Salt, pepper

Procedure: Volume 3, page 155.

Pineapple Glaze

1 dl (1/2 cup) pineapple syrup
8 cl (1/3 cup) wine vinegar
2 dl (3/4 cup) white or red wine
1 L (1 qt) demi-glaze
Roux
Salt, pepper 10-15 g (1/3-12 oz) gelatin per liter (quart)

Procedure: Volume 1, page 224.

Ivoire Sauce

1 L (1 qt) suprême sauce
1-3 tbsp meat glaze made from white veal stock

Gently heat the meat glaze to melt it and add it to the suprême sauce. The meat glaze will give the sauce an ivory color and a deeper flavor.

Poulette Sauce

1 L (1 qt) suprême sauce
1 dl (1/2 cup) mushroom cooking liquid
1 egg yolk
Few drops lemon juice 2-3 tbsp chopped parsley

Add the mushroom cooking liquid to the suprême sauce, then add the egg yolk liaison and the lemon juice and chopped parsley.

Poulette sauce is served with poached poultry, but also with veal poached in a light veal stock.

Bordelaise Sauce

30 g (1 oz) clarified butter
60 g (2 oz) shallots
4 dl (1 2/3 cups) red wine
20 g (2/3 oz) crushed black peppercorns
2 sprigs thyme – 1/2 bay leaf
5 dl (2 cups) rich demi-glaze
Roux (optional)
Salt
45 g (1 1/2 oz) butter

Chop the shallots finely and cook them in the clarified butter until soft but not brown. Deglaze with the red wine. Add the crushed pepper, the thyme, the bay leaf and reduce the mixture by half.

Add the demi-glaze and reduce by one-third. Add some roux if a thicker sauce is desired. Strain through a conical sieve and mount with the butter.

Bordelaise sauce is served with grilled or sautéed beef.

Bercy Sauce

30 g (1 oz) clarified butter
60 g (2 oz) shallots
2.5 dl (1 cup) dry white wine
5 dl (2 cups) demi-glaze
2 tbsp meat glaze
100 g (3 1/2 oz) butter
2 tbsp chopped parsley

Chop the shallots finely and cook them in the clarified butter until soft but not brown. Add the white wine and the demi-glaze. Reduce by one-third. Add the meat glaze and bring the sauce to a boil. Mount with butter then add the chopped parsley.

The Bercy sauce is served with many beef preparations.

Madeira Sauce

4 dl (1 2/3 cup) madeira
1 L (1 qt) demi-glaze
Roux (optional)
45 g (1 1/2 oz) butter
Mushrooms (optional)

Reduce the madeira by half. Add the demi-glaze and reduce by one-third. If a thicker sauce is desired, add a little roux. Strain the sauce through a conical sieve and mount it with butter. If desired, add the mushrooms that have been diced and cooked.

Madeira sauce is served with many meat dishes, especially beef, pork and variety meats.

Port Sauce is made by replacing madeira with port in the previous recipe. The procedure is the same.

Piquante Sauce

30 g (1 oz) clarified butter
60 g (2 oz) chopped shallots
2 dl (3/4 cup) dry white wine
2 dl (3/4 cup) wine vinegar
7.5 dl (3 cups) demi-glaze
Cooked roux (optional)
40 g (1 1/4 oz) butter
3 tbls chopped cornichons (tart pickles)
Parsley, chervil, tarragon, chopped

Cook the chopped shallots in the butter until soft but not brown. Deglaze with wine and vinegar. Reduce by half. Add the demi-glaze and reduce. Whisk in roux if necessary. Pass through a fine conical sieve before mounting with butter and adding the pickles and herbs.

Piquante sauce is served with beef, pork and certain offal dishes.

Pineapple " Gastrique "

2 dl (3/4 cup) pineapple syrup
5 cl (1/4 cup) wine vinegar
1.5 dl (2/3 cup) dry white wine
1 1/4 L (5 cups) demi-glaze
Roux
Salt, pepper
10-15 g (1/3-1/2 oz) gelatin per liter (quart)

Procedure: Volume 4, page 27.

Sweet and Sour Sauce

100 g (3.5 oz) sugar
5 cl (1/4 cup) wine vinegar
4 strips of orange zest
80 coriander seeds
3 dl (1.5 cups) dry white wine
2 L (2 qts) demi-glaze
Cooked roux
10-15 g (1/3-1/2 oz) gelatin per liter (quart)

Procedure: Volume 4, p.

Chasseur Sauce

45 g (1 1/2 oz) clarified butter
50 g (1 3/4 oz) shallots, finely chopped

150 g (5 oz) mushrooms, finely chopped
2.5 dl (1 1/4 cups) dry white wine
2.5 dl (1 1/4 cups) tomato sauce
5 dl (2 1/2 cups) demi-glaze
Cooked roux (optional)
100 g (3 1/2 oz) butter
1 tbsp chopped chervil
1/2 tbsp chopped tarragon
Salt, pepper

In a skillet, combine the butter, shallots and mushrooms over medium heat. Cook until soft; do not color.

Deglaze with the wine and cook until reduced by half. Add the tomato sauce and demi-glaze and bring to a boil. Boil for several minutes.

Skim any impurities and strain. Whisk in the butter, bit by bit, until thoroughly incorporated.

Add the chervil and tarragon.

This sauce may be served with meat dishes (beef, veal, poultry and certain offal).

Diable Sauce

40 g (1 1/2 oz) clarified butter
100 g (3 1/2 oz) shallots, finely chopped
2 dl (3/4 cup) dry white wine
2 dl (3/4 cup) wine vinegar
6.5 dl (3 1/4 cups) demi-glaze
Cooked roux (optional)
Salt, cayenne pepper

In a skillet, combine the butter and shallots over medium heat. Cook until soft; do not color. Deglaze with the wine and vinegar and cook until reduced by two-thirds.

Add the demi-glaze, bring to a boil and cook to reduce slightly.

Strain and taste for seasoning.

Diable is French for devil, and this highly flavorful sauce gets its punch from the vinegar reduction and cayenne pepper. It is delicious when served with grilled poultry.

Bigarrade Sauce

40 g (1 1/2 oz) sugar
3 cl (2 tbsp) vinegar
Juice of 3 oranges – Juice of 1/2 lemon
7.5 dl (3 cups) well-reduced duck stock

Cooked roux (optional)
Zest of 1 orange, julienned and blanched – Zest of 1/2 lemon, julienned and blanched

In a saucepan, combine the sugar and vinegar and cook to the caramel stage. Deglaze with the orange and lemon juice and cook until reduced by three-quarters. – Add the stock and bring to a boil. Boil for several minutes, and strain.

Add the julienned citrus zests.

This is the classic sauce served with Duck à l'Orange, but it may also be served with pork dishes.

Charcutière Sauce

40 g (1/2 oz) clarified butter
80 g (3 oz) onions, finely chopped
3 dl (1 1/2 cups) dry white wine
7.5 dl (3 3/4 cups) demi-glaze
Cooked roux (optional)
1 tbsp – Dijon-style mustard
100 g (3 1/2 oz) cornichon pickles, julienned – Salt, pepper

In a skillet, combine the butter and onions over medium heat. Cook until soft; do not color.

Deglaze with the wine and cook until reduced by two-thirds.

Add the demi-glaze and cook until slightly reduced. Add roux if necessary.

Strain. Off the heat, whisk in the mustard (do not boil after this point).

Taste for seasoning.

Add the pickles.

This sauce is delicious when served with grilled or pan-fried pork.

Grand Veneur Sauce

40 g (1 1/2 oz) clarified butter
250-300 g (8-10 oz) assorted aromatic vegetables, finely chopped (for example, from the marinade of the meat to be served; drain thoroughly)
1.5 L (6 cups) wine from the marinade – 1.4 L (5 cups) game stock
Cooked roux (optional)
2 dl (3/4 cup) hare blood

In a skillet, combine the butter and aromatic vegetables over medium heat. Cook until lightly colored.

Deglaze with the wine and cook until reduced by two-thirds.

Add the stock, bring to a boil, and reduce slightly.

Off the heat, slowly whisk in the blood.

Taste for seasoning and strain through a fine-mesh sieve.

This flavorful sauce is delicious with marinated game.

If hare blood is unavailable, pork blood may be substituted but the flavor will not be the same.

Once the blood is added, the sauce should not boil or it will separate. The blood acts as a binding agent for the sauce, but it only works if the heat is gentle and constant.

Matelote Sauce

20 g (3/4 oz) clarified butter
40 g (1 1/2 oz) shallots, finely chopped
40 g (1 1/2 oz) mushrooms, finely chopped
1 sprig of thyme
1/2 bay leaf 10 black peppercorns, coarsely crushed
3 dl (1 1/2 cups) red wine
4 dl (1 2/3 cups) fish stock (or red wine)
5 dl (2 1/4 cups) demi-glaze Cooked roux (optional)
40 g (1 1/2 oz) bittersweet chocolate, finely chopped (optional)

In a saucepan, combine the butter, shallots and mushrooms over medium heat. Cook until soft; do not color.

Deglaze with the wine. Add the thyme, bay leaf and pepper. Cook until reduced by three-quarters.

Add the stock and cook until reduced by half.

Add the demi-glaze, bring to a boil and boil for several minutes. Stir in the chocolate, if using.

Matelote is also the name of a fish stew, based on this sauce. It may also be served with simple poached fish.

The chocolate adds color, helps to bind the sauce and adds a delicate flavor.

Sauce à la Moelle

1 L (4 cups) Bordelaise sauce
1 tbsp finely chopped flat-leaf parsley
150 g (5 oz) bone marrow

Prepare the Bordelaise sauce, but omit the butter.

Stir in the parsley.

Finely chop the marrow and poach in a light consommé (or white stock, or salted water). Add to the sauce.

Sauce à la Moelle may be used interchangeably with Bordelaise Sauce.

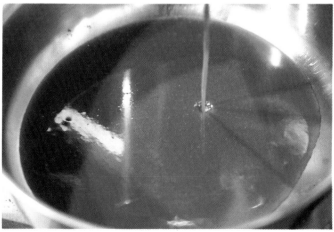

Cold Emulsified Sauces

Emulsified sauces are made by holding the elements in suspension and blending to create a homogenized mixture.

The basic ingredients are divided into two groups:

Fatty element (oil for cold emulsions, egg yolk)

Watery element (includes all liquids)

An emulsion occurs when these two elements are held together by an emulsifier, which in these sauces is the lecithin in the egg yolk. The fat molecules are broken apart and bound together combined with liquid molecules.

Mayonnaise is the best example of a cold emulsified sauce and many derivitives can be made using mayonnaise as a base.

Procedure for Making Mayonnaise

Making mayonnaise is simple if you follow a few important guidelines:

• Use fresh egg yolks.

• Use a perfectly clean bowl and whisk.

• Bring all the ingredients to the same temperature.

Once the mayonnaise is made it should not undergo a drastic change in temperature which would cause the ingredients to separate.

In a large bowl, place the egg yolk(s) with an equal amount of mustard. Turning the whisk in one direction, pour the oil in a thin stream. Whisk constantly as the emulsion " takes ", once the mixture looks a little thick and creamy, whisk in the oil more quickly.

Note: The sauce becomes thicker as more oil is added. The yolk will absorb about 1 cup of oil.

Season to taste with salt and pepper. The mayonnaise will be more stable (will not separate with a change of temperature) by whisking in a little hot vinegar at the end.

Basic mayonnaise can be flavored with a myriad of aromatic seasonings.

Examples:

Green Sauce: mayonnaise + cream + chopped herbs

Chantilly Sauce: mayonnaise + whipped cream

Mayonnaise has many uses: as an ingredient in other sauces, as a glaze when blended with aspic (chaud-froid), as a spread, and binding ingredient.

Herb, Saffron, Tarragon, Tomato and Curry Mayonnaise Sauces are made from a classic mayonnaise to which the different flavorings, herbs and spices are added.

Cocktail Sauce

150 g (5 oz) mayonnaise
Dash of vodka
2 dl (3/4 cup) ketchup
Salt
Pinch of cayenne pepper

Procedure: Volume 3, page 261.

Andalouse Sauce

1/2 L (2 cups) mayonnaise
8 cl (1/3 cup) ketchup
3 cl (2 tbsp) vodka
2 dl (3/4 cup) whipped cream
10 g (1/2 oz) cooked red bell pépper, cut in fine dice
50 g (1 3/4 oz) salmon eggs
Salt, cayenne pepper

Procedure: Volume 2, page 185.

Curry and Anchovy Sauce

3 cl (2 tbsp) olive oil
8 anchovy fillets
4 lemon slices (rounds)
2 tsps curry powder

Procedure: Volume 2, pages 192-193.

Chantilly Sauce

1/2 L (2 cups) mayonnaise
Few drops lemon juice
2 dl (3/4 cup) whipped cream
Salt, cayenne pepper

Make a very thick mayonnaise, using lemon juice instead of vinegar. At the last minute, add the stiffly whipped cream, incorporating it carefully so the mixture is smooth but maintains its volume. Taste and correct seasoning.

This sauce is very versatile; it is a good accompaniment to cold fish, mixed vegetables, and egg dishes.

Green Sauce

1/2 L (2 cups) mayonnaise
Few drops lemon juice
2 dl (3/4 cup) whipped cream
Salt, cayenne pepper
1 tbsp finely chopped chervil
1/2 tbsp finely chopped tarragon
1tbsp finely chopped chives

Follow the steps for Chantilly Sauce, adding the herbs at the end.

Italian Sauce

125 g (4 oz) calves' brain (or beef or lamb)
1 L (4 cups) lemon mayonnaise
2 tbsp finely chopped parsley

Poach the calves' brain; drain and dry thoroughly. Force through a fine-mesh sieve. Add the mayonnaise to the brain puree in batches, blending thoroughly between each addition. Adjust seasoning and add parsley.

Italian sauce is best when served with cold meats.

Tartar Sauce

6 hard-boiled egg yolks
1 L (4 cups) oil
1 cl (2 tsp) vinegar
1 tsp Dijon-style mustard
80 g (30 z) onions, finely chopped
60 g (20 z) cornichon pickles, finely chopped
30 g (1 oz) small capers (optional)
3 hard-boiled egg whites
2 tbsp assorted finely chopped herbs (parsley, chervil, chives)
Salt, pepper

Crush the egg yolks. Slowly pour in the oil, stirring constantly, until thoroughly blended. Stir in the vinegar and mustard. Add the onions and pickles, and capers if using. Force the egg whites through a fine-mesh sieve and add to the sauce. Stir in the herbs.

Tartar sauce may be served with meat, poultry and seafood dishes, and it is also suitable for beignets.

Aïoli Sauce

60 g (2 oz) garlic
50 g (1 1/2 oz) boiled potatoes, peeled (optional)
3 egg yolks
5 dl (2 1/2 cups) olive oil
Few drops lemon juice
Salt, pepper

If necessary, degerm the garlic (this facilitates digestion). In a mortar, grind to a fine paste. Add the potato if using and blend thoroughly. Stir in the egg yolks and season. Slowly pour in the oil, stirring constantly with the pestle, until thoroughly blended. Add the lemon juice. If the sauce is too thick, add a few drops of cold water to thin.

This sauce is similar to mayonnaise both in texture and preparation.

As for mayonnaise, Aïoli that has separated may be fixed by adding additional egg yolks.

Aïoli sauce is flavorful, and is a suitable accompaniment to cold meats, especially pork and lamb. It may also be used as a salad dressing and to accompany certain vegetables.

"Rouille" Sauce

40 g (1 1/2 oz) garlic
1/4 tsp hot pepper sauce (or cayenne pepper)
Pinch of coarse salt
40 g (1 1/20 z) crustless white bread
3 tbsp fish stock
2.5 dl (1 1/4 cups) olive oil

If necessary, degerm the garlic (this facilitates digestion). In a mortar, grind to a fine paste. Grind in the hot sauce. Soak the bread in the fish stock to soften and add to the garlic mixture. Slowly pour in the oil, stirring constantly with the pestle, until thoroughly blended. Adjust seasoning. If the sauce is too thick, thin with a few drops of broth from fish soup.

Rouille, which is the French word for rust, is named for its color. It is the classic garnish for fish soup, but it may also be served with certain poached fish or shellfish.

Zucchini Mousse Sauce

35 g (1 oz) clarified butter
40 g (1 1/2 oz) butter
100 g (3 1/2 oz) onions
3 garlic cloves
450 g (15 oz) zucchini
150 g (5 oz) spinach
Bouquet garni: bay leaf,
1 sprig thyme,
4 parsley stems, tied in a leek green
1/2 L (2 cups) white or chicken stock
40 g (1 1/2 oz) flour
2 dl (3/4 cup) heavy cream
Salt, pepper
10 g (about 1/2 oz) gelatin (5 sheets) per liter (quart) of mixture

Procedure: Volume 2, page 200.

Hot Emulsified Sauces

Introduction

Hot emulsified sauces like their cold counterparts use the lecithin in the egg yolk to emulsify the various ingredients.

However it is the watery element (reduced wine or vinegar, water) which is bound with the lightly cooked egg yolk.

The " poaching " of the eggs should be done over low or medium heat. Proceed as for a sabayon, whisking as the egg yolks and liquid element heat through. Do not overcook which would cause the eggs to become scrambled.

The oily element (clarified butter) is warm when blended into the cooked yolks, and the sauce thickens as the butter is absorbed.

Season to taste at the end of the procedure.

Keep the sauce warm in a water bath until service.

There are two basic hot emulsified sauces:

Hollandaise Sauce made with a little water blended with the yolks and seasoned with salt and pepper.

Bearnaise Sauce: made with reduction of vinegar blended with the yolks and seasoned with salt, pepper, and tarragon.

It is best to make hot emulsified sauces at the last moment and they can be held for a short period in a water bath or poured into a thermos bottle which keeps the sauce at a constant temperature. This method is ideal for catered events when it would be difficult to make the sauce on-site.

It is not recommended to make them in advance and reheat.

Hollandaise Sauce

2 cl (4 tbls) dry white wine
5 cl (1/4 cup) water
8 egg yolks
500 g (8 oz) clarified butter
Few drops lemon juice
Salt, coarsely gound pepper, cayenne
    pepper

Reduce the white wine and water with the coarsely ground pepper.

Lower the heat, whisk in the egg yolks.

Beat the eggs over low heat until warm and thickened.

Off the heat, whisk in the warm, clarified butter.

Season to taste and strain through a fine-meshed conical sieve.

Hollandaise is delicious with most fish and vegetable dishes.

Bearnaise Sauce

60 g (2 oz) finely chopped shallots
1.5 dl (2/3 cup) dry white wine
1.5 dl (2/3 cup) wine vinegar
15 g (1/2 oz) chopped tarragon
15 g (1/2 oz chopped chervil
1 tsp coarsely ground pepper
Salt
8 egg yolks
500 g (8 oz) clarified butter
2 tbls finely chopped tarragon
2 tbls finely chopped chervil
Cayenne pepper

Combine the the wine, vinegar, herbs and pepper in a saucepan and reduce by 1/3.

Lower the heat and whisk in the egg yolks and continue to beat over low heat until warm and thickened.

Off the heat whisk in the warm, clarified butter in a thin stream.

Season to taste then strain through a fine-meshed conical sieve.

Stir in the finely chopped herbs.

Bearnaise sauce is served with all grilled meats.

Recipes: Hollandaise Derivatives

Chantilly Sauce

Hollandaise Sauce +
1.5 dl (2/3 cup) whipped cream
Salt, cayenne pepper

Prepare the hollandaise sauce in advance. Just before serving, fold in the firmly whipped cream. Season, and serve immediately.

This sauce is a lighter version of hollandaise and may be served with the same dishes.

Maltaise Sauce

Hollandaise Sauce +
Juice of 1 blood orange
About 2 tbsp grated blood orange
   rind
Salt, pepper

Prepare the hollandaise and stir in the orange juice and rind. Adjust seasoning if necessary.

Maltaise sauce may be served with certain fish and vegetables, and it is particularly suited to aspargus. It may also be served with beignets and mignonnettes.

Mikado Sauce

Hollandaise Sauce +
Juice of 1 tangerine
About 2 tbsp grated tangerine rind
Salt, pepper

Follow steps for Maltaise Sauce.

The tangerine flavor of this sauce makes it a suitable accompaniment to certain fish dishes.

Mustard Sauce

Hollandaise Sauce +
1 tsp Dijon-style mustard

Stir the mustard into the finished hollandaise. The amount of mustard can vary according to its strength and the use of the sauce.

Mustard sauce can be served like plain hollandaise. It adds a spicy note to the finished dish.

Recipes: Bearnaise Derivatives

Paloise Sauce

Bearnaise Sauce +
Fresh Mint

Replace the tarragon in a classic bearnaise with fresh mint. It is added to the vinegar reduction and chopped fresh and added to the finished sauce.

This sauce goes very well with lamb dishes.

Tyrolienne Sauce

Dry white wine
Vinegar
Tarragon-Chervil
Coarsely ground pepper
2 egg yolks
5 dl (2 cups) oil
2 tbls tomato paste
Cayenne pepper

Proceed like for a classic bearnaise. Oil replaces the clarified butter.

Strain the sauce, then stir in the tomato paste and cayenne. No herbs are added at the end.

This sauce is delicious with grilled or pan-fried meats.

Choron Sauce

Bearnaise Sauce +
2 tsp tomato paste or reduced tomato
   sauce

Follow the same procedure as classic bearnaise. Instead of adding the freshly chopped herbs into the finished sauce, stir in the tomato paste (2 tsp of tomato paste needed for a "batch" of bearnaise using 200 g (7 oz) butter).

The consistency remains the same.

This sauce is delicious with meats and grilled fish. It does not hold well once the tomato is added.

Foyot Sauce

Bearnaise Sauce +
5-10 cl (1/4-1/2 cup) meat glaze

Stir the meat glaze into the finished sauce. The amount depends on the taste of the chef and the character of the final dish.

This sauce is served with grilled or pan-fried beef.

Custards

Introduction

Custard is the basic filling in quiches and " croustades ".

The same formula can be used for quiches of all sizes; bite-size hors d'œuvres, individual first courses, or for large quiches that are sliced into 6-8 portions.

The classic custard is a mixture of egg yolks with an addition of crème fraîche, heavy cream and/or milk (used in varying combinations to obtain custards of different textures).

The custard can be seasoned with a myriad of flavorings; curry, safran, fresh herbs, etc..

Note: Crème fraîche is a heavy cream, rich in butterfat, thickened naturally by lactic fermentation. In France it is readily available and its rich, slightly " cheesey " taste is ideal for quiche custards. When it is used, fewer egg yolks are necessary to achieve a thick, rich custard.

Heavy cream or whipping cream, similar to the French " crème fleurette " can be used wherever crème fraîche is indicated in these recipes. An extra egg yolk can be added if needed.

Procedure

Making custards is very easy. The eggs and cream are blended and passed through a fine sieve to homogenize the mixture.

When the ingredients are whisked together, the mixture should not be beaten too much which incorporates air and creates undesirable bubbles in the custard. The sieved custard is seasoned with salt, pepper and usu-

ally nutmeg. Other seasonings can be added to personalize the quiche and marry the taste with the other ingredients (curry with mussels, basil with tomatoes etc.).

Cooking and Storage

Quiches cook in a medium oven (200 °C (375 F). The custard sets quickly, in about 20-30 minutes. The eggs in the mixture puff slightly making the custard light and creamy.

The pastry crust should be blind-baked in advance so that it is thor-

oughly cooked and crispy when the custard is set. Be careful to not overcook the custard. The custard can be blended in sizeable batches and stored for 1-2 days in the refrigerator.

Note: For recipes using " crème fraîche " and milk, combine the amounts and substitute heavy cream if crème fraîche is not available.

Roquefort Custard

125 g (4 oz) roquefort
2.5 dl (1 cup) " crème fraîche "
2 dl (3/4 cup) milk – 5 eggs

Salt, pepper, nutmeg

Procedure: Volume 2, page 307.

Custard for Mussel Croustade with Saffron

3 dl (1 1/3 cups) " crème fraîche "
1.5 dl (2/3 cup) mussel juice
5 cl (1/4 cup) mushroom essence
5 eggs
1 tbl chopped herbs (chervil, chives, dill)
Salt, pepper, saffron

Procedure: Volume 3, pages 26-27.

Custard for Quiche Lorraine

2 dl (3/4 cup) milk
3 dl (1 1/3 cup) " crème fraîche "
5 eggs – Salt, pepper, nutmeg

Procedure: Volume 2, page. 300.

Custard for Vegetable Croustade

1/4 L (1 cup) milk
1/4 L (1 cup) " crème fraîche "
5 eggs – Salt, pepper

Procedure: Volume 2, page 315.

Custard for Endive Croustade

1/2 L (2 cups) heavy cream
5 eggs
Salt, pepper

Custard for " Trianon " Croustade

2 dl (3/4 cup) milk
2 dl (3/4 cup) " crème fraîche "
5 eggs – Salt, pepper

Procedure: Volume 2, page 304.

Custard for Leek " Flamiche "

2 dl (3/4 cup) milk
2 dl (3/4 cup) " crème fraîche "
6 eggs – Salt, pepper

Procedure: Volume 2, page 309.

Custard for Asparagus and Frogs' Legs Croustade

2 dl (3/4 cup) milk
2 dl (3/4 cup) " crème fraîche "
5 eggs
8 chives, chopped
Salt, pepper, nutmeg

Procedure: Volume 3, page 18.

Custard for Mussel and Pesto Croustade

3 dl (1 1/3 cup heavy cream)
5 eggs
Salt, pepper, safran

Procedure: Volume 3, page 28.

Custard for Mushroom Croustade

3 dl (1 1/3 cup) heavy cream
5 eggs – Salt, pepper, nutmeg

Procedure: Volume 3. page 34.

Custard for Cheese Croustade

3 dl (1 1/3 cup) milk
3 dl (1 1/3 cup) " crème fraîche "
5 eggs – Salt, pepper, nutmeg
Paprika (optional)

Procedure: Volume 3, page 45.

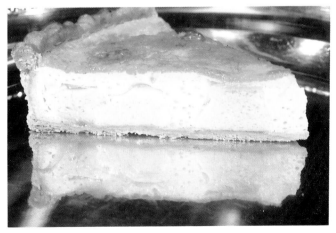

Chaud-froid Sauces

Introduction

Chaud-froid sauces are made in different ways and are usually used to glaze a cold individual portion of meat or a large elaborate presentation.

They can be flavored with herbs, spices, port, sherry, etc. to marry the taste with the dish.

They can be divided into three groups:

Chaud-froid made with mayonnaise and aspic:

The ratio is about 2/3 aspic to 1/3 mayonnaise.

The stock that the aspic is made from can vary to marry the taste of the chaud-froid to the dish. For example poultry aspic for a chaud-froid to glaze Chicken with Truffles "Demi-Deuil" or fish aspic for Stuffed Filets of Sole.

Chaud-froid made with a classic sauce and gelatin:

Almost any sauce can be set with gelatin and used to glaze a cold version of a classic dish such as Canard à l'Orange or Beef "Perigeux".

Chaud-froid made cooking liquid:

The cooking or deglazing juices from a meat dish can be strained and thickened (reduction + roux) then set with gelatin and used to coat dishes such as Noisettes of Venison or Braised Beef "Bourgeoise".

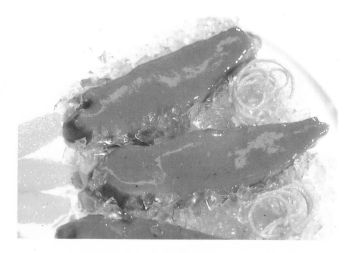

Note: The amount of gelatin varies with the consistency of the sauce to which it is added, the nature of the dish to be glazed and the weather (in warm weather, more gelatin is needed).

The average amount is 10-15 g (about 1/2 oz) per liter (quart) of liquid.

Glazing with Chaud-froid

Depending on the dish and consistency of the chaud-froid the glaze can be applied in three ways:
- With a soft-bristled pastry brush.
- With a spoon (for individual portions).
- With a ladle (for larger presentaions).

The amount of chaud-froid used to coat a dish should be in proportion to the size of the dish.

Chaud-froid plays a very important role in making cold dishes for buffets. They not only protect the meat and keep it fresh and moist but these sauces also add a wonderful flavor and make the dish smooth and shiny.

Therefore it is important to marry the taste of the chaud-froid to the flavor of the dish.

Poultry Chaud-froid

1/2 L (2 cups) mayonnaise
1 L (4 cups) poultry aspic

Procedure: Volume 3, page 292.

Fish Chaud-froid

1/4 L (1 cup) mayonnaise
1/2 L (2 cups) fish aspic
1/4 L (1 cup) aspic for final glazing)

Herb Chaud-froid

1/3 mayonnaise, 2/3 aspic, chopped chervil, tarragon, chives, sherry

Procedure: Volume 1, page 208.

Curry Chaud-froid

1/3 mayonnaise, 2/3 aspic, curry powder, salt, pepper

Paprika Chaud-froid

40 g (1 1/4 oz) clarified butter
100 g (3 1/2 oz) onions
1 dl (1/2 cup) dry white wine
1.5 dl (2/3 cup) medeira
1l (1 qt) demi-glaze
1.5 dl (2/3 cup) cream
Cooked roux (optional)
Salt, pepper, paprika
10-15 g (1/2 oz) gelatin per liter (quart)

Procedure: Volume 1, page 212.

Chaud-froid " Perigueux "

Madeira sauce, demi-glaze, truffle essence, roux, gelatin, salt, pepper, truffles

Chaud-froid with Ketchup

Ketchup, gelatin, tarragon, tomato paste, aspic

Chaud-froid for Duck à l'Orange

5 cl (1/4 cup) dry white wine
20 g (3/4 oz) sugar
Zest of 1/2 lemon
Zest of 1 orange
3 cl (6 tbls) orange juice
2 cl (4 tbls) lemon juice
3/4 l (3 cups) duck stock
50 g (1 3/4 oz) cooked roux (optional)
12-14 g (1/2 oz) gelatin

Procedure: Volume 3, pages 305-306

Vinaigrette

Introduction

Vinaigrettes are easy to make and a variety of ingredients can enter into their composition.

They are primarily used as dressings for salads but can be used to season other dishes as well.

They are distinguished by their lively acidic flavor.

The basic recipe has three parts:
• The acidic element
• The oil
• Seasonings

To this basic formula, one can add other ingredients like cream, egg yolks and essences (truffle for example).

Ingredients

The Acidic Element

Vinegar

Wine vinegars, plain or flavored (herbs, garlic, shallots, etc.), cider vinegar, honey vinegar, fruit vinegars (raspberry), champagne vinegars.

Citrus fruits

Lemons and limes

Mustards

Strong, mild and flavored mustards

The oil

Corn, peanut, sunflower, walnut, hazelnut, olive. Sometimes stronger oils are mixed with bland ones for a balanced taste.

Seasonings

Salt, pepper, garlic, onions, shallots, herbs, spices....

The seasonings are very important and their taste should always marry with the other dressing ingredients and the makeup of the salad or other dish (truffle essence with a foie gras salad for example).

The proportion of the ingredients can vary according to the strength of the vinegar, taste of the oil and the flavor of the dish.

The dressing is usually mixed into the salad just before it is served. The vinaigrette causes the greens to wilt very quickly.

In some cases, the vinaigrette is added in advance to marinate the dish as in a potato or shellfish salad or a cold vegetable dish.

Storage is also variable. Some dressings must be made at the last moment while others can be made in advance and kept refrigerated in closed containers.

Procedure Making vinaigrettes is easy. Blend together the acid and mustard (if using) and whisk in the oil, add the seasonings.

Soy and Ginger Dressing

1/2 lemon
8 cl (1/3 cup) oil
1 cl (2 tsp) soy sauce
Salt, pepper, ginger
(Uses: see Vol. 2 P. 12)

Basic Vinaigrette

1 1/2 tbsp vinegar
1 tsp Dijon-style mustard
8 tbsp corn oil
Salt, pepper

Dressing for Mediterranean Salad

1 1/2 tsp wine vinegar

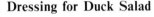

4 tbsp olive oil
4 tbsp corn oil
1 tsp Dijon-style mustard
Salt, pepper

Dressing for Méli-Mélo Salad

1/2 lemon
4 tbsp olive oil
4 tbsp peanut oil
1 tsp Dijon-style mustard

Dressing for Chinese Salad

1 tbsp soy sauce
2 tbsp sesame oil
3 tbsp sunflower oil
Salt, pepper

Dressing for Cinderella Salad

1 tbsp wine vinegar
1 tsp Dijon-style mustard
4 tbsp corn oil
Salt, pepper

Dressing for Exotic Salad

1/2 lemon
6 tbsp olive oil
1 tbsp Dijon-style mustard
Salt, pepper

Dressing for Brazilian Salad

2 tbsp sherry vinegar
10 tbsp olive oil
1/2 tbsp Dijon-style mustard
Dash of Tabasco
Salt, pepper

Dressing for Taboulé

1 lemon
Olive oil
Salt, pepper
Dash of Tabasco

Dressing for Seafood Salad

1 lemon
1/2 tbsp Dijon-style mustard
12 tbsp corn oil
Salt, pepper

Dressing for Haddock Salad

2 tbsp well-reduced Américaine
  sauce
2 egg yolks
1/2 tbsp Dijon-style mustard
1 tbsp crème fraîche or sour cream
4 tbsp oil
Salt, pepper

Dressing for Pasta and Seafood Salad

1 dl (1/2 cup) crème fraîche or sour
  cream
2 egg yolks
1/2 tsp Dijon-style mustard
6 tbsp olive oil
3 tbsp corn oil
Salt, pepper

Dressing for Chicken and Sweet-breads Salad

1 tbsp honey vinegar
3 tbsp hazelnut oil
3 tbsp corn oil
Salt, pepper

Dressing for Foie Gras Salad

1/2 tbsp sherry vinegar
7 tbsp corn oil
1 tbsp truffle essence (liquid from
  preserved truffles)
Salt, pepper

Dressing for Duck Salad

1/2 tbsp sherry vinegar
7 tbsp hazelnut oil
Salt, pepper

Dressing for Country-Style Beef Salad

1/2 tbsp vinegar
9 tbsp corn oil
1/2 tbsp Dijon-style mustard
Salt, pepper

Basic Vinaigrette with Chives

2 tsp wine vinegar
8 tsp oil
6 chives
Salt, pepper

Ravigote

1.5 dl (2/3 cup) vinegar
1 tsp Dijon-style mustard
5 dl (2 cups) oil
Salt, pepper
40 g (1.5 oz) chopped parsley
40 g (1.5 oz) chopped chervil, tarragon, chives
70 g (2.5 oz) chopped onions
50 g (1.75 oz) small capers

Make a well-seasoned vinaigrette. Add the chopped herbs and onions. The capers are small and agreeable to eat.

This spicy sauce is often served with offal; poached brains, tongue, calves' feet or calves' head.

Compound Butters, Mousses, Cream-based Sauces and Spreads

Compound Butters

For the caterer, compound butters are mainly used in the making of canapés. They are either spread in a very thin layer on the bread base, or piped out in designs on the finished canapé. In a few cases (trout butter for example), the compound butter is one of the main ingredients on the canapé.

Compound butters are made by blending butter with other ingredients (herbs, anchovies, mustard, tomato etc.).

Mousses

These savory mousses are also used to coat the bread base of canapés. As a sauce, they accompany cold, light dishes like fish terrine.

The basic ingredients of these light preparations vary:
- Butter, " fromage frais " (substitute sieved cottage cheese), crème fraîche (or sour cream)
- Fish
- Liver purée with cream, butter, egg yolks
- Purée of vegetables with gelatin

The chef can use his imagination to create different mousses to accompany light dishes.

Cream-based Spreads

These creamy spreads are also used to coat canapés. They are very light and can be made with various ingredients:
- Compound butter + cream
- Parmesan sauce + cream (for hot hors d'œuvres)
- " Fromage frais ", crème fraîche + seasoning

These base ingredients are all creamy and light. They are usually applied in a thin layer on a solid base. For example, in addition to being a spread for canapés, they are fillings for stuffed crêpe canapés and sand-

wiches and are served warm (parmesan sauce) when spread on a layer pastry.

Recipes: Compound Butters

Compound butters serve two purposes:

• As a spread or accompaniment, they are used to coat the bread base of canapés, piped out as decoration or chilled in a roll and sliced to serve as a simple accompaniment to meats or vegetables.

• As an ingredient, they are whisked into sauces to add flavor. For example shrimp butter reinforces the flavor of a shrimp-based sauce.

Note: the butter used in these recipes should always be unsalted. The salt is then added to taste.

Maître d'hôtel Butter

250 g (8 oz) butter
2 tbls chopped parsley
Few drops of lemon juice
Salt, pepper – 1 tsp Dijon-style mustard (optional)

Cream the butter. Stir in the parsley and lemon juice. Season with salt and freshly ground pepper. Add a little mustard which adds a tangy flavor. This butter is served with grilled or pan-fried meats and can be used to flavor sauces.

Tarragon Butter

80 g (3 oz) tarragon leaves
200 g (7 oz) butter – Salt, pepper

Blanch the tarragon leaves briefly in boiling water and refresh in cold water, drain and dry on a paper towel. Crush the tarragon in a mortar with salt and freshly ground pepper. Add the butter a little at a time, continuing to work the mixture with the pestle. Pass through a fine-meshed sieve, pressing to extract all the flavor. This flavorful butter is used as a spread or ingredient in sauces.

Shallot Butter

150 g (5 oz) shallots
150 g (5 oz) butter – Salt, pepper

Peel the shallots and blanch them briefly in boiling water. Refresh in cold water, drain and dry. Crush the shallots in a mortar with salt and freshly ground pepper. Add the butter a little at a time, continuing to work the mixture with the pestle. Pass through a fine-meshed sieve, pressing to extract all the flavor.

Shallot butter has many uses: spread for canapés, accompaniment to meats, ingredient in sauces.

Horseradish Butter

50 g (1 3/4 oz) fresh horseradish
250 g (8 oz) butter – Salt, pepper

Grate the horseradish. Crush it in a mortar and add the butter a little at a time. Season to taste. The horseradish has a very strong flavor which is not suited to all dishes. This butter is delicious with certain fish and meats and can be used as a spread.

Bercy Butter

30 g (1 oz) clarified butter
20 g (3/4 oz) finely chopped shallots – 2 dl (3/4 cup) dry white wine
1 tbl crème fraîche (or heavy cream)
200 g (7 oz) butter
Salt, pepper – Few drops lemon juice
250 g (8 oz) beef marrow (poached in consommé, cut in pieces)

This compound butter sauce which is flavored with dry white wine is named for the former Bercy wine warehouse in southeast Paris.

Melt the clarified butter in a saucepan, add the shallots and cook until soft but not brown. Deglaze with dry white wine and reduce by half. Add the cream and bring to a boil. Off the heat, whisk in the butter a little at a time, continuing to whisk until it is completely incorporated.

Add a little lemon juice and the poached beef marrow. (This sauce is not strained.) This sauce is served to accompany meat dishes.

Marchand de Vin Butter

20 g (3/4 oz) calrified butter
30 g (1 oz) finely chopped shallots
2 dl (3/4 cup) red wine
5 cl (1/4 cup) light meat glaze
150 g (5 oz) butter
Few drops lemon juice
1 tsp chopped parsley

Heat the clarified butter and cook the shallots until soft but not brown. Deglaze with red wine and reduce by half. Season with salt and freshly ground pepper and stir in the meat glaze (if it is very strong, reduce the amount). Mount the sauce with butter. Stir in the lemon juice and parsley. " Marchand de vin " is a wine merchant, hence this sauce made with red wine. Meat dishes (grilled or pan-fried beef) that are served with this sauce use the name as well.

Seasoned Butter

1 kg (2 lb) butter, softened
1/4 L (1 cup) warm water
1 tbsp Dijon-style mustard
Salt, pepper

Slowly whisk the water into the butter. Whisk in the mustard and seasoning.

This lightly seasoned butter is used as a canapé and sandwich spread.

Variations:

Roquefort and Walnut Butter
Foie Gras Mousse/Cream of Foie Gras
Egg Salad Spread
Salmon Mousse
Sardine Butter: equal quantities sardines in oil and softened butter
Smoked Eel Butter: 1/5 smoked eel to 4/5 butter
Aurora Butter: 100 g (3 1/2 oz) butter; 20 g (3/4 oz) tomato concentrate; dash of Cognac or Vodka; salt, pepper, paprika
Anchovy Butter: 1/5 anchovy fillets to 4/5 butter
Tarama: 200 g (7 oz) cod roe; 1 cl (2 tsp) lemon juice; 3 cl (2 tbsp) oil; 6 cl (1/4 cup) crème fraîche or heavy cream; salt, pepper
Smoked Trout Mousse
Duck Mousse: 250 g (8 oz) cooked duck breast; 2 cl (4 tsp) duck glaze; 3 cl (2 tbsp) crème fraîche or heavy cream
Gorgonzola Cream: 100 g (3 1/2 oz) gorgonzola; 25 g (1 oz) crème fraîche; 25 g (1 oz) butter
Munster Cream: 100 g (3 1/2 oz) munster; 25 g (1 oz) crème fraîche; 25 g (1 oz) butter
" Fromage Frais " Mousse with Chives: 200 g (7 oz) fromage frais; 50 g (1 3/4 oz) crème fraîche or heavy cream; 100 g (3 1/2 oz) butter; salt, pepper, chives
" Fromage Frais " Mousse with Walnuts and Raisins Roquefort Cream : 50 g (1 3/4 oz) roquefort; 100 g (3 1/2 oz) Parmesan sauce *" Fromage Frais " with Herbs:* 200 g (7 oz) fromage frais; 3 cl (2 tbsp) crème fraîche or heavy cream; 2 tbsp assorted chopped fresh herbs (chervil, tarragon, chives)
" Fromage Frais " Mousse with Paprika: 200 g (7 oz) fromage frais; 50 g (1 3/4 oz) crème fraîche or hevay cream; 100 g (3 1/2 oz) butter; salt, pepper, paprika
Snail Butter: (for 12 snails) 250 g (8 oz) butter; 25 g (1 oz) flat-leaf parsley; 20 g (3/4 oz) garlic; 10 g (1/2 oz) shallots; salt, pepper, nutmeg; dash of anise-flavored liquor
Stuffed Clam Butter: 200 g (7 oz) butter; 5 cl (1/4 cup) heavy cream; 1 tsp chopped flat-leaf parsley; 20 g (3/4 oz) garlic; 20 g (3/4 oz) chopped walnuts; 1 cl (2 tsp) vermouth; salt, pepper
Stuffed Mussel Butter: 200 g (7 oz) butter; 5 cl (1/4 cup) reduced mussel cooking liquid; 20 g (3/4 oz) chopped flat-leaf parsley; 50 g (1 3/4 oz) chopped dill; 10 g (1/2 oz) shallots; 10 g (1/2 oz) garlic; pepper

Note: Sour cream can be subsituted for crème fraîche in these recipes. To make a product close in taste and texture to " fromage frais ", pass cottage cheese through a fine sieve.

Other Sauces

Tomato Sauce

Recipe A

5 cl (1/4 cup) olive oil
150 g (5 oz) onions, finely chopped
50 g (1 3/4 oz) shallots, finely chopped
250 g (8 oz) tomato concentrate
40 g (1 1/2 oz) garlic, degermed and crushed
30-60 g (1-2 oz) flour
1 L (4 cups) consommé, stock or water

Bouquet garni: thyme, bay leaf and parsley stems, tied in a leek green
20 basil leaves
Salt, pepper, sugar

Preheat the oven to 180 °C (350 F). In a saucepan, combine the oil, onions and shallots over medium heat. Cook until soft; do not color. Stir in the tomato concentrate, garlic and flour. Transfer to the oven and bake, 5 to 8 minutes.

Return to the stovetop, add the consommé, bouquet garni, and basil. Season, and simmer gently in the oven or over low heat, 15 to 30 minutes. Strain.

The thickness, or thinness, of the sauce may be adjusted to suit the dish it will accompany.

Recipe B

5 cl (1/4 cup) olive oil
150 g (5 oz) onions, finely
    chopped
50 g (1 3/4 oz) shallots, finely
    chopped
2.5 kg (5.5 lbs) tomatoes, peeled,
    cored, seeded and chopped
40 g (1 1/2 oz) garlic, degermed
    and crushed
Bouquet garni: thyme, bay leaf and
    parsley stems, tied in a leek
    green
20 basil leaves
Salt, pepper, sugar

In a saucepan, combine the oil, onions and shallots over medium heat. Cook until soft; do not color.

Stir in the tomatoes, garlic, bouquet garni and basil. If necessary, add some tomato concentrate to intensify the color and flavor. Taste for seasoning. Cover, and simmer gently (in the oven, if desired). When the tomatoes have given off their liquids, remove the cover and cook until most of the liquid has evaporated.

Discard the bouquet garni. Process in a food processor.

This sauce is best when prepared from fresh tomatoes at the height of the season. Alternatively, it may be made year-round from canned, peeled tomatoes.

This sauce may be used with any dish that calls for tomato sauce.

Tomato Sauce for Pizza

2 dl (3/4 cup) olive oil
3 kg (6.5 lbs) onions, finely
    chopped
3 kg (6.5 lbs) tomatoes, peeled,
    cored, seeded and chopped
100 g (3 1/2 oz) garlic
250 g (8 oz) tomato concentrate
Bouquet garni: thyme, bay leaf and
    parsley stems, tied in a leek
    green
Marjoram
Salt, pepper, sugar

In a saucepan, combine the oil and onions over medium heat. Cook until soft. Add the tomatoes, garlic, tomato concentrate, bouquet garni and marjoram. Taste for seasoning. Cover, and simmer gently (in the oven, if desired). When the tomatoes have given off their liquids, remove the cover and cook until most of the liquid has evaporated. Refrigerate until needed.

The quantity of tomato concentrate will depend upon the color and flavor of the fresh tomatoes; add only as needed.

This recipe may be prepared with canned peeled tomatoes. Use fresh or dried marjoram depending upon availability.

The required thickness of the sauce will vary according to the type of pizza base being used.

Cumberland Sauce

This sauce of British origin is classic accompaniment to game dishes.

20 g (3/4 oz) shallots, finely
    chopped
Zest of 1/2 orange, julienned-
    (short and thin)
150 g (5 oz) red currant jelly
3 cl (2 tbsp) Port
1/4 tsp Dijon-style mustard
Pinch of cayenne pepper
Pinch of powdered ginger

Separately blanch and drain the shallots and orange zest. Strain the jelly through a fine-mesh sieve. Stir in the Port. Add the shallots and orange zest.

Add the mustard, pepper and ginger.

Marinades

Marinades play many different roles in the caterer's kitchen:

Brine is used in charcuterie to salt and conserve hams and other pork products.

" Instant Marinades " are used primarily for thin slices of seafood that are eaten raw. The marinade " cooks " the flesh slightly and flavors it as well. They are usually a blend of oil, seasonings and sometimes vinegar or citrus juice.

Marinades for meat and venison serve two functions: to flavor the meat and to tenderize the meat.

These marinades are often used to braise or baste the meat then are strained and thickened to make a sauce.

They can be applied two ways:

- Cold: the process takes about 12-24 hours

- Hot: marinade time is shorter

Ingredients: red wine, white wine, oil, cognac, seasonings and aromatic vegetables (parsley, thyme, bay leaf, peppercorns, coriander, juniper berries, carrots, onions, shallots, garlic, celery).

Chap. 4 - Planning, organization and execution of Buffets and Receptions

Catering : Food + Service

" The Professional Caterer Series " describes in detail a large assortment of dishes that are suitable for catered events.

The caterer's job is to combine the many dishes in his reperatoire to create menus that are right for each client, taking into consideration budget, location, theme and season.

General Advice for Organizing Buffets and Receptions

The Caterer's Different Responsibilities and Subcontracting

The professional caterer must be capable in many areas : in addition to being a qualified chef, the caterer must be a good business man. He should also be an effective organizer and be able to oversee the service end of the business.

Services provided by the Caterer	Caterer Provides	Sub-contract
Establish menu/Take order	YES	–
Visiting the location (for large receptions, meet with sub-contracters)	YES	–
Set-up of buffet (according to the plan)	YES	YES
Tablecloths/napkins (table liners; simple or fancy linens)	YES	YES
Decorations (created for this event/particular theme)	YES	YES
Rental (tableware, equipment, platters, etc.)	YES	YES
Delivery (set-up: hot and cold items)	YES	YES
Chef on-site (final preparation)	YES	–
Supply beverages (ice buckets, ice, refrigeration)	YES	YES
Servers (black pants, white shirt; tailcoat)	–	YES
Other personnel (coat check, doorman)	–	YES
Sound system	–	YES
Disc-jockey (podium, music microphone)	–	YES
Orchestra (classical or modern)	–	YES
Photographer (publicity, album)	–	YES
Speaker	–	YES
Invitations (RSVP, tickets)	–	YES
Flowers	–	YES

The caterer's first responsibility is to meet with the client, present a choice of menus and services and coordinate the event within the limitations of the client's budget. If the client has not chosen a location, the caterer can suggest several possibilities that would be suitable.

In some cases it will be necessary to visit the location of the reception to decide on the rental (size of tables, etc.), verify kitchen facilities, check the lighting etc..

It is important to outline exactly what the caterer's responsibilities are which can range from the delivery of a simple cold buffet on disposable trays to the total organization of a luxurious banquet.

Being fully in charge means that the caterer coordinates all the details with his kitchen and service personnel as well any subcontracters. Although this is a big responsibility, it gives the caterer more control to present his food under the best possible circumstances.

The full-service caterer must be prepared to take responsibility for personnel, rental, flowers, beverages, music, sound system and lighting, photographers, tents and reserving special locations. Impeccable organization is needed to coordinate all the details.

Some caterers have a commercial attaché who makes the preliminary arrangements with the client. In smaller businesses, it is usually the owner, his assistant or the head chef who works directly with the client.

Personnel: Serving the Needs of the Client

Some clients will pick-up their order and either serve the food themselves or hire their own server. It is therefore important to package the food so it will stay fresh, label all containers and provide detailed descriptions of each dish as well as instructions for last minute preparation.

For small events one trained server can deliver as well as arrange the food and serve. Clear labeling and detailed instructions will make his job easier.

For larger events, the caterer will often take charge of the final preparation in the on-site kitchen and oversee the service himself.

Delivery

The caterer must be equipped to deliver the food efficiently. Catastrophes can be avoided if the proper precautions are taken.

Cases that stack are very convenient. Also useful are boxes outfitted with shelves that will hold the baking sheets and cooling racks from the kitchen.

Platters of food prepared in the caterers kitchen should be covered with plastic wrap to protect the dish from odors and dirt.

Containers are available with a refrigerated unit or room to put an ice pack or dry ice. The temperature should be carefully controlled because too low a temperature can ruin the taste and appearance of some dishes (in aspic for example). Caterers who do a volume business usually have refrigerated delivery vans.

Heated containers rarely become too hot for the dishes transported in them.

Some delicate dishes are better if transported in small containers arranged on platters or assembled in the on-site kitchen (canapés and fancy garnishes, etc.).

The person loading the delivery van should take into account the weight and fragility of each dish. A large damp mat made of sponge can keep platters from sliding during transport.

Containers should be stacked with care to avoid breakage and damage to the preparations.

A well equipped delivery van can be very versatile and used by the caterer for small and large events. It should be kept impeccably clean at all times.

Advance Preparation

Important : get the work done on schedule

There are many details to coordinate even for the simplest reception. It is recommended to use check listes and do as much of the work in advance as possible.

Organization is the key to the smooth operation of a caterer's business.

The " mise en place " (assembly of the various elements of a preparation or event) is an important aspect of the caterer's work.

An efficient " mise en place " allows the caterer to orchestrate large receptions with a minimum of work the day of the event.

Most events require that the preparation be scheduled over a 5 day period.

The various preparations are divided between the different kitchen personnel. One chef or department is usually responsible for all the doughs and desserts while another will prepare the meats, stocks, sauces, etc.

Each chef should have a detailed check list so that no detail is forgotten and that the head chef can see the progress at a glance.

It is preferable to prepare as much as possible by qualified personnel in the caterer's kitchen which is well-equipped.

Example :

Day 1 : Make the breads for canapés and surprise breads, stocks.

Day 2 : Prepare certain meats, galantines, terrines, pastry bases for tartes.
   Order beverages.

Day 3 : Make cookies, ice creams and sorbets, glazes, puff pastry (cut out and freeze), cakes and presentation bases.

Day 4 : Assemble surprise breads.
   Make brioche for various preparations.

Day 5 : Cream puff pastry, pastry creams, certain canapés, filled crêpes.
   Slice and glaze certain meats.
   Prepare salad ingredients.
   Set up tables.
   Set up preparation area.

Day of the event:

   Final preparation of meat dishes.
   Make canapés.
   Make mignonnettes, filled brioches, tartes.
   Check the order and deliver.

The Food Cost and the Price

The price charged to the client is usually based on the cost of the food (the food cost multiplied 2 to 3 times to arrive at the price).

Dishes using more expensive ingredients such as lobster or prime rib are usually multiplied by 2 whereas salads, canapés and pastry hors d'oeuvres are multiplied by 3.

More elaborate presentations and service which require more on-site personnel will be more expensive. Fancy receptions, with additional decorations and dishes that demand attention to detail may require up to three on-site chefs which must be reflected in the price.

How can the price be adjusted ?

If the caterer proposes a price per person which is too high for the customer, a few adjustments can be made to bring the price down :
• Offer fewer items per person or propose dishes that use less expensive ingredients.
• Examine all the details : smaller flower arrangements (or none), stainless steel or disposable platter instead of silver.

Explain to the client that there are many elements that contribute to the price (personnel, equipment, ingredients...)

Quantity Control

To keep food cost stable, each chef should control the quantity of items that are produced from each loaf of bread, each standard batch of dough, etc.

Material Organisation

Cliché OPTIONS

When the caterer is in charge of all details, he must contact the necessary subcontracters well in advance to receive estimates for the client then remain in contact as the event approaches and confirm that all is in order.

Equipment and Rental

Equipment Belonging to the Caterer

The caterer usually owns a supply of serving platters, chafing dishes, ice buckets, and presentation bases that are used for serving the food on the buffet at no extra charge to the client.

Rental

The dishes, glasses etc. are usually rented from a company that delivers and picks up.

When subcontracted by the caterer, the rental fee and charge for breakage/damage is added to the bill. If the caterer supplies the tableware himself, the rental is calculated and added to the bill. Additional platters may also need to be supplied by the rental company.

It is important for the servers to take inventory and verify the rental at the beginning of the reception and again after the reception to register all breakage/damage. All of these charges are listed separately on the bill.

If possible, the final inventory should be approved by the client himself or a responsible representative of the client.

Choice of Rental

The choice of plates, glasses, simple or ornate platters, candlesticks etc. is the choice of the client and is a function of taste, the atmosphere of the event and the budget.

For most functions, only two kinds of glasses are used. Water glasses are used for water, fruit juice, mixed drinks and stemmed wine glasses are used for the aperatif and wine.

Wine glasses with short, solid stems can be an all-purpose glass for all beverages.

Logistics

Items to be delivered

Each reception is a little different; small or large, elaborate or fancy and requires serving pieces, decorations and tableware suited to the particular event.

For a large fancy reception, for example, all tableware, chairs etc. is rented from a subcontracter, so that it is all co-ordinated.

The rental company delivers and puts all containers etc. in a convenient place so that the servers can set up the tables. The rental should be verified before set-up (for quantity, breakage) and marked on a checklist which is used after the event to verify loss or breakage during the reception.

The caterer delivers all the prepared food items with any needed equipment for storage on-site and final preparation. The kitchen is staffed with qualified personnel to set up the food.

Depending on the distance and the quantity of items to be transported, the caterer will use a delivery van or refrigerated truck.

Setting up the Buffet

Simple dishes (canapés, pastry hors d'oeuvres) can be arranged on platters by the servers. More elaborate presentations are done by a chef or server with kitchen experience.

Disassembling the Buffet

Disassembling the kitchen equipment is done by the chef in charge and his assistants, with further assistance by the service staff if necessary. The reception room is returned to order by the servers and they are also in charge of replacing all rental dishes etc. back in the right containers and preparing it for pick-up.

Delivery Vehicles

Special delivery vans are available with insulated or refrigerated compartments, and racks for easy storage of containers and trays.

Delivery is added separately to the bill. The charge is by zone within the city and by the mile for greater distances.

The mileage of the personnel's cars is also calculated and charged to the client. In general, count on 3-4 persons per car.

Communication

It is important to remain in close communication with all subcontracters involved with each event. Caterers depend on the services of rental companies, florists, light and sound specialists, beverage and ice suppliers etc. and must co-ordinate time of delivery and pick-up.

Keeping Items Hot and Cold on the Buffet

Cold Items

Refrigeration plays an important role in the serving of buffets. Not only is refrigeration necessary for preventing spoilage, it keeps the food fresh looking and tasting. The work on-site is facilitated by proper refrigeration; foods slice more easily and more neatly, presentations need less last minute attention...

A cold temperature can be obtained in different ways depending on the circumstances:

Ice: Used primarily for chilling beverages. Bottles of Champagne, and white wines are placed in buckets with ice and the cubes are added to drinks in the glass.

Ice Packs, Dry Ice: Different methods are available to keep small items chilled. Placed in a closed container with dry ice or ice packs, foods will remain cold for short periods of time.

Refrigerated Delivery Van: This is the best way of keeping all foods at a constant cold temperature.

Refrigerators: When on-site kitchens have a refrigerator, space can be made for a few items.

Insulated Containers: Label insulated containers with a detailed list of contents so that they do not need to be opened unnecessarily.

Ice

Ice is used by the caterer in two forms:

Blocks of ice weighing 15-20 kg (about 30-45 lbs), Large blocks of ice are used exclusively for cooling beverages. The blocks need to be broken up on-site which is extra work. It is used in this form only when the caterer must travel a long distance to the reception or during very hot weather. It occupies less room in the delivery van and it melts more slowly than ice cubes.

Ice cubes are available in different forms and in sacks of varying sizes. They are used in ice buckets and in glasses to cool individual liquid refreshments. This form of ice is the easiest to use.

For a reception with 60 guests, the average amount needed is 20-25 kg (about 45-55 lbs) to cool the beverages.

Cold Storage

The amount of on-site cold storage needed depends on several details:
• The size of the reception.
• The type of dishes on the menu.
• The season (beverages can be cooled outdoors, for example.)
• The temperature of the kitchen (air-conditioned?)

Transporting Cold Food

All food items, with the exception of pastry hors d'œuvres, cookies, and hot items being transported a short distance, should be transported in insulated containers equipped with dry ice or ice packs.

It is recommended to only pack similar items in one container so that the oders and tastes do not mingle (no sweet with savory, no fish with cheese...).

Specially made containers come in many sizes and are available in plastic, stainless steel, and aluminum. Metal ones hold the cold better if refrigerated in advance.

Refrigerated delivery vans ensure that foods remain at a constant temperature. In all cases, it is important that food does not undergo a change of temperature during transport. Label each container clearly to avoid having to open it unnecessarily. Transfer cold items from the kitchen refrigerator directly into insulated containers.

Items that freeze well can be removed from the freezer shortly before delivery and finish thawing in transit.

Hot Items

Food is transported hot only when the reception is taking place nearby.

Individual hot dishes (bouchées for example) are more easily reheated in the on-site kitchen. The prepared filling is transported, chilled in containers and the pastry bases are arranged in airtight boxes.

Some large meat presentations do not reheat well and are difficult to cook in the on-site kitchen. These more substantial dishes can be cooked shortly before delivery and transported hot then reheated just before service, if necessary.

The hot item is kept warm in an insulated container. Food in pastry will become soggy when the steam collects in the container.

When the on-site kitchen is well equipped, it may be possible to transport prepared items and finish the cooking on-site.

Delicate sauces that do not reheat well can be transported in thermos bottles.

Items Reheated in the On-site Kitchen

Before including a hot item on a menu, check that the on-site kitchen is adequate for reheating (or that there is room to install a portable oven and/or hotplate). Remember that microwaves tend to make pastry soft and chewy.

Items Cooked in the On-site Kitchen

Some items are easily cooked with minimal equipment (certain " mignonnettes ", shellfish..). Verify that the necessary equipment is in working order and that the chef or server who does the cooking has detailed instructions.

Beverages for Buffets and Receptions

Alcoholic Beverages

Champagne

Champagne is the most popular liquid refreshment, at receptions in France, accounting for about 80 % of all alcoholic beverages. Dry Champagne is appropriate to serve throughout the reception, from cocktails to dessert. It is enjoyed by a wider range of guests than other alcoholic beverages.

Count on one bottle for 4-5 guests.

Wines

For a classic reception, it is recommended to not offer many wines, but to select a wine that is appropriate for all the dishes and can be served throughtout the reception.

For a dinner buffet, the client may wish to serve a white and a red wine.

It is highly recommended to serve only top quality wines. Good wines are available in a range of prices (moderate to expensive) and the cost of other items can be adjusted to accomodate the cost ot the wines.

Cocktails

In France, the assortment of drinks offered before a meal is usually limited.

Whisky is popular, as are strong wines such as Port and Sherry.

Service

Usually two types of glasses are used to serve beverages ; a water glass for juice and mixed drinks and a stemmed glass for Champagne and wines.

The beverages are served from the buffet and/or passed on trays.

Champagne should be chilled in ice about one hour before service.

Large containers with ice can be placed under the buffet to hold many bottles with a few ice buckets placed on the buffet table.

The servers in charge of beverages should check the supply periodically to make sure enough is on hand and chilled as needed.

If one type of beverage runs out, the server should discreetly make another suggestion.

If the server anticipates a shortage during the event, he should consult with the client to work out a solution.

It is recommended to have a back-up supply to avoid running out.

Ordering Beverages

When the menu is finalized, the ordering of the beverages is determined.

• The client may choose to supply the beverages himself. In this case, the caterer provides only the ice. The client will save money and the caterer has one fewer detail to tend to.

• The caterer is often responsible of all beverages, ice, ice buckets, etc...

The caterer should suggest a wine that is appropriate for the menu.

Examples of beverages for a classic reception

Alcoholic Beverages

1 bottle of Champagne per 4-5 guests
1 bottle Whisky per 25 guests
1 bottle Port (or other strong wine) per 35 guests
Ricard (anise-flavored drink) (optional)
Gin, Vodka if requested by client
1 bottle wine per 4-5 guests (served in a small keg for less formal events)

For less formal receptions the wine can be light and less sophisticated (Beaujolais for example).

For receptions with several courses, red and white wines are selected.

It is recommended to not mix too many wines.

Non alcoholic Beverages

1 L (1qt) orange juice for 8-10 guests
If another fruit juice is offered, substitute about one fourth of the orange juice.

Tomato juice (in small bottles)
Carbonated water (about 1 large bottle per 20 guests) often served with whiskey
Water : 1 large bottle per 15 guests
Soft drinks : colas and other soft drinks are rarely served at receptions in France.

Non-Alcoholic Beverages

Water

In France, bottled water is served, carbonated (usually Perrier) and " still " (Evian, Vittel, etc.)

Fruit juice

Orange juice is the most popular, followed by grapefruit juice.

The juices can be freshly squeezed or purchased in bottles.

Juices are served alongside other beverages on the buffet.

It is recommended to have a back-up supply.

Example of a rental checklist for a medium-sized reception

1 buffet table of 6 meters (about 18 feet)
1 buffet tables of 3 meters (about 9 feet)
1 table liner for each table
1 table cloth of 8 meters (about 24 feet)
1 table cloth of 5 meters (about 15 feet)
150 papier napkins
6 handtowels
1 table runner
1 large container for ice
1 warming oven
30 whiskey glasses
30 stemmed glasses
12 ashtrays
2 pitchers for juice
72 dessert plates
60 luncheon plates
48 coffee cups and saucers
2 small serving dishes
1 tiered serving dishes
1 small tray for passing
5 large platters
2 medium platters
1 ice bucket with tongs
1 sugar bowl
1 creamer
48 forks (with cutting edge)
48 teaspoons
1 serving spoon
1 serving fork
1 serving knife

16 Sample menu combinations

Choosing items for a menu

When planning a buffet, the caterer must consider three important points:

1. *Number of guests*
2. *Budget*
3. *The location and atmosphère*

Keeping these three points in mind, the caterer plans the event:
• Choose a menu and propose it to the client.
• Plan the preparation of each item.
• Arrange all details for delivery and service.

It is indispensable to work methodically. Denis Ruffel describes 16 sample menu combinations for different occasions. Each event is broken down into separate steps to show how to organize different kinds of receptions.

CLIENT .... Dossier N°

If company
Person in charge ....

Address
for billing ....

Method of payment ....

Tel. ....
Fax ....

Number guests

Budget

Place and address
of the reception ....

Set-up and atmosphere of reception room   Preparation facilities

RENTAL EQUIPMENT ☐ Furnished by us
(Check)   (Dossier N° ....)

Rented ☐ from ....

BUFFET   Menu finalized
by ....

BEVERAGES ....

Ice ....

TRANSPORTATION ....

Flowers ....

Musique ....

Other ....

RECEPTION SCHEDULE

Reception ....

Food
delivery ....

Food
pick-up ....

Rental
delivery ....

Rental
pick-up ....

(Other) ....

PERSONNEL

Additional information ....

Budget Guests	Category + **Low**	Category ++ **Medium**	Category +++ **High**	Category ++++ **Very high**
Category **A** **15 à 25**	**Bridge Club Party**	**Engagement Party**	**Directors' Meeting**	**Golden Anniversary**
Category **B** **40 à 60**	**Baptism**	**Informal wedding Reception**	**Boutique Inauguration**	**Reception on bateau-mouche**
Category **C** **120 à 150**	**Awards Ceremony**	**Officers Reserve Ball**	**Chamber of Commerce Reception**	**Formal Wedding Reception**
Category **D** **300 à 500**	**Reception at City Hall**	**Business School Ball**	**New car Promotion**	**Factory Opening**

Catering for a Variety of Events

A+ (P. 222) Annual Bridge Club Party

A++ (p. 228) The Engagement Party

B+ (p. 246) The Baptism

B++ (p. 252) The Informal Wedding Reception

C+ (p. 270) Awards Ceremony

C++ (p. 276) Officers Reserve Ball

D+ (p. 294) Reception at City Hall

D++ (p. 300) Business School Annual Ball

The 16 Sample Menus of Denis Ruffel

A+++ (p. 234) Board of Directors' Meeting

A++++ (p. 240) The Golden Anniversary

B+++ (p. 258) Designer Boutique Inauguration

B++++ (p. 264) Public Relations on " Bateau Mouche "

C+++ (p. 282) Retirement Reception/Chamber of Commerce

C++++ (p. 288) Formal Wedding Reception at a Château

D+++ (p. 306) Promoting the New Car Model

D++++ (p. 312) Factory Opening

The Annual Bridge Club Party

A small town bridge club is holding its annual party. The club members usually pool their resources to provide food and drink for this event, but in honor of this year's club building facelift, they have decided to call in a professional caterer to make the occasion extra special.

Details

This gathering is always a time for old and new members to interact: old friendships are renewed and new friendships are started. This year's party will also include the election of a new club council and a formal ceremony to introduce the new members.

Location

The party will be held in the municipal gym. Prior to the main event, the introductry cocktail will be held in the adjacent club room, which has tables that will later hold the buffet items.

CLIENT _Bridge Club_ .... _Wed April 16_ .... Dossier N° | _A+_ |

If company
Person in charge .... _Mr SCHLEM, Secretary_ .... Tel. _XX XX_ .....

Fax ------/------

Address
for billing .... _Bridge Club_ ....

.... _Community Center, Charnas_ ....

| Number guests |
| 25 |
| Budget |
| _Low_ |

Method of payment .. _By check, upon receipt of bill_ ....

Place and address
of the reception ..... _Charnas Community Center_ ....

.... _12, place de la Mairie   07340 CHARNAS_ ....

Set-up and atmosphere of reception room

In Community Center ....

Preparation facilities

.... _Not necessary_ ....

RENTAL EQUIPMENT | _X_ | Furnished by us
(Check)   (Dossier N° .... | _7_ |)

Rented |__| from ....

RECEPTION SCHEDULE

Reception ..... _8:00 pm to 9:30 pm_ ....

Food
delivery .... _16:00 pm_ ....

BUFFET   Menu finalized
             by .... _April 10_ ....

Food
pick-up .... _No_ ....

BEVERAGES ... _Supplied on site_ ....

Rental
delivery .... _No_ ....

Ice .... _Supplied on site_ ....

Rental
pick-up .... _No_ ....

TRANSPORTATION ... _Small van or_ ....
                    station wagon ....

(Other) ..... _platters, plates, etc._ ....
.... _all disposable_ ....

Flowers ... _Furnished by customer_ ....

Musique ... _No_ ....

Other ...... _No_ ....

PERSONNEL

... _no professional personnel_ ....

Additional information .. _The buffet is presented entirely on disposable platters_ ....

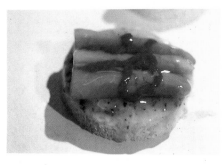

Suggested Menu (Example A+)

Savory Items

Savory Hors d'œuvres

- 25 Savory Almond Hors d'œuvres (1 item per person)
- 25 Cheese Matchsticks (1 item per person)

Total of 50 Savory Hors d'œuvres (2 items per person)

Filled Rolls

25 Mini Brioches with Foie Gras Mousse (1 item per person)

Canapés

- 10 Lumpfish Egg Canapés
- 10 Hard-Boiled Egg Canapés
- 10 Dry Sausage Canapés
- 10 Asparagus Tip Canapés
- 10 Parmesan Canapés

Total of 50 Canapés (2 items per person)

Centerpieces for Buffets

One Surprise Bread with Salami
Total of 25 sandwiches (1 per person)

Sweet Items

- 25 Fruit Tartelettes
- 25 Mini Cream Puffs
- 25 Decorated Fruit

Total of 75 sweet items (3 per person)

Grand Total of 225 items (9 per person) :

- 6 Savory Items
- 3 Sweet Items

Comments Menu Conception (Example A+)

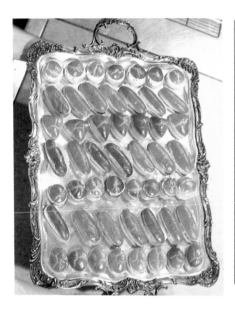

Savory Items

This is a simple menu that does not require a great deal of time, complicated set-up, or an oven for reheating.

Emphasis is placed on light, savory hors d'œuvres that may be served at room temperature.

Attractive platter presentations may be achieved by combining the various canapés (fish, meats, vegetables and cheese) made from inexpensive ingredients.

The Surprise Bread serves as a copious item that is sure to please all, while heightening the overall presentation.

Sweet Items

To determine the number of sweet and savory buffet items, professional caterers follow the ratio of (for 10 items):

- 7 Savory Items
- 3 Sweet Items

This buffet menu respects the standard division of 2/3 savory to 1/3 sweet.

Tartelettes are always a welcome item, the variety of mini cream puffs add a touch of color, and the decorated fruit adds a touch of gaiety.

Preparation

Advance prepartion for the savory items includes: the bread for the canapés, the puff pastry, the brioche dough for the surprise bread and sandwich assembly.

Advance preparation for the sweet items includes: the sweet pastry, the cream puffs, and the decorated fruit, which is an assortment of dried fruits, like prunes and dates; and nuts like walnuts and hazelnuts; all garnished with colored marzipan.

Be sure to shop in advance, and alot time for final preparations and finishing touches.

Other Considerations

The main problems with this buffet menu arise during delivery. Due to a small budget and a small number of guests, the items are delivered prearranged on disposable trays that are put in place by the delivery person.

The buffet should be in place before the beginning of the event.

Organization (Example A+)

For a reception without a serving staff, the entire buffet must be arranged in the caterer's kitchens on disposable trays.

The caterer should arrange platters for each of the savory items: puff pastry hors d'œuvres, an eye-catching assortment of canapés, and the filled rolls.

Decorate the surprise bread with a bright ribbon tied around the middle.

Savory Items

Savory Hors d'Œuvres

Prepare each item in advance and freeze uncooked. Defrost and bake several hours before delivery.

Canapés

Bake the bread well in advance to facilitate cutting. Do not assemble the canapés too far in advance or the bread will dry out.

Filled Rolls

Be sure the rolls are thoroughly cooled before filling. The bread must be very fresh.

Surprise Bread

Choose a small loaf of bread that marries well with the salami.

Sweet Items

Fill and glaze the tartelettes at the last minute.

The decorated fruit, may be coated by rolling in sugar or dipping in a sugar syrup.

Organization and Layout of the Buffet

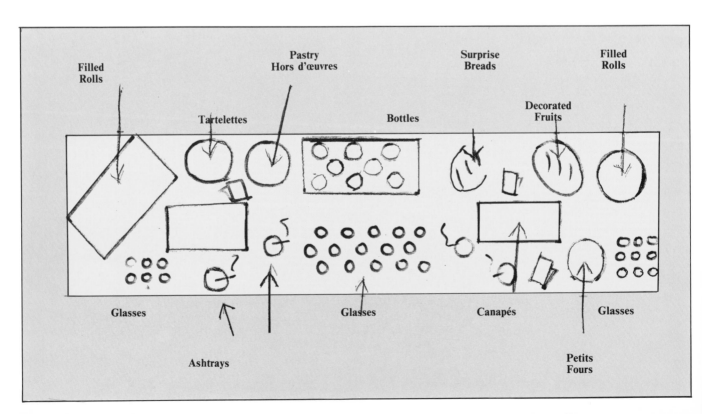

General Information and Advice

How much to serve per person ?

It is very difficult to determine exactly how much food to serve per person. Each event is a little different but with a few guidelines the caterer can estimate the amount.

For a classic stand-up buffet lasting 1 1/2 - 2 hours, count on about 8-12 pieces per person. The size of the portions is an important consideration.

Usually, the ratio is 2/3 savory items and 1/3 sweet items. This ratio can be modified : for a cocktail buffet, there are more savory items ; a buffet for younger guests may feature more sweet items.

The location and circumstances must be considered. A short reception that takes place in the office following work will require fewer items per person than an event where the guests do not have engagements following the reception.

Receptions with a very large number of guests require fewer items per person.

It is useful to know the " makeup " of the group (athletes, secretaries, business men).

The temperature plays a role as well. Guests tend to eat more in cold weather than in hot weather.

The quantity of food on the buffet is also determined by the budget and desires of the client.

The rapport budget/items per person

The price per person will be determined by the ingredients used. The menu can be composed of dishes made with reasonably priced ingredients and also with luxurious items such as caviar and lobster.

The caterer can combine menu items to suit every client's budget.

What makes one portion?

Depending on the style of buffet (cocktail, dinner) the portions will vary from a bite-size hors d'œuvre to an individual dish.

The Engagement Party

This is a special day for the Martin family. The oldest daughter, Véronique, is announcing her engagement. All the family members on both sides have been invited, and for this happy event (to take place in the month of June), the Martin's have chosen to celebrate at a lovely countryside inn.

Details

This is to be an intimate family gathering. The atmosphere must be pleasant and festive as it will be the first meeting of the two families, and the Martins want things to go as smoothly as possible.

Location

The owners of this beautifully restored country inn have a hall that they often rent for this type of gathering. It is a pictoresque setting, and the inn is well isolated and located directly next to a stream.

CLIENT .... *Mr & Mrs MARTIN* .... *Sat, June 12* .... Dossier N° | *A++* |

If company
Person in charge ..../............. Tel. ...*XX XX*......

Fax ...*XX XX*......

Address
for billing ...... *Mr & Mrs MARTIN* ....

.... *344, bd de la République ... 75004 Paris* ....

Number guests
25

Method of payment ... *By check, upon receipt of bill* ....

Budget
Average

Place and address
of the reception ..... *Moulin du Vert-Galant* ....

.... *Hameau des Gâtines ... 44301 SERRES-DU-HAUT* ....

Set-up and atmosphere of reception room   Preparation facilities

... *Old mill, restored for reception* .... *Furnished by customer* ....

RENTAL EQUIPMENT |___| Furnished by us
(Check)   (Dossier N°.../............. |___|)

Rented |___| from ..../...........

.............................../............

RECEPTION SCHEDULE

Reception .... *12:30 pm to 7:00 pm* ....

Food
delivery .... *11:00 am* ....

BUFFET   Menu finalized
       by .... *June 1* ....

Food
pick-up ...... *No* ....

BEVERAGES ... *Find local supplier* ....

Ice ....

Rental
delivery .... *No (furnished by Moulin)* ......

Rental
pick-up .... *No* ....

TRANSPORTATION ... *Refrigerated van* ....

(Other) ....

Flowers.... *Furnished by Moulin* ....

Musique ... *arranged by Moulin & customer* ..

Other... *None* ....

PERSONNEL

...... *1 server* ....

    Additional personnel furnished by Moulin

Additional information ..... *Not much more than a simple delivery* ....

       Careful to take full account of the distance

Suggested Menu (Example A++)

Savory Items

Savory Hors d'Œuvres
- 10 " Croque Monsieur "
- 10 Pâté Hors d'œuvres
- 10 Tartelettes of Juilienned Vegetables
- 10 Mini Pizzas
- 10 Mini Quiches

Total of 50 items

Canapés
- 10 Smoked Salmon Canapés
- 10 Lumpfish Egg Canapés
- 10 Cocktail Mignonettes
- 10 Quail Egg Canapés
- 10 Green Bean Canapés

Total of 50 items

Centerpiece
- Stuffed Crêpe Hedgehog, crab mousse filling, grapefruit base (25 crêpes)
- Surprise Bread, Walnut and Raisin Loaf (25 sandwiches)

Total of 8 items

Presentation Item
Chicken in Chaud-Froid (25 pieces)

Mixed Salad
Méli-Mélo Salad (25 servings)

Cheese Platter
Cheese cubes with toothpicks, served with walnut bread

Total of 225 Savory Items

Sweet Items

- 1 Croquembouche Centerpiece (1 cream puff per person)

- Sherbet Cups (1 per person)

- Assorted Cookies: tuiles, cigarettes and palmiers (1 per person)

Comments on the Menu Selection (Example A++)

Savory Items

Although this buffet is destined for a small lunchtime gathering, we chose to serve an assortment of substantial hors d'œuvres, which are made from a variety of doughs: bread dough, basic pie pastry and puff pastry.

The same holds for the five sorts of canapés, which bring a touch of color to the presentation by varying the ingredients (fish, eggs, meats and vegetables).

The Stuffed Crêpe Hedgehog is always a crowd pleaser. The small number of guests permits a single filling for the crêpes, and this helps to keep costs down.

The hedgehog centerpiece is built around a grapefruit.

A long, thin walnut raisin loaf is most suitable for the surprise bread for this size gathering.

Chicken in chaud-froid is ideal for a small buffet. It has universal appeal and it heightens the overall presentation.

The Méli-Mélo Salad is the ideal accompaniment, adding a touch of freshness to the menu.

Sweet Items

In keeping with French tradition, an engagement party buffet includes a croquembouche.

The sherbet cups are a refreshing item, and the assorted cookies may be served with the sherbet or the coffee.

Others Considerations

The family of the bride organized the event.

They chose a charming reception spot, but it is about 60 miles outside of town and they insist that their favorite in-town caterer prepare the buffet.

All of the necessary equipment will be furnished by the the reception hall: tables, tablecloths, tableware, ice and a sound system.

It is the caterer's responsiblity to contact the hall and arrange the buffet organization, i.e. table set-up, buffet presentation, etc. The caterer should organize in advance any special equipment necessary to the buffet.

Make sure that both the checklist and order form have been thoroughly filled out. For out-of-town events, be sure to calculate travel time, leaving a large buffer for unexpected occurences like traffic jams or flat tires.

Also note local weekend business hours in case of last-minute shopping needs.

Organization (Example A++)

This is a fairly simple menu. The components of this buffet require a minimum of preparation and the volume is small. The crucial tasks are delivery and on-site preparation.

Savory Items

Hors d'Œuvres

The pastry hors d'œuvres may be prepared up to several days in advance and frozen before cooking.

They should be baked the day of the event, but not so soon that freshness suffers and never at the last minute.

Placing piping hot hors d'œuvres in boxes for transport keeps all the steam inside and the food arrives soggy.

The julienned vegetable tartelettes are best assembled on-site to avoid damage during transport.

Canapés

Prepare the white bread three days in advance to facilitate slicing.

The toppings may be prepared the day before: seasoned butters, quail eggs, etc.

Assembly, decoration, and aspic glaze are all done the day of the event.

Stuffed Crêpe Hedgehog

The crêpes may be prepared and stuffed one day in advance. To facilitate transportaion, the hedgehog should be assembled on-site.

Surprise Bread

The bread is prepared at the same time as the canapé bread.

Filling and assembly may be done one day in advance; wrap the sandwiches in plastic and refrigerate.

Chicken in Chaud-Froid

Cook the chicken two days in advance, and coat with the chaud-froid one day in advance.

Glaze with aspic just prior to delivery, or on-site.

Mixed Salad

All the ingredients are prepared one day in advance. Prepare the dressing separately and toss on-site.

Cheese Platter

The cheese cubes may be prepared, with toothpicks, one day in advance. Store under plastic wrap. The walnut bread may be baked one day in advance.

Sweet Items

Croquembouche

Prepare the cream puffs one day in advance, and the pastry cream on the day of the event.

If using a nougatine base, it may be prepared and cut several days in advance if stored in a cool, dry place.

A croquembouche is very fragile and it is best to assemble on-site, and this is mandatory when the event requires long-distance delivery. For on-site delivery, fill the cream puffs and glaze one day in advance.

Be sure to include the ingredients and material necessary to assembly, as well as the ornaments (pulled or blown sugar decorations).

Sherbet Cups

The sherbet cups may be prepared several days in advance with the proper equipment. This includes a freezer for storage and well-insulated ice chests with dry ice for transport.

The sherbet should be taken out in sufficent time to soften slightly before serving (it should be about 40 to 45 F/5 to 7 °C). Be sure to instruct the serving staff on timing.

Assorted Cookies

These may be prepared several days in advance if stored in airtight containers. Presentation should be done on-site by serving staff.

The caterer's job ends after delivery and on-site preparations. From this point on, it is up to the serving staff to assure smooth transition between the courses.

Preparation and Layout
of the Buffet

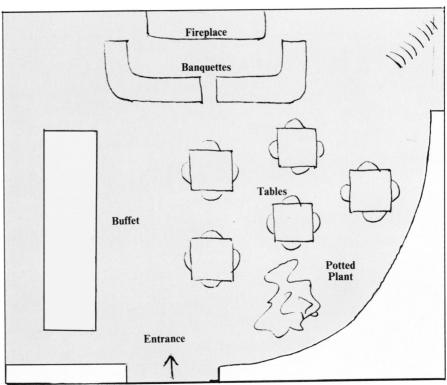

Fireplace

Banquettes

Buffet

Tables

Potted
Plant

Entrance

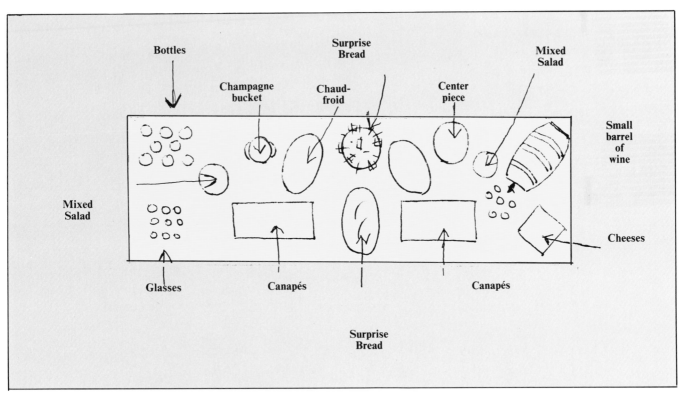

Bottles

Surprise
Bread

Mixed
Salad

Champagne
bucket

Chaud-
froid

Center
piece

Small
barrel
of
wine

Mixed
Salad

Cheeses

Glasses

Canapés

Canapés

Surprise
Bread

The Board of Directors Meeting

A successful international engineering corporation will be holding its annual board meeting. This year's meeting is particularly important as the directors of the new Japanese and Brazilian subsidiaries will be present.

Details

The meeting will begin at 9:00 a.m. and is scheduled to last through till noon. The caterer has been asked to provide a cocktail buffet to be held outdoors, followed by a buffet luncheon.

Location

The director's meeting is held at the corporation's main office, which is located in a skyscraper. The top floor is reserved for executive gatherings and the main room has sliding glass doors that open on to a rooftop garden.

CLIENT _INTERNATIONAL TECHNOLOGY RESEARCH, INC._ _May 24_   Dossier N° |A+++|

If company
Person in charge __Mr Charles__   Tel. _XX XX_

Fax _XX XX_

Address
for billing ___I.T.R., INC___

_____11, rue Jacques-Tourbleux___45300 La Chapelle_____

Number guests
25

Method of payment __By check, 30 % in advance, balance upon receipt of bill__

Budget
High

Place and address
of the reception ____I.T.R.___

_____11, rue Jacques-Tourbleux___45300 La Chapelle_

Set-up and atmosphere of reception room	Preparation facilities
__Terrace for drinks buffet__	__Small off reception hall kitchen__
__Reception hall for lunch buffet__	

RENTAL EQUIPMENT |X| Furnished by us
(Check) (Dossier N° _____|27|)

Rented |X| from __OPTIONS__

BUFFET Menu finalized
by _____May 19

BEVERAGES ___Champagne, whisky, Porto,___
__mineral water, St-Emilion, Chablis__

Ice __1 x 40 lbs__

TRANSPORTATION _Small delivery van_

Flowers_1 centerpiece for buffet_

Musique __None__

Other__ _None_

RECEPTION SCHEDULE

Reception ___1:00 pm to 3:30 pm_

Food
delivery_____11:00 am

Food
pick-up _____4:30 pm

Rental
delivery _____9:00 am

Rental
pick-up _____5:00 pm

(Other) ____flowers at 12:00 noon

PERSONNEL
2 servers
1 chef

Additional information _____

Suggested Menu (Example A+++)

Savory Items

Savory Hors d'Œuvres
- 25 Mini Pizzas
- 25 Gougères

Total of 50 items

Canapés
- 10 Sole Medallion Canapés
- 10 Quail's Eggs Canapés
- 10 Sautéed Zucchini Canapés
- 10 Cherry Tomato Canapés
- 10 Baby Corn Canapés

Total of 50 items

Mignonnettes
- 25 Langoustine Fritters
- 25 Belgian Endive Leaves with Foie Gras

Total of 50 Mignonnettes

Centerpiece
Stuffed Crêpe Hedgehog with assorted fillings, on toothpicks (25 crêpes)

Fish Presentation
Galantine of Salmon in Aspic (25 slices)

Meat Presentation
Beef Tenderloin " Perigueux " in Aspic (25 servings)

Poultry Presentation
Pâté of Duck à l'Orange in Aspic (25 slices)

Mixed Salad
Brazilian Salad (25 servings)

Cheese
Assorted Cheese Platter, with walnut bread rolls (25 servings)

Sweet Items

- 25 Mini Tartelettes
- 25 Assorted Mini-Pastries
- Basket of Fresh Fruit (1 per person)

Grand Total of 375 items

Comments on the Menu Selection (Example A+++)

This menu is particulary suitable for stand-up affairs because each item is served separately.

Savory Items

The client requested two separate savory courses :

The first course is a cocktail buffet. The small size of the gathering calls for a restricted number of items, but they may be copious, which is perfect for the flavorful mini-pizzas and the more neutral cheese gougères.

The Mignonnettes add elegance: the langoustine fritters are served with a tartare sauce, and the Belgian endives with foie gras are delicious. The the combination of fish and foie gras balances out the flavor distribution.

The Crêpe Hedgehog adds volume to the menu and it is always a welcome addition to the buffet table.

The assortment of five canapés is equally distributed between fish, eggs and vegetables for a well-balanced finish to the first course.

The second course of the buffet is reserved for the main dishes. Begin with the duck pâté, and follow with the salmon galantine and the beef tenderloin. The salad may be served either with the fish or the meat, or on its own, before the cheese.

The savory course ends with the cheese platter. The cheeses are presented whole, and pieces are cut by the serving staff and served with walnut rolls.

Sweet Items

All the dessert items are served individually to facilitate stand-up dining.

This course is comprised of assorted tarts and pastries, made from a variety of flavors and using a range of different colored ingredients.

The fresh fruit basket adds a note of freshness to the buffet, and fruit is always appreciated at the end of a meal.

Preparation

All ingredients may be purchased several days in advance. Prepare the white bread, walnut rolls, pizza dough and gougère pastry several days in advance. The fritter batter must be made at the last minute.

Make thorough preparations for the sweet items to speed up assembly.

The buffet table is prepared by the serving staff and the chef about 30 minutes to 1 hour prior to the event.

Other Considerations

It is difficult to calculate the exact time at which this sort of buffet will begin, so be sure that delivery and set-up are well organized.

While the cocktails are being served, the chef should warm the hors d'œuvres. The chef may help the staff serve this course, which is a pleasant and original enhancement to any buffet.

The chef must prepare the langoustine fritters on-site.

As a matter of safety, all cooking elements must be electric. Also, the on-site kitchen space is limited, which requires a great deal of organization.

Organization (Example A+++)

This is the standard menu for this type of gathering, however it does require extra supervision because the caterer will be supplying only the food and not the equipment. Be sure that the company responsible for supplying the tableware has received the proper instructions.

Set-up for this buffet is standard due to the small volume.

Savory Items

Hors d'Œuvres

The pizzas and gougères may be prepared one day in advance and refrigerated. Reheat just before serving.

Canapés

Bake the bread three days in advance. Prepare all the toppings one day in advance, i.e. seasoned butter, quail eggs, etc. For maximum freshness, canapés should always be assembled the day of the event

Mignonnettes

The langoustines (salt water crayfish) may be prepared and marinated up to one day in advance.
The fritter batter is prepared on-site, just prior to serving (be sure to include oil for frying).
The Belgian endive leaves should be prepared and glazed the morning of the event to ensure maximum freshness. Store under plastic wrap.

Stuffed Crêpe Hedgehog

Prepare, stuff, and roll the crêpes one day in advance and refrigerate.
Assemble the hedgehog on the day of the event, or assemble on site.

Pâté of Duck à l'Orange in Aspic

Prepare the pâté several days in advance and refrigerate.
Slice and arrange on platters before delivery or on site. For on-site assembly, be sure to include all the necessary ingredients: diced aspic, orange slices, etc.

Galantine of Salmon in Aspic

Same as Pâté of Duck.

Beef Tenderloin " Perigueux " in Aspic

The tenderloin is cooked one day in advance and refrigerated.
Slice, glaze, and arrange on platter before delivery. Protect with plastic wrap.

Brazilian Salad

Prepare all the ingredients separately one day in advance, and refrigerate. Assemble on-site, just prior to serving to prevent the salad from becoming soggy by sitting too long in the dressing.

Cheese Platter

Order a prepared platter from a specialty cheese shop, or assemble before delivery. Cover with plastic wrap to keep the odors away from the other items.

Walnut Rolls

Prepare one day in advance, or order from a bakery or specialty shop.

Sweet Items

Plan ahead so that the assorted pastries are worked into the daily baking schedule.

Fruit Basket

Order from a specialty shop, or arrange fruit in an attractive basket before delivery.
Just prior to serving, spray with a mist of water (use a plant sprayer, for example). The drops of water enhance the presentation and make the fruit appear even more refreshing.

Specifics

The head waiter should be on-site when the tableware and set-up equipment is delivered to ensure that nothing is misssing, and to organize the set-up. Another waiter should arrive just prior to the beginning of the event.

The caterer's responsibilities include: on-site preparations, cleanliness of the site before and after the event, and verification of any damage to rented material.

Verify one day in advance that the proper quantity and assortment of drinks has been provided. Refrigerate any drinks to be served cold, and verify the serving temperature of the wines.

Order the floral centerpiece several days in advance, to be delivered to the caterer.

Organization and Layout of the Buffet

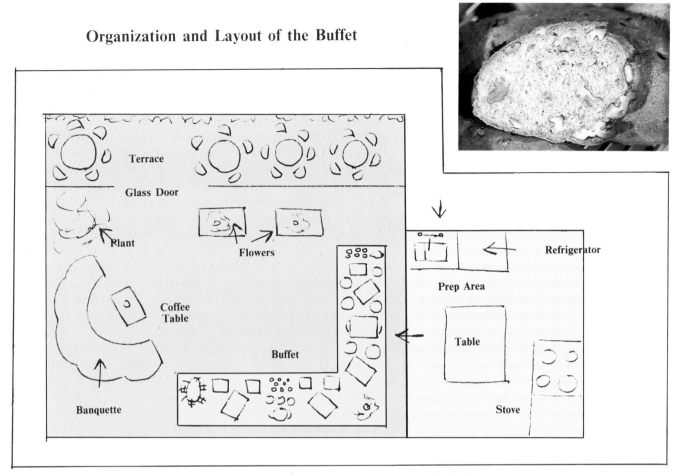

General Information and Advice

Fruits

Fruits serve a dual purpose on a buffet table:

• Taste: Fruit can accompany other desserts or can be the only dessert.

• Decoration: A presentation of fruit with a wide variety of colors and shapes can be a veritable work of art.

Choosing the Fruits

For large arrangements, choose fruits with a variety of forms and colors that create a harmonious display. Cherries, strawberries and currants can be served without silverware.

Other fruits should be small so that they are easy to handle.

Some fruits are expensive and cannot be used if the budget is limited. For best flavor and price, choose the fruits that are in season.

Presentation

Fruit presentations can range from a simple basket of small whole fruits (decorated with leaves and a ribbon) to more elaborate displays that can serve as a centerpiece for the buffet table. These larger presentations could include a wicker cornucopia overflowing with fruits of every color or other dramatic base.

Large fruits can be cut into portions and arranged with whole uncut fruits within a display (pineapples cut in cubes or slices and arranged on the " shell ").

The caterer can purchase the fruits and arrange them himself or order a dazzling display from a specialty shop. Fruit presentations can be as fresh and colorful as the prettiest floral bouquet.

Fruit Salad

For some occasions the fruit is best served as a salad. A large bowl of several fruits cut into bite-size pieces is a refreshing dessert. The fruit is usually combined with a flavorful sugar syrup (cinnamon, fruit liquer, etc.) to give a wonderful flavor and keep the fruit from turning brown.

In France one popular combination is a medley of several red berries. A variety of exotic fruits also makes a delicious salad.

The fruit is spooned into small bowls or ramekins by a server which makes it easy to eat at a stand-up buffet.

The Golden Anniversary

A well-to-do elderly couple will celebrate their fiftieth wedding anniversary. They have invited all of their friends and family.

Details

The party will be held on a Saturday afternoon in the couple's luxuriously decorated apartment. The caterer has been asked to provide a sumptuous dinner buffet.

Location

The tables will be set up in the large dining room, and guests will be allowed to wander into the adjacent salon that opens on to a garden.

CLIENT _Mr Charles-Henri BRACHMUTZ_ _Sat June 21_ Dossier N° $\boxed{A+++}$

If company
Person in charge

Tel. _XX XX_

Fax

Address
for billing _Mr & Mrs BRACHMUTZ_

46, Quai André 75002 PARIS

Method of payment _By check, upon reception of bill_

Number guests
25
Budget
Very high

Place and address
of the reception _Same as above_

Set-up and atmosphere of reception room	Preparation facilities
Luxury apartment	_Fully equipped kitchen_
Dining room and terrace	

RENTAL EQUIPMENT $\boxed{X}$ Furnished by us
(Check) (Dossier N° $\boxed{33}$)

Rented $\boxed{X}$ from _S.L.M.T._

BUFFET Menu finalized
by _May 5_

BEVERAGES _Customer's own wine cellar_

Ice _1 x 40 lbs bag_

TRANSPORTATION _Small delivery van_

RECEPTION SCHEDULE

Reception _3:30 pm to 10:00 pm_

Food
delivery _1:30 pm_

Food
pick-up _after reception_

Rental
delivery _11:30 am_

Rental
pick-up _Monday, am in presence_
of caterer's representative
(Other)

Flowers _by customer_

Musique _No_

Other _No_

PERSONNEL

1 servers
1 chef

Additional information _Take care not to damage antique furniture._
Pay special attention to flaver of food

241

Suggested Menu (Example A++++)

Savory Items

Savory Hors d'Œuvres
- 25 Crab Canapés
- 25 Caviar Canapés
- 25 Foie Gras Canapés

Total of 75 canapés

Mignonnettes
25 Belgian Endive Leaves with Smoked Salmon

Hot Hors d'Œuvres
- 25 " Feuilletés " with Asparagus Tips
- 25 " Feuilletés " with Crayfish
- 25 " Croustades " of Sweetbreads

Total of 75 Hot Hors d'Œuvres

Fish Presentation
Sea Bass in Chaud-Froid (25 servings)

Brochettes
- 25 Shellfish Brochettes
- 25 Ham and Pineapple Brochettes

Total of 50 brochettes

Centerpiece
Surprise Bread (25 sandwiches)

Beignets
- 25 Breaded Salmon Beignets with Green Beans
- 25 Breaded Oyster Beignets

Total of 50 beignets

Poultry Presentation
25 Quails with Foie Gras in Aspic (25 servings)

Mixed Salads
Cinderella Salad (25 servings)

Cheese
Platter of Assorted Cheeses (25 servings)

Sweet Items

- Birthday Cake (25 servings)
- 25 Tartelettes
- 25 Mini-pastries
- 25 Chocolate Covered Candied Orange Rind
- 25 Sorbet cups
- Basket of Fresh Fruit

Grand Total of 550 items

Comments on the Menu Selection (Example A++++)

The client has ordered a luxurious banquet with high-quality products for a family gathering. There will be a handful of small tables for this sit-down affair, with silverware and porcelain dishes. There will be a head waiter.

Both the cocktail and the main course buffets will be presented by the head waiter on a main dining table, with tablecloth.

Savory Items

The Cocktail Buffet

For a formal affair, this course is just as important as the main course. In this case, it will last about 2 hours, and the items should be substantial.

The chef prepares the hot hors d'œuvres, which are served by the head waiter. This requires perfect timing.

The chef also prepares the beignets, which are to be served piping hot. It is best to prepare these in small batches.

The canapé assortment includes a variety of elegant ingredients: crab, caviar and foie gras. The Belgian endives with salmon appeal to all.

The brochette combinations – shellfish, and ham and pineapple – are delicious, and they help to lighten up the menu.

For this event, be sure to serve the surprise bread on a silver platter.

The Main Buffet

The main buffet menu consists of fish, poultry, salad and cheese.

At the close of the cocktail buffet, the head waiter begins organizing the main course buffet. All of the courses should be in the kitchen and ready to go.

The sea bass is the ideal fish for an elegant occasion. Depending upon the size of the fish and the number of guests, serve either one or two sea bass.

The boned quail stuffed with foie gras are also an appropriate choice when a client asks for refined ingredients.

The small number of guests makes this dish particularly simple to serve.

The Cinderella salad is best when the ingredients are in season, and in keeping with the tone of the occasion, prepare it with fresh asparagus tips and artichoke bottoms. The salad may be served separately, or to accompany the fish or the quail.

For an elegant finish, the head waiter should serve the cheese course, offering slices from the assorted cheeses presented on a wicker tray decorated with ribbons.

Sweet Items

The centerpiece should be the birthday cake. Display prominently, with adequate decoration.

Arrange the tartelettes, assorted pastries, and orange slices on platters.

The head waiter will serve the sorbet cups.

The fruit basket should be set on the main table and the guests allowed to serve themselves.

Preparation

All purchases may be made several days in advance.

Be sure that all advance preparation is thoroughly executed:

Bake the pastry for the feuilletés and the croustades; and cook the asparagus and the crayfish.

For the sweetbreads, prepare the sauce and reheat just before serving, or as requested by the guests.

Cook the green beans. Prepare the fritter batter, and shuck the oysters. Fry at the last minute, or as requested by the guests.

Prepare the Belgian endive leaves with smoked salmon.

Bone and cook the quail.

Prepare all the ingredients for the salad.

The following items may be prepared several days in advance:

Bread for the canapés, surprise bread, bread for the cheese course, puff pastry, birthday cake, tartelette pastry dough, dough for assorted pastries, and sorbet.

Be sure that all the reception material is of the best quality and includes: silver platters, champagne buckets, silverware, crystal glasses, high-quality fabric tablecloths, elegant baskets, etc.

Other Considerations

Although the guest list is small, the client requested a large variety of items. All the items should correspond to the formality of the event, taking into account the age spectrum of the guests. There should be a sufficient number of items, with enough to please young and old alike.

Space is limited and there is a great deal of antique furniture that cannot be moved.

The client would like the cocktail buffet to be outdoors, but there is a chance of bad weather.

Formal events require a great deal of on-site, last minute preparations.

Organization (Example A++++)

The success of this buffet, although small, depends on a great deal of organization.

Savory Items

Hot Hors d'Œuvres

The feuilletés are shaped up to several days in advance, and frozen uncooked.

Bake the day of the event to ensure maximum freshness. Assemble on site and reheat just prior to serving.

The croustade molds may be lined one day in advance. Bake the day of the event and reheat before serving.

Beignets

When handling perishable ingredients like salmon, green beans, and oysters, it is best to prepare them the day of the event, just prior to delivery. These are prepared and arranged on platters on-site. Be sure that all the necessary equipment is provided for both cooking and serving.

Canapés

The bread may be prepared several days in advance, but because the toppings are made with perishable ingredients, it is best to assemble the day of the event, just prior to delivery.

Belgian endive leaves

The salmon may be prepared on the day of the event, but assemble just prior to delivery to ensure maximum freshness.

Brochettes

Preparation and assembly should be done the morning of the event. Cover with plastic wrap and refrigerate. Glaze with aspic and arrange on platter just prior to delivery.

Surprise Bread

Prepare the loaf for the surprise bread four days in advance.

Prepare the sandwiches and assemble one day in advance. Cover with plastic wrap and refrigerate (about 7 °C (40 F).

Sea Bass in Chaud-Froid

Cook the fish 48 hours prior to the reception, and refrigerate.

Assemble and coat with the chaud-froid up to one day in advance. Coat with aspic just prior to delivery to ensure a shiny and appealing glaze.

Quail

Prepare, stuff, and cook the quail 48 hours in advance. Store in the refrigerator.

Decorate and coat with aspic before delivery, platter arrangement is done on-site.

Be sure to include the garnish and necessary decoration ingredients.

Cinderella Salad

Because the ingredients of this salad discolor easily, it is best prepared on the day of the event and assembled on-site. Dress just before serving.

Cheese Platter

Order the cheeses from a specialty shop and arrange on a platter. Cover securely with plastic wrap for delivery to ensure that the odors do not permeate the other dishes.

The head waiter is in charge of serving the cheeses at the proper temperature.

Sweet Items

Birthday Cake

Prepare two to three days in advance, and decorate according to client instructions.

Organize the cake's display in advance as it is the center of attraction for this event and should be prominently and attractively displayed.

If using presentation stands, be sure that they are delivered well in advance so that the rest of the buffet may be set up around them.

However, do not deliver the cake too far in advance, especially if it requires refrigeration.

Accompaniments

The preparation of the tartelettes, pastries, and chocolate covered candied orange zest should be worked into the daily baking schedule.

Sorbet Cups

Prepare one day in advance and store in deep-freeze. Transport in well-insulated ice chests.

The head waiter should oversee their temperature, and ensure that they are served at the proper temperature, about (6 °C (45 F)).

Fruit Basket

Arrange on-site, or order a fruit basket arrangement from a specialty shop.

Just prior to serving, spray a light mist of water on the fruit to add an attractive sheen.

Specifics

Be sure that all the requested equipment is delivered on time.

The head waiter should have some

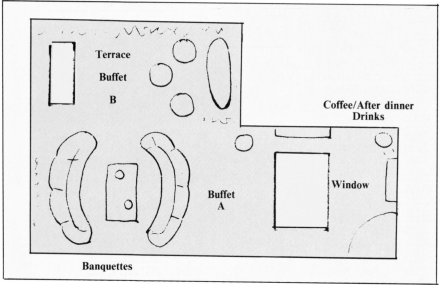

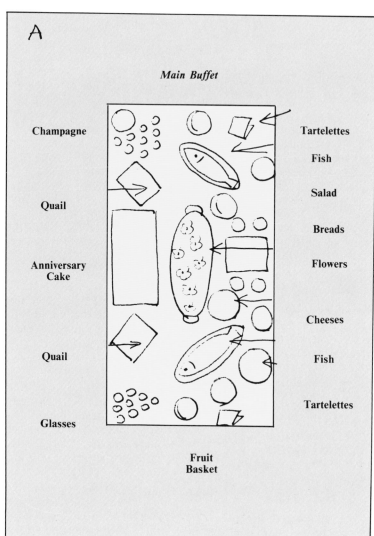

A

Main Buffet

Champagne

Tartelettes

Fish

Salad

Quail

Breads

Flowers

Anniversary
Cake

Cheeses

Quail

Fish

Tartelettes

Glasses

Fruit
Basket

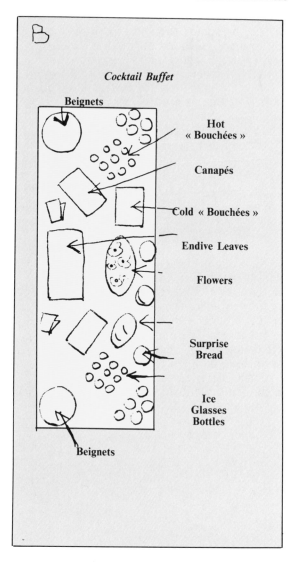

B

Cocktail Buffet

Beignets

Hot
« Bouchées »

Canapés

Cold « Bouchées »

Endive Leaves

Flowers

Surprise
Bread

Ice
Glasses
Bottles

Beignets

experience with apartment receptions as the space will be limited.

Arrange the choice of wines and flowers with the clients well in advance.

Outline the tasks for the serving staff to ensure that no aspect is overlooked.

Check the rented material and equipment after the reception to note any damage.

Assure a total clean-up, and take out all the trash.

If necessary, after clean-up, ask the clients to verify that all has been arranged to their satisfaction.

Arrange in advance any post-reception services the client may require, such as returning furniture to its original place and distributing floral arrangements.

A Baptism

The Richard's will be celebrating the baptism of their newborn son. The young couple has decided to organize a small family gathering, and they hired a caterer to take care of all the details.

Details

Because the Richard's recently moved into their current home, they would like the event to double as a sort of housewarming and an occasion to show off the new house to their family.

Location

The event has been scheduled for midsummer, which will allow for an outdoor buffet in the Richard's well-shaded backyard. The Richard's will provide tables, with umbrellas, as well as a long table for the children.

CLIENT _____ *Mr & Mrs J.-C. RICHARD* _____ *Sundy july 21* _____ Dossier N° | *B+*

If company
Person in charge _____ Tel. _*XX XX*_____

Fax __*XX XX*_____

Address
for billing _____ *45, Villa des Hirondelles* _____

Number guests

| *60* |

_____ *78000 Le Vésinet* _____

Method of payment ___ *By check, upon presentation of bill* _____

Budget

___ *limited* _____

_____ *on the day of the reception* _____

Place and address
of the reception _____ *45, Villa des Hirondelles* _____

Set-up and atmosphere of reception room

___ *On lawn in rear of private home* _____

Preparation facilities

_____ *Kitchen in cellar not well equipped* ____

RENTAL EQUIPMENT | *X* | Furnished by us
(Check)   (Dossier N° _____ | *12* |)

Rented | *X* | from __*AKTUEL*_____

BUFFET   Menu finalized
                by _____ *July 10* _____

BEVERAGES ___ *Furnished by customer* _____

Ice ___ *2 x 40 lbs bags* _____

TRANSPORTATION ____ *Van*_____

_____ *Small delivery van* _____

Flowers ___ *By customer* _____

Musique _*By customer*_____

Other ___ *None*

RECEPTION SCHEDULE

Reception _____ *3:30 pm* _____

Food
delivery _____ *11:30 am* _____

Food
pick-up _____ *After reception* _____

Rental
delivery _____ *Saturday afternoon* _____

Rental
pick-up _____ *Monday morning* _____

(Other) _____

PERSONNEL

___ *2 servers* _____
___ *1 chef* _____

Additional information ___ *Make sure delivery is on time. Do not exceed budget.* _____

Contingency plan inside in case of rain.

Suggested Menu (Example B+)

Savory Items

Savory Hors d'Œuvres

- 12 Parmesan Canapés
- 12 Pâté Canapés
- 12 Anchovy Canapés
- 12 Ham Crescents
- 12 Dry Sausage Canapés
- 12 Mini-Pizzas
- 12 Gougères
- 12 Salmon Tartelettes
- 12 Mushroom Tartelettes
- 12 Tartelettes of Julienned Vegetables

Total of 120 items.

Mini-Sandwiches

- 30 Ham Sandwiches
- 30 Lettuce and Cucumber Sandwiches

Total of 60 Sandwiches

Canapés

- 12 Monkfish Medaillon Canapés
- 12 Lumpfish Canapés
- 12 Liver Mousse Canapés
- 12 Tomato Wedge Canapés
- 12 Radish Canapés
- 12 Broccoli Canapés
- 12 Green Bean Canapés
- 12 Baby Corn Canapés
- 12 " Fromage Frais " and Chive Canapés
- 12 Mini Goat Cheese Canapés

Total of 120 assorted canapés.

Centerpieces

2 Surprise Breads (Brioche Mousseline) of 30 sandwiches each. Filling: Crab Mayonnaise with Chervil.
Total of 60 items.
Grand Total of 360 savory items.

Sweet Items

- One cake, such as a " Fraisier ", (Strawberry Genoise) (60 servings)
- Assortment of 30 Decorated Fruit and Macerated Fruit (30 items)
- 30 Macaroons
- 30 Mini Almond Butter Cakes (Financiers)
- 60 Mini Eclairs; 30 coffee and 30 chocolate

Comments on the Menu Selection (Example B+)

This is an informal outdoor garden reception for 60 guests.

The clients would like to keep the costs down. The caterer should choose inexpensive but high-quality ingredients that respect the budget while still providing a substantial and attractive buffet.

There is no need for any large centerpiece items. This buffet will center around a selection of cocktail items with universal appeal as there will be many children.

Savory Items

For the cocktail buffet, there will be 120 items comprised of 10 different varieties with many ingredients (cheese, meat, pizza, fish and vegetables), including hot items.

Next are the 60 sandwiches, an assortment of lettuce and cucumber, and ham, which complete the cocktail buffet.

The next course is the assortment of varied canapés, 120 items in all, which add a festive element.

To enhance the presentation, the two brioche mousseline surprise breads should be decorated with brightly-colored ribbons and served on separate, adjacent tables.

Sweet Items

The centerpiece is a Fraisier cake, decorated specially for this event (a baptism). Spring is the perfect season for this cake, and it is sure to please old and young alike.

An assortment of sweets is served alongside the cake: decorated fruit, mini almond butter cakes, macaroons, and chocolate and coffee mini-eclairs.

Preparation

Shopping is relatively easy for this type of buffet.

Advance preparation may be done for the: puff pastry, white bread, brioches, cake batters, decorated fruit, choux pastry.

Deliver the goods before the church ceremony, while the clients are still at home. Set up the kitchen in the garage, with sawhorses and boards for work surfaces.

It is often best to arrive well in advance to allow for on-site preparation, which also facilitates delivery. This generally improves the presentation because the dishes look brighter and fresher.

All of the finished or semi-finished dishes should be transported in well-insulated ice chests. Be sure to label each container with its contents to facilitate unloading and on-site organization. This also prevents unnecessary opening and closing of the ice chests.

Arrange for the rental material: stainless steel platters, standard tableware and glassware, eating utensils and tablecloths.

Other Considerations

Weather: For outdoor events, always be sure to have an alternate plan, regardless of the weather forecasts, to ensure that the reception is pleasant, whether outdoors or in.

Delivery: Be sure to arrive before the family has left for the ceremony.

Refrigeration: Have plenty of ice chests, with ice packs on hand to keep the dishes at the proper temperature for the duration of the event. The client's refrigerator may not be big enough.

Organization (Example B+)

Because this buffet menu is made up of small items, everything should be prepared before delivery. On-site preparations will be reheating and presentation.

The substantial dessert course should also be prepared before delivery.

Overall, this buffet is simple to prepare and present.

Savory Items

Hors d'Œuvres

The puff pastry hors d'œuvres may be prepared in advance and frozen before cooking. Bake the day of the event to ensure fresh, crispy hors d'œuvres.

Prepare the pie crust shells one day in advance; fill and bake the day of the event.

The gougères may be prepared one day in advance, and reheated just before serving.

Mini Sandwiches

Prepare the ham sandwiches one day in advance. Cover in plastic wrap to prevent the sandwiches from drying out, and refrigerate.

To prevent the bread from becoming soggy and the lettuce from wilting, the cucumber sandwiches should not be made any earlier than the day of the event.

Canapés

Prepare the bread for the canapés up to three days in advance. One day in advance, slice the bread, wrap in plastic and refrigerate. The canapé ingredients may be prepared one day in advance: cook the sole fillets, the quail eggs, etc, and refrigerate. Prepare the seasoned butter one day in advance but be sure to bring to room temperature before assembly to facilitate spreading.

Assemble the canapés the day of the event. Depending on the season, the canapés may be stored placed on moistened parchment paper (to keep the bread fresh), then wrapped in plastic and refrigerated until time of delivery. The head waiter should unwrap and arrange on platters on-site.

Surprise Bread

Prepare the brioche two days in advance. Prepare the filling and assemble the day of the event. This is a perishable item, which is best prepared at the last minute and refrigerated. Wrap in moistened parchment paper, then in plastic and chill.

Refrigerate before and after delivery. Platter arrangement should be done on-site.

Sweet Items

Fraisier The cake may be prepared one day in advance. For square cakes without side frosting, trim the day of the event to ensure an even and attractive edge.

To heighten the presentation, the cake may be served on a stand and decorated with pulled sugar or marzipan flowers.

Decorated Fruit Prepare two days in advance and glaze the day of the event.

Mini Eclairs Fill and glaze the day of the event. Take all the necessary precautions to ensure the freshness of the pastry cream, which is highly perishable (especially for an outdoor, afternoon event).

Allow sufficent time to make two deliveries, if necessary, to ensure that all the products receive adequate refrigeration.

Specifics

When setting up the tables, take into account these factors: shade and

General Information and Advice

Tableware

The tableware should be chosen to coordinate with the formality of the buffet. Plates, glasses and silverware are available in a variety of styles.

It is also important to have the tableware necessary to easily consume the items chosen for a given menu. For example, a stand-up buffet featuring primarily "finger-foods" will not require silverware. More substantial dishes for a stand-up buffet should be portioned in small pieces that can be handled with just a fork.

For a dinner buffet, tables are set up and the necessary tableware (fish knives, dessert spoons, etc.) are made available to the guests.

sunlight over the course of the afternoon, gusts of wind, and plants or trees that may have overpowering or unpleasant odors.

In the event of bad weather, prepare an alternate plan for indoor set-up that includes the actual transfer.

The buffet tables should be well protected by shade umbrellas.

For outdoor events, do not set-up the buffet too far in advance: warm weather is not favorable for perishable ingredients, and cool weather may require a last-minute transfer indoors.

The head waiter should verify that all rental material is accounted for at the end of the reception. Because outdoor events tend to cause more damage to material, it is in the caterer's best interest to have the clients sign an inventory sheet after the event. This prevents any misunderstandings when it comes time to reimburse the rental company for the damaged or missing material.

Organization and Layout of the Buffet

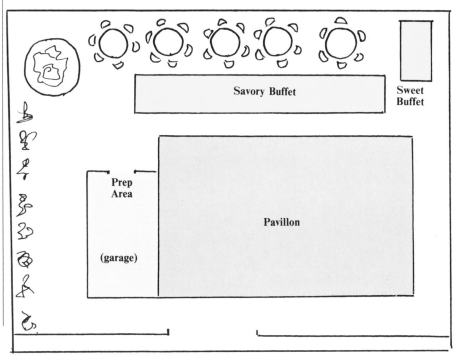

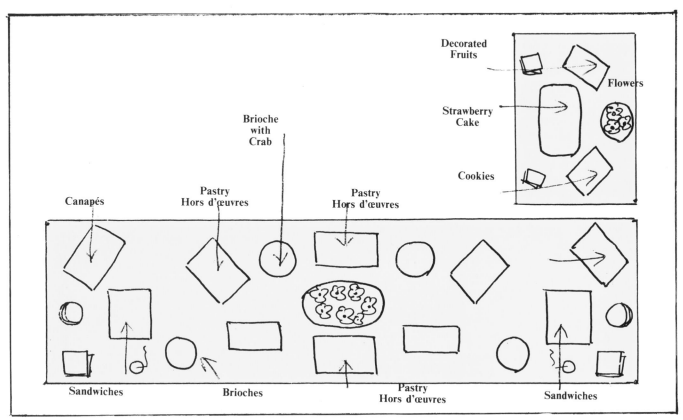

Table Linens

A choice of table linens is available to the caterer: either a classic straight tablecloth with paper napkins or pleated, draped tablecloths, in different weights and colors, with cloth napkins.

The buffet table can be decorated with different items – light fixtures and candlesticks, silver bowls, crystal bowls, porcelain vases. These decorative items must of course be billed to the client.

Other specialty decorations might include items made from molded and glazed bread dough, such as rosebud candleholder or napkin ring.

An Intimate Wedding Reception

The family of the bride has organized the reception for this joyous occasion, to be held not far from their home. The guest list is made up primarily of family members.

Details

A local countryside inn is run by one of the family members, who has closed his facilities to the public for one day to be the site of the wedding festivities. The caterer will have full use of the restaurant kitchens and whatever equipment he requires.

Most of the guests will be staying at the reception site.

Location

The reception will be held in the main dining room. The tables have been rearranged, leaving room at one end for a dance floor.

CLIENT ..... _Mr & Mrs LEROY_ .... _July 7_ .... Dossier N° |_B++_|

If company
Person in charge ..../..................... Tel. .._XX XX_.....

Fax ..._XX XX_....

Address
for billing ...... _Mr & Mrs LEROY_ ....

............_11, square Monet_ ... _95300 GIVERNY_.............

Number guests
60

Method of payment ..._By check, upon receipt of bill_ ....

Budget
..._Average_...

Place and address
of the reception .... _Auberge du Cheval Blanc_ ....

................_27220 MARLY_.................

Set-up and atmosphere of reception room	Preparation facilities
...._Dining room of restaurant_............	........_Professional kitchen_........
......_(closed to public on 7/7)_............	

RENTAL EQUIPMENT |_X_| Furnished by us
(Check)   (Dossier N° ....|_32_|)

Rented |__| from ....

RECEPTION SCHEDULE

Reception ...... _5:30 pm until dawn_ ....

Food
delivery ...._3:30 pm_..........

BUFFET   Menu finalized
by ...._June 15_............

Food
pick-up ...._Following afternoon_..............

BEVERAGES _Furnished by Auberge_...........

Rental
delivery ..../...............

Ice ..._Furnished by Auberge_..........

Rental
pick-up ..../...............

TRANSPORTATION ...._Van_...............

(Other) ....

......_Small delivery van_...............

Flowers..._By customer & restaurant_............

Musique _By customer & restaurant_............

Other _By customer & restaurant_...........

PERSONNEL

......_3 servers in shifts_............

......_2 kitchen personnel_............

......_(1 chef, 1 assistant)_............

Additional information ...._Contact restaurant manager and confirm important issues_..............

Suggested Menu (Example B++)

Savory Items

Savory Hors d'Œuvres
- 30 Sliced Almond Hors d'Œuvres
- 30 Chorizo Hors d'Œuvres
- 30 " Chipolatas " Hors d'Œuvres
- 30 Stuffed Olive Hors d'Œuvres
- 30 Onion/Roquefort Tartelettes
- 30 Mussel Tartelettes
- 30 Pissaladières

Total of 210 Savory Hors d'œuvres

Centerpieces
- 1 Bouquet of Crudités
- 1 Canapé Hedgehog (60 items, on toothpicks)
- 1 Stuffed Crêpe Hedgehog (60 items)

Total of 180 items

Individual Cold Dishes
- 30 Glazed Eggs with Curry Chaud-Froid
- 30 Glazed Eggs with Tomato Sauce

Total of 60 glazed eggs

Fish Presentation
- 30 Salmon Steaks in Aspic
- Hake in Aspic (30 items)

Total of 60 items

Poultry Presentation
- Chicken with Truffles in Aspic (30 items)
- Duck à l'Orange in Aspic (30 items)

Total of 60 items

Mixed Salads
- Russian Salad (30 servings)
- Exotic Salad (30 servings)

Total of 60 servings

Cheese
Assorted cheeses (60 servings) with walnut rolls

Sweet Items

- 1 Croquembouche (60 servings)
- Assorted Petits Fours Secs (macaroons, florentines, financiers)
- Basket of Fruit (60 items)

Grand Total of 780 items

Comments on the Menu Selection
Example B++

The originality of this reception is that it will take place over the course of two days, with the following courses: the wedding day buffet, onion soup served early the next morning, and breakfast and lunch of the next day.

Savory Items

Cocktail Buffet

An attractive and colorful Bouquet of Crudités will be served at the beginning of the reception.

It will be followed by the two Hedgehog centerpieces, which will provide original presentations and substantial items.

Finally the assortment of 210 hot hors d'œuvres will be served, marking the end of the cocktail buffet.

Main Course Buffet

The head waiter is responsible for setting up the tables, with full meal place settings: plates, glasses and silverware.

Because the buffet location provides a fully-equipped kitchen, the caterer may prepare sophisticated and dishes, like the glazed eggs and the fish in aspic, which are always appreciated.

As a meat course, the guests have the choice of chicken or duck. And, these items help to keep costs down.

There is also a choice of salads: the Russian Salad would be suitable with the fish dishes, and the refreshing Exotic Salad may be served with the meats.

The head waiter will serve the cheeses, on a platter, accompanied by the walnut rolls.

Sweet Items

A beautifully decorated croquembouche is mandatory at traditional French wedding buffets. Follow it with assorted petits fours served with the coffee.

The fruit basket will be appreciated by those who prefer a light and refreshing element for dessert.

Preparation

All the ingredients may be ordered in advance.

Prepare the following in advance: white bread, puff pastry, walnut rolls, cream puff dough, petits fours.

Arrange to meet with the owners of the reception site well before the day of the event to determine the equipment available. Any additional equipment or tableware materials should be rented.

The advantage here is that the location provides the caterer with ideal working conditions: a fully-equipped kitchen, complete with adequate refrigeration space.

All that is required is standard kitchen organization. The remainder of the work is carried out by the chef during the reception.

For the dessert buffet, the croquembouche is assembled on-site (pastry cream filling, cream puffs and decorations are delivered in well-sealed containers).

The petits fours are prepared in advance and delivered to the reception site. Arrange on platters prior to serving.

The chef must alot time for the onion soup service, and breakfast and lunch preparations: defrosting, and rising and baking time for the morning pastries.

For the second-day lunch, arrange to serve the leftovers from the reception buffet, or with items on-hand (to be arranged with the reception site owners).

Other Considerations

Since the event will be lengthy (two days), and most of the guests will be staying at or near the reception location, the caterer has been requested to provide dishes for both days (early morning snack, breakfast and lunch).

Service on the second day will most likely be less formal, and the caterer should be prepared to serve as requested rather than forsee an organized buffet.

Organization (Example B++)

This is a standard wedding reception buffet, which is simplified by adequate on-site facilities. Most of the work may be done in advance, leaving only pre-service platter arrangements for the last minute.

Savory Items

Bouquet of Crudités

To ensure maximum freshness, prepare the vegetables the morning of the event and refrigerate until needed. Assemble on-site.

Canapé Hedgehog

Prepare the canapé bands one day in advance, cover in plastic wrap and refrigerate.

Cut, insert toothpicks and assemble on-site.

Stuffed Crêpe Hedgehog

Prepare and stuff the crêpes one day in advance. Cover in plastic wrap and refrigerate.

Trim and assemble on-site.

Hot Hors d'Œuvres

The doughs may be prepared several days in advance. Refrigerate or freeze.

The hors d'œuvres may be garnished and baked one day in advance, but they must be reheated on-site.

Glazed Eggs

Poach the eggs one day in advance, drain thoroughly on paper towels and refrigerate. Glaze the morning of the event.

Assemble and coat with aspic on-site.

Be sure that all the necessary ingredients will be on-site: liver mousse, bread and aspic.

Salmon Steaks

Prepare the salmon roll one day in advance and refrigerate. Cut, decorate and glaze the morning of the event.

Just prior to service, coat with a final layer of aspic and arrange on platters.

Do not forget decoration ingredients.

Hake in Aspic

Same as above.

Chicken with Truffles in Aspic

Cook the chickens up to two days in advance. Refrigerate.

Assemble and glaze the day of the event.

Just prior to service, coat with a final layer of aspic and arrange on platters.

Do not forget decoration ingredients.

Duck à l'Orange in Aspic

Same as above.

Mixed Salads

All salad ingredients may be prepared, separately, one day in advance. Cover with plastic wrap and refrigerate.

For maximum freshness, assemble and dress on-site.

Do not overlook dressing ingredients in the delivery.

Cheese

Two assorted cheese platters are assembled on-site by the caterer.

Bake the walnut rolls in advance, or order from a bakery. Be sure to serve the rolls thinly sliced.

Sweet Items

Croquembouche It is best to assemble the croquembouche on-site.

Bake the cream puffs one day in advance. Prepare the pastry cream on the morning of the event, allowing enough time to cool before filling. Glaze before delivery.

Be sure to include decoration items: pulled sugar decorations, bride and groom figurines, and nougatine base (which may be prepared several days in advance if stored in a cool, dry place).

The preparation of the assorted petits fours should be worked into the daily baking schedule.

Basket of Fruit This may be ordered from a speciality shop, or prepared on-site. Be sure to include a colorful assortment of festive, seasonal fruits.

For a more appealing and refreshing appearance, include a small sprayer to spray a light mist of water on the fruit just before serving.

Organization and Layout of the Buffet

Specifics

Include all the ingredients necessary for preparation of the second day meals.

Arrange for an all-night chef to man the reception-site kitchen. The breakfast pastries may be prepared in the caterer's kitchen in advance and reheated on-site just prior to service.

Assign one staff member the task of accounting for all material after the reception to avoid a mix-up of catering and reception-site equipment.

Provide a thorough clean-up of the reception-site kitchens before departing.

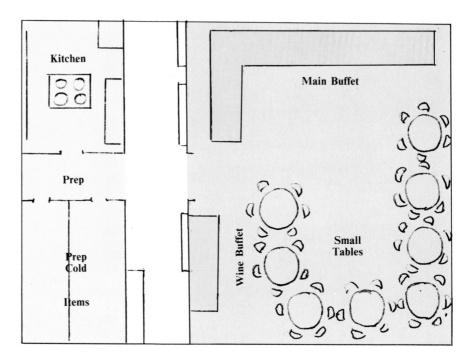

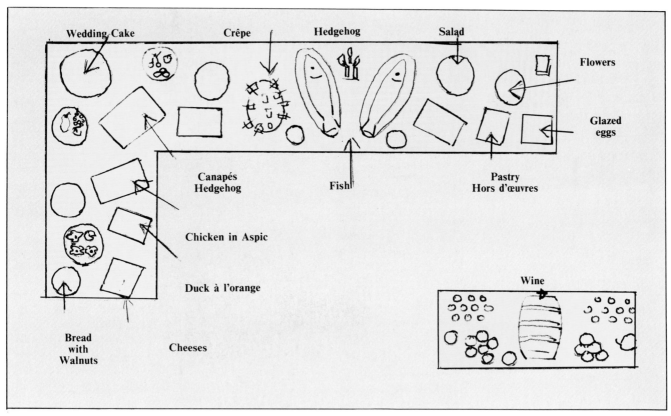

General Information and Advice

Disposable Items

High quality disposable paper napkins are used commonly at many catered functions. Other disposable paper and plastic items are available as well but are appropriate only for informal affairs, such as picnics and other casual outdoor parties.

Paper tablecloths come on a roll or in square sheets.

Paper plates are often plastic coated; a variety of plastic utensils are available, as well as cups and glasses, but none of these items is really desirable except from a practical point of view.

Another disposable item available is a paper serving tray, often coated with plastic. These look better when dressed with a paper doily. If these items are used, they must be billed to the client.

Again, other than paper napkins, paper and plastic items should be used only for very informal parties or parties in which the number of guests or the location makes it impossible to provide china and silver.

The Inauguration
of a Designer Clothing Boutique

A well-known fashion designer is opening a new store in the heart of the most elegant shopping district. Many of the buildings in this area are old and have been tastefully restored to house the trendy shops. This particular boutique is located in one of the nicest buildings and will provide a pleasant reception spot.

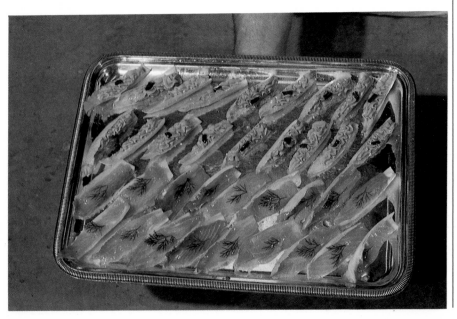

Details

The press attaché, Julie Alsina, is responsible for organizing the event. The inauguration ceremony will double as a fashion show for the new collection.

Location

The store is divided between two floors: the first floor will be the reception hall and the collection will be displayed on the second floor. There will be very little room to set up tables, and the buffet must be split between the two levels (the main buffet will be served upstairs).

CLIENT	CHIC-MODE	Wednesday, Sept 17	Dossier N°	B+++

If company
Person in charge ..... *Julie Alsina, Press attaché* .....

Tel. ..*XX XX*.....

Fax ..*XX XX*.....

Address
for billing .... *CHIC-MODE* .....

.... *229, rue St-Honoré   75001 Paris* .....

Method of payment ..*30 % in advance, balance on receipt of bill* .....

Number guests
60

Budget
Generous

Place and address
of the reception ..... *CHIC-MODE* .....

.... *229, rue St-Honoré   75001 Paris* .....

Set-up and atmosphere of reception room	Preparation facilities
Upseale ready-to-wear boutique	*Difficult in hallway and courtyard of building*

RENTAL EQUIPMENT |X| Furnished by us
(Check)   (Dossier N° .... |21|)

Rented |X| from *AKTUEL Co* .....

RECEPTION SCHEDULE

Reception .... *6:30 pm to 9:30 pm* .....

Food
delivery ..... *5:00 pm* .....

BUFFET   Menu finalized
              by .... *SEPT 1* .....

Food
pick-up ..... *10:30 pm* .....

BEVERAGES ... *Champagne, whisky*
..... *orange juice, Perrier* .....
Ice ... *2 x 40 lbs bags* .....

Rental
delivery ..... *4:30 pm* .....

Rental
pick-up ..... *8:30 next morning* .....

TRANSPORTATION ... *Small delivery van* .....

(Other) ..... *Caterer pick up own* .....
.... *equipment at 10:30 pm* .....

Flowers ... *By customer* .....

Musique ... *By customer* .....

Other ... *Red carpet for entrance (doorman)* .....

PERSONNEL

3 servers

2 kitchen personnel

1 doorman

Additional information ... *Notify and get agreement of super intendant* .....
              for setting up facilities. The press will be there. .....

Suggested Menu (Example B+++)

Savory Items (cocktail)

Mignonnettes
- 60 Veal Sausage on Toast with Apples
- 60 Stuffed Prunes in Canadian Bacon

Total of 120 Mignonnettes

Centerpiece
Stuffed Crêpe Centerpiece, in the form of a fish (60 items)

Savory Items (main course)

Aspic Canapés
60 Aspic Canapés with Crayfish

Mignonnettes
- 60 Langoustine Fritters
- 60 Belgian Endive with Smoked Salmon
- 60 Broccoli Fritters
- 60 " Paupiettes " of Sole in Aspic

Total of 180 Mignonnettes

Centerpiece
" Drakkar ", with 120 assorted sandwiches and canapés

Cold Brochettes
60 Chicken Brochettes with Herb Chaud-froid

Sweet Items

- 60 Assorted Tartelettes
- 60 Assorted Pâte à Choux Petits Fours
- 60 Macaroons
- 60 Assorted Decorated Fruit and Macerated Fruit

Grand Total of 960 items

Comments on the Menu Selection
(Example B+++)

Mignonnettes and filled crêpes on toothpicks will be served for the cocktail buffet.

For the main course buffet: The following items should be heated and served as ordered: langoustine fritters, broccoli fritters.

The Drakkar centerpiece should be placed on the central buffet and drinks table, allowing the guests to help themselves to the sandwiches and canapés.

The guest count is rarely exact for this type of event, so be sure to overestimate rather than run short.

Savory Items

The guests at this public relations event attend many such buffets, hence the importance of an impeccable presentation and high-quality ingredients, but especially an original menu. It is in the caterer's best interest to use this kind of event as a showcase for his talents.

For both the cocktail and main course buffets, the waiters will circulate among the guests with platters.

In keeping with the elegance of the occasion, all of the dishes should be small and easy to consume at a stand-up event. Quality is far more important than volume.

Sweet Items

The dessert buffet is an appealing assortment of high-quality items, which are easily consumed at a stand-up event.

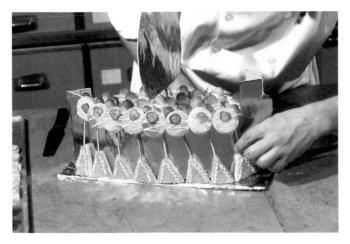

Preparation

All shopping may be done in advance. Advance preparation includes: white bread, tartelette pastry dough (prebake), pâte à choux and nougatine decor, decorated and macerated fruit.

There will be limited on-site facilities (only reheating and platter arrangement), so all preparations must take place in the caterer's kitchens. All dishes should be prepared in full before delivery and packed in well-insulated ice chests for transport. Be sure to label each ice chest with its contents to avoid any unnecessary opening and closing of the containers.

Other Considerations

The lack of kitchen facilities requires a great deal of organization.

The luxurious setting requires extra attention to prevent damage.

Be sure to serve items that do not require silverware, and avoid sauces or ingredients that are not easily contained on a toothpick.

Specifics

Before delivery, the caterer should visit the reception site to ensure that all is in place and the proper precautions have been taken to protect the surroundings.

Use this time to set-up the work space and arrange heating elements.

Keep an open schedule the day of the event to allow for any last-minute demands by the client.

Foresee ice chests to keep the drinks chilled.

The serving staff should arrive well in advance to ensure a smooth set-up.

Install the welcome carpet at entrance.

Ensure that there will be adequate parking facilities for the delivery trucks.

Be sure that all the necessary arrangements have been made to return the rental equipment, and that any damages are noted.

Organization (Example B+++)

Because this is a formal event in a limited space, organization is of the utmost importance.

Savory Items

Mignonnettes

Prepare one day in advance, wrap in plastic and refrigerate.

Crêpes

Prepare, stuff and roll one day in advance. Wrap in plastic and refrigerate.

Slice and assemble before delivery.

The veal sauasages and stuffed prunes will be reheated on-site.

Langoustine Fritters

Prepare and marinate the langoustine the day of the event. Drain and dry thoroughly before delivery. Fry on-site (include necessary ingredients, sauce, and equipment).

Broccoli Fritters

Clean and steam broccoli before delivery.

Same cooking requirments as the langoustine fritters.

Belgian Endive with Smoked Salmon

Prepared and glazed before delivery; platter presentation on-site.

Ham and Pineapple Brochettes

Prepared the day of the event. Refrigertae until delivery; platter presentation on-site.

Aspic Canapés

Prepare one day in advance and refrigerate in the molds. Assemble before delivery.

Canapés and the " Drakkar "

Prepare the bread three days in advance and prepare the garnishes one day in advance.

Assemble the Drakkar before delivery but arrange the canapés around the sides on-site.

" Paupiettes " of Sole in Aspic

Prepare the sole two days in advance. Wrap securely and refrigerate. Glaze the day of the event, and arrange on platters before delivery.

Sweet Items

Assorted Pastries Bake on the day of the event and refrigerate.

Macaroons Prepare well in advance as these may be frozen up until delivery.

Arrange the items on platters before delivery, when possible, given the limited space at the reception location.

Organization and Layout of the Buffet

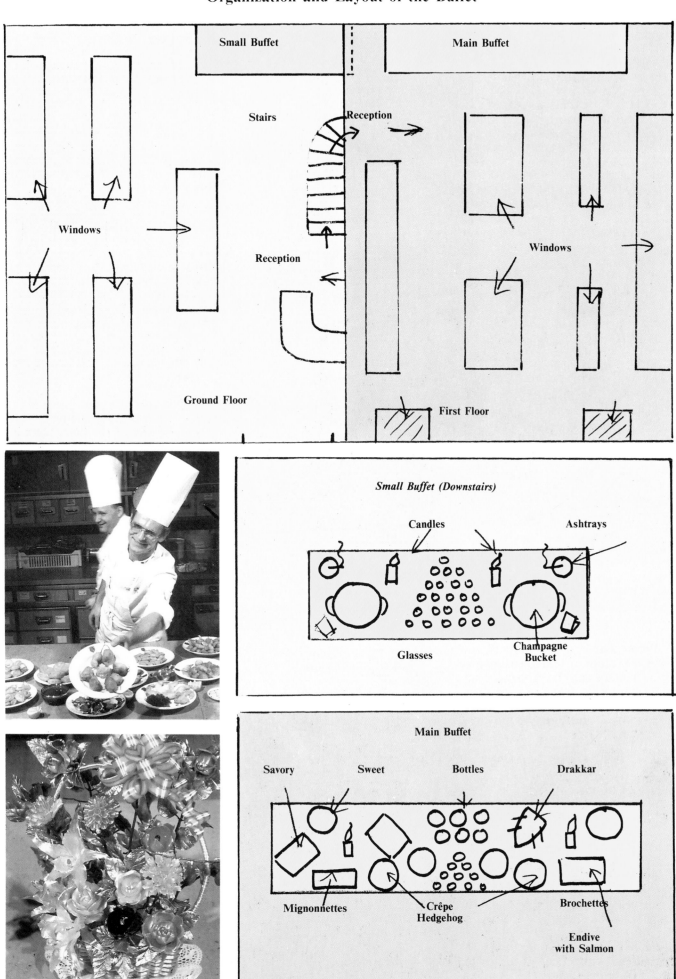

Small Buffet

Main Buffet

Stairs

Reception →

Reception

Windows →

Ground Floor

Windows

First Floor

Small Buffet (Downstairs)

Candles   Ashtrays

Glasses   Champagne Bucket

Main Buffet

Savory   Sweet   Bottles   Drakkar

Mignonnettes   Crêpe Hedgehog   Brochettes

Endive with Salmon

Public Relations Event:
A Nautical Reception

A small yacht-building firm has decided to launch its latest model with panache by holding a publicity party on a boat. The yacht will be displayed to the guests on land, and the reception will be held aboard a boat rented for the occasion.

Details

The event has been organized as a publicity event, and the firm would like to make a good impression on the journalists invited.

A cocktail buffet will be held before the boat leaves the dock, where the press packets will be distributed. The main buffet will be held as the boat cruises the river.

Location

The buffet will be divided into two parts: the cocktail will be held in one location, while the main buffet will be set up in the dining room.

CLIENT	Port Authority	February 13	Dossier N°	B+++

If company
Person in charge ..... Mr. J. DUVAL

Tel. XX

Fax XX

Address
for billing ..... Port Authority

Method of payment ..... 30 % in advance, balance upon receipt of bill

Number guests
60

Budget
High

Place and address
of the reception ..... Bateau Mouche Port Bir Hakeim Paris

Set-up and atmosphere of reception room	Preparation facilities
Small Bateau Mouche (Tour boat operating on the Seine river in Paris)	Very small kitchen on board

---

RENTAL EQUIPMENT ..... [X] Furnished by us
(Check) (Dossier N° ..... 127)

Rented [X] from ..... NILSSON

RECEPTION SCHEDULE

Reception ..... 11:30 am

Food
delivery ..... 10:00 am

BUFFET Menu finalized
by ..... January 15

Food
pick-up ..... 4:30 pm

BEVERAGES Customer will specify

Rental
delivery ..... 9:00 am

Ice ..... 45 lbs

Rental
pick-up ..... 5:00 pm

TRANSPORTATION Small delivery van

(Other) .....

Flowers ..... Submit proposal

Musique ..... Provided by bateau mouche

Other ..... None

PERSONNEL
One server (tailcoat)
One kitchen person

Additional information ..... Don't forget anything. Schedule to be followed precisely Tallcoats

Suggested Menu (Example B++++)

Savory Items

Canapés
- 20 Pickled Herring Canapés
- 20 Salmon Egg Canapés
- 20 Duck Mousse Canapés
- 20 Heart of Palm Canapés
- 20 Sweet Pepper Canapés
- 20 Munster Cream Canapés

Total of 120 canapés

Mignonnettes
- 60 Marinated Shrimp
- 60 Stuffed Grape Leaves

Total of 120 Mignonnettes

Hot Hors d'œuvres
- 60 Croustades with Sweet Pepper Compote
- Croustades of Bay Scallops with Chervil Sauce

Total of 120 hot hors d'œuvres

Beignets
- 60 Beignets made with Brains
- 60 Breaded Red Mullet Beignets

Total of 120 beignets

Centerpieces
- 1 Canapés Hedgehog; 30 Smoked Salmon Sandwiches and 30 Parma Ham Sandwiches
- 1 " Drakkar " of 120 assorted vegetable-filled sandwiches

Total of 180 items

Fish Presentation
Salmon in Aspic (60 servings)

Meat Presentation
- Leg of Lamb with Mint (30 servings)
- Breast of Veal with Dried Fruit (30 servings)

Total of 60 servings

Mixed Salads
- Russian Salad (30 servings)
- Vegetables à la Grecque (30 servings)

Total of 60 servings

Cheese Platter
Assortment of cheese cubes, on toothpicks (60 servings).

Sweet Items
- 60 Cookie Cups filled with Ice Cream
- 60 Assorted Tartelettes
- 60 Assorted Pastries (choux pastry, with nougatine)
- 60 Lace Tuiles
- 60 Macaroons

Comments on the Menu Selection
(Example B++++)

When an event is held in an unusual location, such as a boat, be sure to visit before determining the menu. It will be necessary to plan the dishes according to the space and equipment available. For this event, the client has requested an elegant menu, which must be organized around the kitchen limitations.

Savory Items
Cocktail Buffet

Begin with the mignonnettes: the shrimp served on toothpicks and the stuffed grape leaves.

Follow with the hot hors d'œuvres. The sweet pepper croustades may be assembled and reheated just before serving. The bay scallop croustades are served with a sauce; assemble and reheat on-site.

The fritters and beignets may be prepared in advance but they should be cooked on-site in small batches.

Next comes the canapé assortment, all served on toothpicks, and made from a variety of ingredients: fish, eggs, meat, vegetables and cheese.

Serve the eye-catching centerpiece as the grande finale to the cocktail buffet. The Drakkar is especially suited to the nautical theme of the event and it may be personalized by placing the company logo on the sail. Decorate with an assortment of light vegetable-filled sandwiches.

Savory Items
Main Course Buffet

This buffet is comprised on several attractively presented dishes: Salmon in Aspic, Leg of Lamb with Mint and Breast of Veal with Dried Fruit.

The Russian salad would be best served with the fish and the Vegetables à la Grecque should be served with the meats, but this is optional.

Follow with the cheeses course of assorted cheese cubes served on toothpicks.

Sweet Items

This course is comprised of a wide variety of assorted pastries and sweets that combine many flavors and textures, and are sure to please all.

Presentation

All shopping may be done in advance.

Catering an event on a boat requires extra organizational efforts. Be sure that all necessary ingredients and equipment are on board because once the boat has left port it will be too late!

The pre-reception visit of the facilities is vital. This is the only way to determine what equipment needs to be brought and how the work should be organized in such a small space.

Be sure to prepare a complete and thorough checklist.

The following items may be prepared in advance for delivery to the boat: Stuffed Grape Leaves

Prebaked shells and fillings for sweet pepper and bay scallop (with sauce) croustades

Beignets and fritters

Canapés

Sandwiches for the Drakkar

All dessert items

Arrange the prepared items in well-insulated ice chests and label clearly on the outside.

Organization (Example B++++)

The most effective way to organize a buffet for a site with limited kitchen space is to prepare as many dishes as possible before delivery.

Savory Items

Marinated Shrimp

Peel, devein and marinate the shrimp one day in advance. Drain and insert toothpicks before delivery.

Stuffed Grape Leaves

Assemble one day in advance. Marinate overnight, covered securely with plastic wrap.

Drain and arrange on platters before delivery.

Hot Hors d'Œuvres

Line the tartelette molds several days in advance and refrigerate or freeze. Fill and cook up to one day in advance; reheat before serving.

Beignets and Fritters

Prepare the day of the event. Cover securely and refrigerate. Fry on-site (include necessary ingredients and equipment).

Centerpiece

Prepare canapés one day in advance. Wrap securely in plastic film and refrigerate. Slice and assemble the day of delivery.

Canapés

Prepare the white bread three days in advance.

Prepare the canapé toppings one day in advance.

Assemble the day of delivery. Wrap securely with plastic film to avoid stale bread. If necessary, wrap first in moistened parchment paper. Refrigerate.

The Drakkar

Prepare the sandwich fillings one day in advance. Assemble the day of the event. Wrap securely in plastic film and refrigerate.

Assemble before delivery, but at the last possible moment to keep the vegetable fillings as fresh as possible.

Salmon in Aspic

Poach the slamon one day in advance and refrigerate.

Decoration and aspic glaze should be done the day of the event and refrigerated.

For extra sheen, give a final coat of aspic just prior to delivery and arrange on platter.

Leg of Lamb with Mint

Cook the lamb one day in advance

Slice and glaze the day of the event. Arrange on platter before delivery, but garnishes may be added on-site to facilitate transport.

Breast of Veal with Dried Fruit

Same as above.

Russian Salad

Prepare all the ingredients and refrigerate in separate, well-sealed containers.

Toss just before delivery for maximum frehsness.

Place in a well-sealed container for transport.

Vegetables à la Grecque

Follow instructions for Russian Salad.

Cheese

Cube the cheese and insert toothpicks the day of the event. Cover with plastic wrap to maintain freshness and to prevent the other foods from absorbing the odors. Unwrap just before serving.

Serve the cheese with thinly sliced bread (baked one day in advance).

Sweet Items

Cookie Cups filled with Ice Cream

Assemble one day in advance and store in deep-freeze.

Be sure to allow time for softening to ensure that the ice cream is the proper consistency, and not too hard, when served.

Pastries and Sweets Bake up to one day in advance, or fit into regular baking schedule.

Organization and Layout of the Buffet

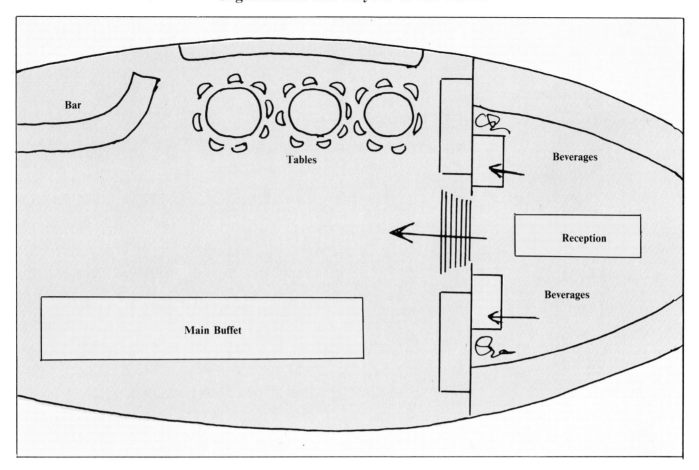

Bar

Tables

Beverages

Reception

Beverages

Main Buffet

Specifics

A visit to the site well in advance of the event is imperative.

Arrange to rent or transport all necessary equipment not on site.

Organize timing for preparations.

Be sure that all the tables on the boat are sturdy.

Arrange for the floral decorations, but keep it simple due to the location (nothing too tall or unsturdy).

Deliver in two trips: begin with the drinks and kitchen equipment. Deliver all the buffet items in the second trip. The serving staff should arrive at the same time for set-up.

Following the reception, verify rental material for any damages and make note on an inventory sheet.

Make a thorough kitchen and dining room clean-up.

Check List
for Canapé Hedgehog

- 1 loaf of bread (30cm (10 in))
- Creamed butter
- Cured ham, sliced
- Aspic
- Toothpicks
- Small watermelon
- Doily
- Round platter
- Damp towel or plastic wrap

General Information and Advice

Check Lists and Work Sheets

Once the order is finalized for a client, the caterer then divides the work into several categories.

A check list should be drawn up to indicate when each ingredient should be ordered. The caterer should also outline each preparation, who is responsible and the day it is to be completed.

Each worker in the kitchen should have his own work sheet, listing the various dishes to be completed (often in various stages over several days) with step-by-step procedure and dates of completion.

The work sheet should be clearly laid out so that a co-worker can tell at a glance the status of the work.

To help organize the work sheet system, columns can be made next to all procedures using symbols to indicate the different steps (for example " * " to indicate that the dish is in progress, " = " to indicate that the dish is finished, " + " to indicate that the dish has been inspected by the head chef and delivered).

Sheets of different colors can be used to signify savory or sweet preparations etc..

An efficient system, that is closely followed by all members of the staff ensures a successful caterering operation.

Awards Ceremony

An important corporation is holding a reception in honor of its employee awards ceremony.

All of the company directors will be present, as well as the directors of several company subsidiaries.

Details

The awards ceremony is traditionally the occasion for the directors to meet directly with the employees, and the president gives a recognition speech to the entire assembly.

All company employees and their spouses are invited to the event. It is meant to be a festive, yet informal, gathering.

Location

The ceremony is held in the executive dining room, which will be rearranged for the event. Tables will be placed close to the kitchen to facilitate buffet set-up and serving.

Smaller tables for dining have been arranged around the room.

CLIENT ....*Micromechanics, Inc.* .... *January 5* .... Dossier N° │ *C+* │

If company
Person in charge ..... *Mr. Abhoret* ....

Tel. ..... *XX* ....

Fax ..... *XX* ....

Address
for billing .. *Micromechanics, Inc.* ....

.... *110, avenue Petits-Carreaux .. Reims* ....

┌─────────────────┐
│ Number guests   │
│   *130*   │
└─────────────────┘

Method of payment ... *30 % in advance,* ....

.... *balance 30/60 days* ....

Budget
.... *Low* ......

Place and address
of the reception ... *Same as above* ....

....

Set-up and atmosphere of reception room	Preparation facilities
..... *Company*	..... *cafeteria kitchen* ....
.... *cafetaria*	....

RENTAL EQUIPMENT │ *X* │ Furnished by us	RECEPTION SCHEDULE
(Check) (Dossier N° .... │ *10* │)	Reception .... *11:30 am* ....
Rented └─┘ from .. *(on-site kitchen* .... *is fully equipped)*	Food delivery .... *10:00 am* ....

BUFFET	Menu finalized by .... *December 20*	Food pick-up .... *9:00 pm* ....

BEVERAGES .. *Client will supply*	Rental delivery ....
Ice .. *Ice machine in kitchen + 40 lbs*	Rental pick-up ....
TRANSPORTATION .. *1 delivery van*	(Other) ....

Flowers ... *Client will supply*	PERSONNEL
Musique .. *Client will supply*	... *2 servers* .... *1 cook* ....
Other ... ╱	

Additional information .. *Instruct the servers supplied by client* ....

....

Suggested Menu (Example C+)

Savory Items

Savory Hors d'Œuvres

- 15 Hazelnut Hors d'Œuvres
- 15 Chorizo Hors d'Œuvres
- 15 " Chipolatas " Hors d'Œuvres
- 15 " Croque Monsieur "
- 15 Mussel Tartelettes
- 15 Mini Pizzas
- 15 Gougères
- 15 Onion/Roquefort Tartelettes
- 15 Mini Quiches

Total of 150 Hors d'œuvres

Filled Rolls

- 50 Filled Rolls with Foie Gras Mousse
- 50 Filled Rolls with Parma Ham
- 50 Filled Rolls with Cheese Mousse

Total of 150 Filled Rolls

Canapés

- 20 Sardine Canapés
- 20 Crab Canapés
- 20 Shrimp Canapés
- 20 Smoked Salmon Mousse Canapés
- 20 Blood Sausage and Apple Canapés
- 20 Cucumber, Corn and Green Peppercorn Canapés
- 20 Asparagus Tip Canapés
- 20 Heart of Palm Canapés
- 20 Sweet Pepper Canapés
- 20 Macédoine of Vegetable Canapés
- 20 Comtés Canapés
- 20 Munster Cream Canapés

Total of 300 canapés

Centerpiece

- 2 Surprise Breads: 1 Raisin Walnut Loaf (40 items) and 1 Salami Loaf (40 items)

Total of 80 items.

Sweet Items

- 150 Assorted Fruit Tartelettes
- 150 Assorted Pastries (choux pastry) with nougatine (75 of each item)
- 150 Assorted Petits Fours
- 150 Decorated Fruit and Macerated Fruit (75 of each item)

Total of 600 items.

Comments on the Menu Selection Example C+

This is a low-budget reception to be held after an awards ceremony. It will be located in a company dining room.

The client would like an assortment of items, based on quality ingredients, but the budget is limited.

Be sure to choose substantial ingredients for a well-rounded menu.

Savory Items

The savory items consist of 10 varieties of pastry hors d'œuvres and three kinds of mignonettes, including bacon-wrapped bananas, which is the ideal kind of item when funds are limited and the buffet needs substantial items.

The salt cod fritters and the celery with roquefort are both crowd-pleasing items.

For an attractive presentation that is also copious, we propose three varieties of filled rolls and an assortment of 300 canapés divided between 15 kinds (meat, eggs, fish, vegetables and cheese).

Surprise breads are a cost-effective centerpiece and add volume to the buffet.

Sweet Items

Small, easily served items are the best choice for this type of event.

The dessert buffet consists of an assortment of refreshing and attractive fruit tartelettes, assorted pastries and butter cookies as well as decorated fruit.

Preparation

Order all the ingredients in advance.

Prepare the following items well in advance: puff pastry, white bread, surprise bread loaves, brioche, tartelette pastry, cream puff pastry for pastries, butter cookies and decorated fruit.

This simple buffet poses no special organizational problems. All items are prepared in advance and stored in well-sealed containers for delivery. Be sure to keep the containers refrigerated and label all items clearly to facilitate delivery and unloading.

The reception site offers a fully-equipped professional kitchen.

The buffet should be set up before the awards ceremony begins so that the guests may proceed directly to the dining room.

Other Considerations

The entire buffet should be set up no later than 11:30 a.m.

The serving staff is responsible for the table arrangements. Be sure to clear space in the center to allow for dancing later in the afternoon.

Advance organization will make the reception run more smoothly.

Organization (Cas C+)

While this is a fairly simple reception to arrange, it nonetheless requires good organization. The date places it during a busy holiday season, which implies other events to organize, and this buffet is large in volume.

Savory Items

Pastry Hors d'œuvres

To minimize work on the day of the event, prepare the hors d'œuvres in advance and freeze. All that remains the day of the reception is baking.

However, the gougères and the mini-quiches should not be filled any earlier than the day of the event.

Reheat on-site and have the serving staff arrange the platters.

Mignonnettes

Prepare one day in advance, but assemble at the last minute for maximum freshness (especially the bananas, which may discolor).

Filled Rolls

Prepare the bread up to several days in advance and freeze in well-sealed containers (to avoid freezer burn).

Defrost the day of the event. Fill and cover with plastic wrap for delivery.

Canapés

Prepare the bread up to several days in advance. Store in plastic wrap or well-sealed containers (vacuum-packing is ideal).

All canapé toppings may be prepared up to two days in advance, but assemble the canapés no sooner than the day of delivery. Wrap in plastic and refrigerate. If necessary, set on sheets of damp parchment paper to keep the bread moist.

For extra shine, coat with a final layer of aspic just before serving.

Surprise Bread

Prepare up to several days in advance. The fillings keep well if stored in plastic wrap in the refrigerator.

Filled Loaves

Prepare the loaves of bread up to several days in advance.

Prepare the fillings one day in advance.

Because the ingredients are perishable, do not assemble any sooner than the day of the event.

Store in plastic wrap and refrigerate until delivery.

Sweet Items

Plan ahead so that the pastries may be worked into the daily baking schedule.

However, this requires additional organization due to the large volume and busy holiday season.

All pastry doughs may be prepared in advance and frozen before assembly. The butter cookies may be stored for several days if kept in airtight containers. Prepare the decorated and macerated fruit in advance and store well-wrapped.

Specifics

Hire the serving staff well in advance.

Be sure that there are no missing items.

Visit the reception site prior to the event to determine the necessary equipment.

The client is responsible for the drinks and rental equipment at this buffet, which leaves only the kitchen and serving equipment to be provided for by the caterer.

General Information and Advice: Serving Bread

Bread plays a very important role when food is served in France. For many dishes on a buffet, it is an indispensible accompaniment.

Unfortunately, the bread served at receptions is often not of the highest quality. It is very important to choose a good baker who can make a variety of breads to accompany different dishes.

Delicious bread is part of a successful buffet. The type of bread should be chosen with care.

Here are several suggestions for breads that go well with specific foods :

Country style French bread : All dishes (meats, game, poultry, fish, charcuterie, cheeses)

Rye bread : Seafood, fish, cured ham, radishes

Whole wheat bread : Hot dishes, mild cheeses, shell fish

Bread made with apples : Pork, Blood Sausage

Light Rye : Charcuterie, strong cheeses

Bread made with sausage : cold meats

Cumin bread : strong cheeses

Bread made with carrots : Game, hot meat dishes, salad

Herb bread : Cold fish, salad, crudités, mild cheeses

Wheat germ bread : Lean meats

Bread made with oysters : Seafood

Italian bread : Salad, crudités

Bread made with corn : Charcuterie

Close-textured white bread : sandwiches, canapés, toast, croutons

Bread made with hazelnuts : meat terrines

Bread made with almonds : Fish

Bread made with walnuts : Cheeses

Bread made with olives : Meats, poultry, sheep's milk cheeses

Barley bread ; all dishes

Soy bread : Crudités

Surprise Breads

The bread base for surprise breads can be made in a variety of sizes, shapes and flavors.

The breads are hollowed out, cut into slices, spread with fillings, then replaced in the bread " shell ".

Surprise Breads are an easy-to-serve item for buffets.

Often the bread base is made of light rye (rye + white flour combined) which slices well. " Pain de mie ", closely textures white bread and egg and butter enriched brioche are also used.

Fillings :
- Compound Butter: Anchovy, sardines, blue cheese, salmon
- Salami
- Garlic sausage
- Andouille
- Mortadella
- Crudités (cucumbers, tomatoes, carots, celery)
- Fish (salmon, trout)
- Walnuts and raisins
- Onions and watercress
- Ham and Swiss cheese
- Chicken and herb
- Roquefort, cumin and walnut
- Cured ham
- Boiled ham
- York ham
- Sausage

Organization and Layout of the Buffet

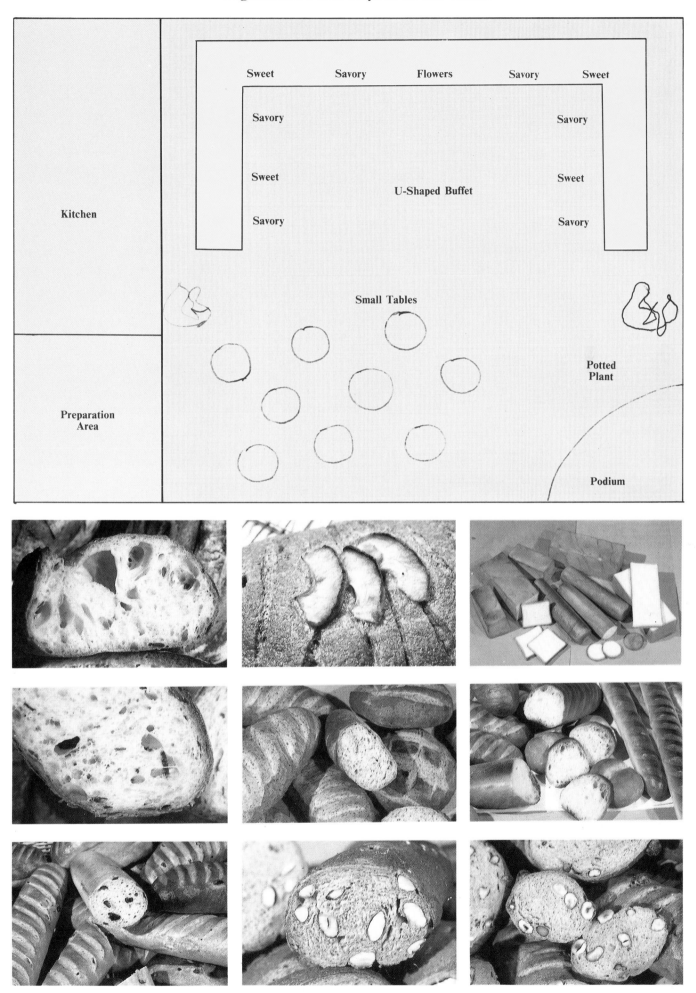

Annual Ball of the Officer's Reserve

One of the most festive occasions in the city of Angoulême is the Annual Officer's Reserve Ball. This event has entered into local tradition, making it one of the most popular local festivities, and the gathering is divided by interest groups: hunting, civic associations, etc.

Details

The guest list includes prominent local military and civilian figures and their spouses. This year's gala will be attended by several guests of honor.

Location

The event is held in the town's Grand Ballroom, and there will be a full orchestra. This is a very formal event and serving staff members should wear tuxedos and white gloves. There are limited kitchen facilities available to the caterer.

CLIENT _Reserve Officer's Association_ _March 21_ Dossier N° | _C++_ |

If company
Person in charge _Captain Choulans_ Tel. _XX_

Fax _XX_

Address
for billing _R.O.A._

Number guests

118 Emile Zola Square _Angoulême_ | _150_ |

Method of payment _50 % in advance,_ Budget

balance on delivery

Place and address
of the reception _Municipal Building, Angoulême_

Set-up and atmosphere of reception room	Preparation facilities
Reception hall of municipal building	_Kitchen in reception hall_

RENTAL EQUIPMENT ☐ Furnished by us
(Check) (Dossier N° ☐)

Rented | _X_ | from _Sterling Rental_
Entrance " B "

BUFFET Menu finalized
by _March 15_

BEVERAGES _We supply_

Ice _120 lbs_

TRANSPORTATION _2 delivery vans_

RECEPTION SCHEDULE

Reception _7:30 pm-1:30 am_

Food
delivery _5:30_

Food
pick-up _Following reception_

Rental
delivery _2:00 pm_

Rental
pick-up _Morning following reception_

(Other) _Follow schedule closely_

Flowers _We supply_

Musique _Orchestra (6 musicians)_

Other

PERSONNEL

4 servers
2 kitchen personnel

Additional information _Large buffet tables needed, clearance needed to park delivery vans_

Suggested Menu (Example C++)

Savory Items

Pastry Hors d'œuvres
- 30 Hazelnut Hors d'œuvres
- 30 Almond Hors d'œuvres
- 30 Parmesan Hors d'œuvres
- 30 Pté Hors d'œuvres
- 30 Anchovvy Hors d'œuvres
- 30 Mini Pizzas
- 30 Mini Croque Monsieurs
- 30 Olive Hors d'œuvres
- 30 Garlic Sausage Hors d'œuvres
- 30 Ham Crescents

Total: 300 Pastry Hors d'œuvres

Filled Rolls
- Rolls with Foie Gras Mousse
- Rolls with Salmon Mousse

Total : 150 Filled Rolls

Canapés
- 30 Sardine Canapés
- Shrimp Canapés
- Egg Salad Canapés
- Parma Ham Canapés
- Dry Sausage Canapés
- Green Bean Canapés
- Artichoke Canapés
- Mushroom Canapés
- " Fromage Frais " Canapés
- Gorgonzola Canapés

Total : 300 Canapés

Buffet Centerpieces
- 8 Surprise Breads with 40 servings each:
  2 Walnut and Raisin Surprise Bread
  2 Bayonne (or Parma) Ham Surprise Bread
  2 Crab Surprise Bread
  2 Roquefort Surprise Bread

Total : 320 servings
- 1 Stuffed Crêpe Hedgehog (assorted flavors)
- Lumpfish Eggs with Salmon Mousse
  Ham with Parmesan Sauce

Cold Brochettes
- 50 Fish and Vegetable Brochettes
- 50 Beef Stroganoff Brochettes
- 50 Lamb with Curry Brochettes

Total: 150 assorted Cold Brochettes

Elaborate Meat Presentations
Cubed Ham with Pineapple and Cherries (70 servings)

Poultry in Aspic
Turkey in Cubes (40 servings)

Sweet Items

- 150 Tartelettes
- 150 Mini Cream Puffs
- 150 Decorated and Macerated Fruits

Total : 450 Sweet Items
Grand Total : 1,970 Items

Comments on the Menu Selection
Example C++

This menu is proposed for the annual Policemen's Ball. The buffet items are classic yet fancy to favorably impress the sophisticated tastes of the guests.

The caterer should pay close attention to the details of this menu for while working with a relatively moderate budget, the caterer does quite a bit of repeat business with this organization.

Since the reception lasts a long time (6 hours) the menu centers around individual, easy-to-eat items that can be efficiently served throughout the reception.

These small items can be arranged to create stunning displays using a variety of presentation platters, mirrors and decorated bases which will give the buffet the festive touch it deserves.

Savory Items

A selection of 10 varieties of pastry hors d'œuvres provides 300 individual bite-size portions.

A superb assortment of 300 canapés featuring 10 different garnishes (including eggs, fish, vegetables, cheese, preserved meats) and 4 different surprise breads are presented on pedestals which gives dimension to the buffet table.

Two kinds of filled rolls (salmon mousse, foie gras mousse) are copious, delicious items that are always well liked. The hedgehog made with slices of stuffed, rolled crêpes attached to a base with toothpicks also adds dimension to the display.

To complete the decoration: 150 assorted cold brochettes (fish, beef, lamb) are presented on shell-shaped bases cut from styrofoam.

Two turkeys and two hams both cut in cubes and reformed are lovely presentations that provide a large number of servings. Guests always enjoy the taste of these lovely decorated centerpieces.

Sweet Items

As with the savory items, all of the sweet items are small individual portions that can be easily served: 450 different items, arranged superbly on tiered silver serving dishes, offer a wide chioce of flavors and colors (fruit tartelettes, miniature cream puffs, decorated and macerated fruits).

Preparation

Be sure to shop in advance for all items and alot time for final preparation and finishing touches.

Advance preparation for the savory items includes: the puff pastry, the white bread, the round loaves for the surprise bread, the brioche dough, basic or sweet pie pastry, the cream puff pastry, the decorated fruits.

All of the preparation is done in advance in the caterer's kitchen. All items arrive in appropriate containers each labeled clearly with a list of the contents.

This menu does not require a large on-site preparation area. The only equipment necessary is a small oven to warm the pastry hors d'œuvres which is done by the maitre d'hotel or a chef.

Even though the budget is not large for this event, the presentation should be outstanding. For the table setting plan on fabric tablecloths, lovely doilies, appropriate decorated bases, silver pedestals and candlesticks.

Other Considerations

The luxurious location and sophisticated tastes of the guests require that the caterer arrange the buffet table with very elaborate presentations.

To give dimension and a touch of drama to the display, large decorative bases can be created from styrofoam to present several of the fancier dishes. Beautifully garnished food arranged on ornate mirrors give a feeling of volume and reflect the lights of the room for a glistening display. Other " special effects " include multi-tiered serving dishes, branches with leaves attached, and pedastals. Remember that the ceiling of the room is very high and height and volume is needed to bring attention to the buffet table.

Organization (Example C++)

The room is very large so the buffet items are displayed on a large table using grand, elaborately decorated presentations. Use centerpiece dishes and presentation mirrors to give a sense of volume.

This gala occasion allows the caterer to express his talents and create displays and decorations that match the grandeur of the location.

The additional platters and bases needed to achieve this stunning buffet must be planned on well in advance. The food should be arranged on the platters on-site so thay do not suffer during delivery.

Savory Items

Pastry Hors d'œuvres

All of the pastry hors d'œuvres can be prepared and shaped in advance and frozen unbaked.

They are freshly baked the day of the event and reheated just before serving.

Canapés

Make the white bread 3 days in advance to facilitate slicing.

One day in advance, prepare the garnishes and refrigerate.

Surprise Breads

The round loaves of rye bread are made three days in advance.

Slice the loaves one day in advance. The walnut, ham and Roquefort surprise breads can be assembled in advance but the one made with crabmeat should be made fresh the day of the event.

Filled Rolls

They are shaped and baked the day before or can be baked several days in advance and frozen.

Prepare the fillings the day before and refrigerate in covered containers.

Pipe the filling into the rolls the day of the event. Cover with plastic wrap and refrigerate until delivery.

Stuffed Crêpe Hedgehog

Make the crêpes one day in advance, fill and roll with the two different preparations.

Cover with plastic wrap and refrigerate.

Shortly before delivery, slice the rolled crêpes, place on toothpicks and assemble the hedgehog.

Cold Brochettes

Prepare the ingredients one day in advance.

Assemble the brochettes the morning of the event and apply one coat of aspic.

Shortly before delivery, glaze a second time. Arrange the platters on-site.

Cubed Turkey

The turkeys are cooked 2-3 days in advance and assembled the day before the event. The day of the event, glaze them first in the morning then a second time shortly before delivery. Arrange on platters and decorate on-site.

Cubed Ham with Pineapples and Cherries

The ham is cut and assembled the day before and the fruits are drained and refrigerated.

The ham is decorated the day of the event to ensure a fresh appearance.

It is glazed shortly before delivery and arranged on a platter on-site and decorated with small pineapple and cherry brochettes.

Sweet Items

The assortment of classic desserts should be worked into the daily baking schedule.

The decorated and macerated fruits are prepared several days in advance. They can be dipped in the clear sugar glaze and kept in a cool dry place.

Organization and Layout of the Buffet

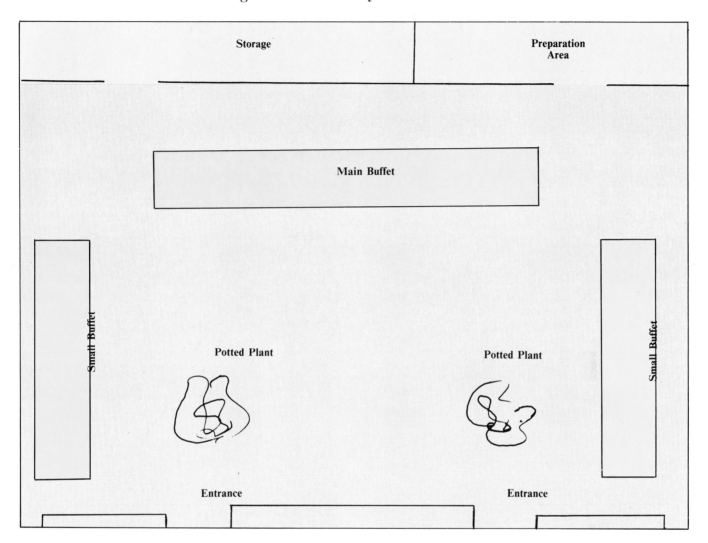

Specifics

Verify that all the rental equipment is delivered and in good working order.

Order large, impressive floral arrangements and confirm delivery.

Procure the large platters and presentation bases and deliver in advance. Remember that the dishes should be arranged on the table at different heights.

Plan in advance for a suitable base to hold the ice sculpture and provide the extra lighting that is necessary.

Plan the delivery schedule so that the ice sculpture, which has been made in advance, arrives at the party in impeccable shape just before the guests arrive.

Insist that the service staff is dressed elegantly in tuxedos and white gloves.

Ask if it is necessary for the service staff to have special clearance to enter the location. Check for permission to park delivery vehicles.

Check that the sound system is adequate for the room and that the orchestra is appropriate for the occasion.

Schedule two servers for the buffet preparation and two additional servers to arrive at the beginning of the reception.

The delivery is done in two stages:
• First the drinks are brought and chilled and the rental equipment is put in place (check that ovens work etc.). The decorations and the items to be reheated are delivered.
• The fresh, refrigerated items and the ice sculpture are delivered shortly before the reception.

Check the location after the event to verify that it is left in perfect order.

Chamber of Commerce Reception

This event is being held to mark the retirement of the president of the Chamber of Commerce and to introduce his successor to the community. The retiring president is an avid hunter and the party has been organized around a hunting theme in his honor.

Details

This Chamber of Commerce is located in the Champagne region. A prestigious Champagne maker will be sponsoring the event, providing the refreshments in exchange for publicity.

Location

The reception will be held in the wine cellar of the Chamber of Commerce building. Because the event coincides with the grape harvest, the caterer should take this into consideration when planning the buffet.

CLIENT _Chamber of Commerce_ _October 16_ Dossier N° $C+++$

If company
Person in charge _Mr. Martin_

Address
for billing _Chamber of Commerce,_

11, place de la Republique, Reims

Method of payment _30 % in advance balance 30/60 days_

Tel. _XX_

Fax _XX_

Number guests
_150_
Budget
High

Place and address
of the reception _Same as above_

Set-up and atmosphere of reception room	Preparation facilities
Champagne cellar	_Kitchen of wine cellar_ _(very well equipped)_

RENTAL EQUIPMENT ☐ Furnished by us
(Check) (Dossier N° ☐)

Rented ☐ _X_ from _Sterling Rental_

RECEPTION SCHEDULE

Reception _5:00 pm_

Food
delivery _3:00 pm_

BUFFET Menu finalized
by _October 10_

Food
pick-up _Following reception_

BEVERAGES _Champagne_
(supplied by client)

Ice _80 lbs_

Rental
delivery _10:30 am_

Rental
pick-up _Day after reception_

TRANSPORTATION _Small delivery van_

(Parking marked " Cellar ")

(Other)

Flowers _We supply_

Musique _No_

Other _Additional lighting_
(indirect/spot lights)

PERSONNEL

4 servers
2 kitchen personnel

Additional information _No hot food, avoid vibration_

Suggested Menu (Example C+++)

Savory Items

Pastry Hors d'œuvres
- 50 Walnut Hors d'œuvres
- 50 Hazelnut Hors d'œuvres
- 50 Matchsticks/Sesame/Poppy
- 50 Cheese Matchsticks
- 50 Olives Hors d'œuvres

Total 300 Pastry Hors d'œuvres

Brioche Mousseline
- 75 Crabmeat Brioche Sandwiches
- 75 Foie Gras Brioche Sandwiches

Total 150 servings

Canapés
- 30 Monkfish Canapés
- 30 Crabmeat Canapés
- 30 Salmon Caviar Canapés
- 30 Smoked Trout Canapés
- 30 Foie Gras Canapés
- 30 Mignonnette Canapés
- 30 Zucchini Canapés
- 30 Broccoli Canapés

Total 300 Canapés

Aspic-Canapés
- 50 Crayfish Aspics
- 50 Tongue Aspics
- 50 Aspics with Lumpfish Eggs

Total 150 Aspic-Canapés

Mignonnettes
150 Belgian Endive with Smoked Salmon

Cold Brochettes
- 75 Seafood Brochettes
- 75 Fish and Vegetable Brochettes

Total 150 Cold Brochettes

Elaborate Meat Dishes
- 50 servings Hare " a la Royale "
- 50 servings Ballotine of Pheasant
- 50 Dodines of Wild Boar

Total 150 servings

Mixed Salads
- 50 servings Meli-Melo Salad
- 50 servings Cinderella Salad
- 50 servings Mixed Salad

Total 150 servings

Cheeses
Cheese Platter of (150 portions)

Sweet Items

- Theme Cake (150 servings)
- 150 assorted Almond Macaroons
- 150 assorted Butter Cookies
- 150 Chocolates (Truffles/Orange Zest)
- 150 servings Champagne Granité

Grand Total 2,400 servings (savory and sweet).

Comments on the Menu Selection Example C+++

This buffet is sponsored by the Chamber of Commerce to celebrate the retirement of its president. The reception takes place in a wine cellar in Champagne.

There are three principle themes that guide the caterer to choose menu items and decorations:

- The retirement of the guest of honor
- Champagne vineyard
- Hunting, the favorite past time of retiree

This is a prestigous event with a high budget. There will be many important people present; members of the Chamber of Commerce, well-known chefs, and the press.

This is a grand occasion when the caterer can express his talents in the making of elaborate and delicious dishes arranged in a perfect display.

This menu includes only cold items because reheating food on-site would raise the temperature of the cellar. Therefore the pastry hors d'œuvres are baked at the last minute and transported fresh to the location.

Savory Items

The savory items include the following:

A selection of six bite-size pastry hors d'œuvres that are easy to eat and do not have to be reheated if freshly baked. The flavors include almond, walnut, hazelnut, cheese, sesame and poppy, olives.

The brioches (with crab, foie gras) are elegant to look at and have a very refined taste.

A wide variety of canapés (10 flavors/300 pieces) offers a refreshing array of tastes and colors.

Three kinds of aspic canapés (crayfish, tongue, lumpfish eggs/150 pieces) also provide a splash of color.

To mark the end of the cocktail hour and the beginning of the buffet itself, a lovely cup of Champagne granité is offered which is refreshing and appropriate for the setting.

The next items to be served are 150 smoked salmon "mignonnettes" and 150 glazed fish brochettes which are appreciated for their delicate flavor and subtle colors.

For the meats, the selection features elaborate dishes using game (hare, pheasant, wild boar). All the dishes, served cold, are sliced in individual portions.

An original selection of three mixed salads (Meli-Melo, Cinderella, mixed) are served with the meat.

The savory buffet ends with a lovely platter of assorted cheeses.

Sweet Items

The main attraction is the cake made especially for the occasion which reflects the theme of the event.

An assortment of almond macaroons, butter cookies, chocolate truffles and chocolate-dipped orange zest, are very easy to eat at the end of the meal and compliment the cake.

Other Considerations

Plan presentations that fill the length of the table but do not stand too high due to the low ceiling of the cellar.

Plan on supplementary lighting: small spotlights or hallogen lamps with indirect light and bring extension cords to reach the outlets.

The wine cellar must be kept at a constant temperature, therefore no items requiring reheating are included on the menu.

Preparation

Shop in advance for all of the ingredients and plan ahead for the preparation of each item.

Savory items that can be prepared in advance include: puff pastry, brioche dough (mousseline), white bread for canapés.

For the sweet items, make the granité and freeze and make the spongecake layers and filling for the cake.

The remainder of the desserts; butter cookies, macaroons, and chocolates should not be made far in advance so that they are perfectly fresh for the event.

Most of the preparation is done in the caterer's kitchen, leaving only a few last minute decorations and finishing touches to be completed on-site.

All the items (except pastry hors d'œuvres) are transported in refrigerated cases with labels that clearly list the contents of each.

Plan ahead for ample ice to keep food items and drinks cold.

The form of the cellar with its rounded ceiling could limit the height of some of the decorations, verify in advance.

Even though no hot food is being prepared, it is recommended to have a chef on duty to oversee the service. He should be dressed in chef's whites which adds a feeling of importance to this prestigous event.

Specifics

Designate someone to install the additional lighting, remembering that certain dishes will be highlighted.

Set the base for the theme cake in place and verify the lighting around it.

Schedule two servers to arrive early and lay out the displays on the buffet table. Two additional servers are needed just before the guests arrive.

Be present the day following the event to verify that all rental equipment is in good order and that the room was properly cleaned.

Organization (Example C+++)

Even though all the items are served cold, a well organized work schedule is imperative. The on-site prep area is very limited so many items must be finished at the last minute in the caterer's kitchen.

Savory Items

Pastry Hors d'œuvres

These hors d'œuvres are prepared in advance, and shaped and frozen unbaked.

Since they cannot be reheated on-site, it is important to bake them fresh shortly before the event so they are crispy.

Brioches Mousselines

The brioche is prepared and baked one day in advance.

The rich, delicate fillings must be applied the day of the event. Cover the assembled brioches with plastic wrap and refrigerate until delivery.

Canapés

The close-textured white bread (pain de mie) is made 48 hours in advance sliced the day before, wrapped in plastic and refrigerated.

The garnishes are assembled and prepared one day in advance. (Quail eggs are cooked, butter left at room temperature to soften, monkfish is poached and chilled.)

The canapés are assembled the day of the event and placed on moistened sheets of parchment paper to keep the bread from drying out. They are covered with plastic wrap and refrigerated until delivery.

Brush on a thin coat of aspic just before arranging them on platters.

Aspic Canapés

They are prepared one day in advance and chilled to set.

They are unmolded onto toast rounds just before delivery and arranged on platters at the location.

Belgian Endive Leaves

The ingredients can be prepared one day in advance.

The leaves are filled the day of the event, glazed once then refrigerated.

They are glazed a second time just before delivery and arranged on platters on-site.

Cold Brochettes

The ingredients can be prepared one day in advance. The brochettes are then assembled the morning of the event, glazed once and refrigerated.

They are brushed with aspic a second time just before delivery and arranged on platters on-site.

Elaborate Meat Dishes

The meats are prepared and cooked 2-3 days in advance.

The garnish ingredients are prepared the day before.

Slicing and glazing the meat, assembling the garnishes and preparing the decorations are done the day of the event.

It is recommended to prepare everything in the caterer's kitchen but to not arrange on platters until delivered as delicate arrangements often suffer damage during delivery. The platters can be coated with a thin coat of aspic in advance and set so the platters are ready to receive the food.

Salads

All of the salad ingredients can be prepared and stored separately covered with plastic wrap and refrigerated.

The dressings are made in advance and refrigerated in air-tight containers.

The dressing is gently tossed with the other ingredients just before delivery and the final seasoning with salt and pepper is done on-site.

Cheeses

The cheeses can be arranged on platters on-site and decorated with colorful autumn leaves or vine leaves or other decorations that reflect the theme.

Sweet Items

The Theme Cake is made 48 hours in advance and refrigerated or frozen depending on the filling. In this case the cake is filled with a champagne mousse accented with grapes and macaroons and served with a raspberry sauce or champagne sabayon.

The decorative base for the cake is made several days in advance. It can be made of pastillage or carved from styrofoam and covered with royal icing and augmented with piped sugar flowers or other edible decorations.

The preparation of the almond macaroons, butter cookies, and chocolates are worked into the daily baking schedule.

The champagne granité is made in advance but rechurned the morning of the event. It is scooped into small cups and frozen solid before delivery.

The granité should be served at a soft consistency and sprinkled with a little champagne or champagne brandy.

Organization and Layout of the buffets

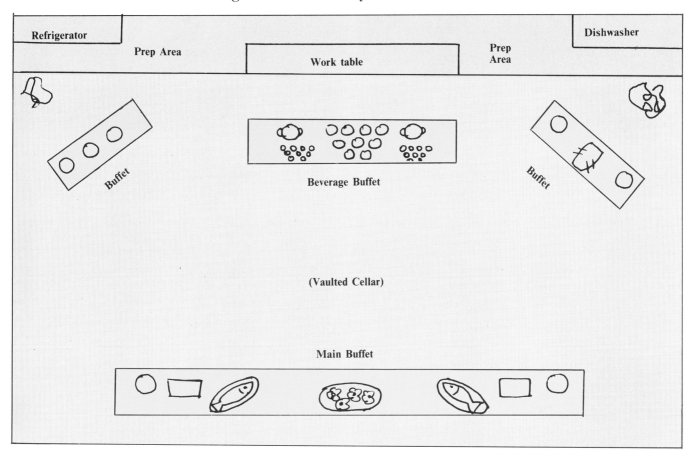

Creating a Theme for a Buffet

Choosing a theme for a buffet gives the client and caterer a central idea to focus on when choosing menu items and decorations. It is a wonderful opportunity for the caterer to express his skill and imagination.

The theme can be carried out in different ways:

• *Dishes and ingredients* chosen to harmonize with the season or the surroundings (Hunting season: game dishes, country-style salads, Nautical theme: fish dishes, Drakkar).
• *A showpiece dessert* can be made for a special event (heart-shaped cake for an engagement party, a croquembouche in the form of a chapel for a first communion).

• *Decorations* can set the mood for the occasion (autumn leaves, decorative branches for a hunt party).

The table decorations can be supplemented by decorative bases created by the caterer on which he arranges certain dishes. The theme can be further expressed in edible decorations used to augment the platter presentations (pulled sugar flowers, models in pastillage...) The possibilities for clever and beautiful decorations are limitless.

287

A Formal Wedding Reception

The Delamour's, a prominent banking family, will hold a reception for the marriage of their youngest daughter. They have rented a château in the countryside just outside of Paris and the wedding will take place on an afternoon in July.

Details

The religious ceremony will be held in the early afternoon. The guests will begin arriving at the château following the photo session on the château grounds.

Location

This château is often rented for just such an event, and both the grounds and the interior have been arranged for formal receptions. The cocktail buffet will be held outdoors. The dinner buffet will be held in the two main dining rooms, one of which will have space for a full orchestra and dance floor.

CLIENT _Mr. and Mrs. Delamour   Saturday 27 July_ Dossier N° |_C++++_|

If company
Person in charge

Tel. _XX XX_

Fax

Address
for billing _____ _Mr. and Mrs. Delamour_

_____ _Bd Malesherbes____75017 Paris_

Number guests
_150_
Budget
High

Method of payment

Place and address
of the reception _____ _Château de Chevreuse_

Set-up and atmosphere of reception room	Preparation facilities
Two large reception rooms	_Large kitchen, ground floor_

RENTAL EQUIPMENT |_X_| Furnished by us	RECEPTION SCHEDULE
(Check) (Dossier N° _____ |_16_|)	Reception _____ _6:00 pm_
Rented |_X_| from _OPTIONS_	
	Food delivery _____ _4:30 pm_
BUFFET Menu finalized by _____ _July 10_	Food pick-up _____ _Following reception_
	Rental delivery _____ _11:00 am_
BEVERAGES _Champagne, whiskey,_ _Perrier, orange and grapefruit juice_	Rental pick-up _Day after reception 8:00 am_
Ice _120 lbs_	(Other) _Everything in order by 9:00 am_ _(another caterer arrives)_
TRANSPORTATION _2 delivery vans_	

Flowers _We supply_	PERSONNEL
Musique _We supply (Orchestra)_	_4 servers_ _2 kitchen personnel_
Other _Fire works, photographer_	

Additional information _We supply everything - flowers, photos, orchestra, fire works, beverages_

Suggested Menu (Example C++++)

Savory Items

Canapés
- 45 Sole Canapés, 45 Salmon Canapés, 45 Monkfish Canapés, 45 Caviar Canapés, 45 Duck Mousse Canapés, 45 Zucchini Canapés, 45 Radish Canapés, 45 Green Bean Canapés, 45 Broccoli Canapés

Total 450 Canapés

Aspic Canapés
- 75 Crayfish Aspics, 75 Chicken Liver Aspics

Total Aspic Canapés

Mignonnettes
- 40 Cocktail Franks in Pastry with Mustard, Blood Sausage in Pastry, 40 Monkfish Fritters, 40 Celery with Roquefort

Total 160 Mignonnettes

Hot Hors d'œuvres
- 40 of each: Quail Eggs on Toast, Snail Bouchées, Mussel Croustades, Mini Brioches with Crab, Feuilletés with Sole, Mini Bouchées à la Reine, Chicken Liver Croustades

Total 280 Hors d'œuvres

Centerpieces for Buffets
- Bouquet of Crudités (150 pieces)
- Stuffed Crêpe " Hedgehog " (150)
- Canapé " Hedgehog " (150 pieces): Salmon canapés and Parma Ham canapés
- 4 Surprise Breads (150 pieces): Wanuts, Raisins, Tongue, Mortadella

Cold Brochettes
- 50 Chicken Brochettes
- 50 Beef Stroganoff Brochettes
- 50 Lamb and Curry Brochettes

Total 150 Cold Brochettes

Fish in Aspic
- Pike Terrine with Asparagus (50 servings)
- Turbot with Salmon Mousses (50 servings)
- Lobsters " en Bellevue " (50 servings)

Total 150 servings

Elaborate Meat Dishes
- Prime Rib with Young Vegetables (50 servings)
- Sliced Decorated Ham (50 servings)
- Galantine of Duck (50 servings)

150 servings

Mixed Salads
- Taboulé (50 servings)
- Cinderella Salad (50 servings)
- Cinese Salad (50 servings)

Total 150 servings

Cheeses
- Platter of Assorted Cheeses (150 portions)

Sweet Items

- Wedding Cake (150 servings)
- 150 Sorbet and Ice Cream Cups
- 150 servings Apple Sorbet with Calvados
- 150 Decorated and Macerated Fruits
- 150 Almond Macaroons and Butter Cookies
- Fruit Basket (150 servings)

Comments on the Menu Selection Example C++++

This menu is for a marriage on a very grand scale. The reception takes place in a château and the client wishes to have a large assortment of dishes presented very elaborately.

The caterer is in charge of every detail: reservation of the château, rental equipment and set up of the rooms (which involves moving funiture out and replacing it after the event). It is necessary to plan ahead for a very functional preparation area to handle the variety of dishes.

The menu is divided into three courses:
- Cocktail Buffet
- Dinner Buffet
- Dessert Buffet

Cocktail Buffet

If the weather permits the cocktail buffet will be set up outdoors.

The first item to be presented is a magnificent bouquet of crudités accompanied by a light sauce. The natural bright colors fit right in with the garden setting.

The mignonnettes and hot hors d'œuvres are served next. The elegant hot hors d'œuvres are reheated a few at a time and passed immediately. The final preparation of these hors d'œuvres is not difficult as long as the assembly is well organized.

Stuffed crêpes, sliced and presented on toothpicks attached to a decorative base give dimension to the buffet. There is a choice of flavors; foie gras, lumpfish eggs, crabmeat mousse, and cheese.

There is also a " hedgehog " made with canapés (smoked salmon and parma ham/150 pieces) which is always enjoyed by guests.

Four surprise breads, filled with crabmeat, walnuts/raisins, tongue and motadella are presented on silver pedestals.

The final item in this course is a selection of aspic canapés (chicken liver, crayfish) which are always appreciated on a luxurious buffet.

To signal the end of the cocktail buffet, a cup of apple sorbet with calvados is served. The guests then move into the dining room for the following course.

Dinner Buffet

The assorted cold brochettes are served first which are refreshing and colorful.

The fish in aspic are presented next. This luxurious array of dishes includes a pike terrine with asparagus which provides beautiful slices and is arranged on decorated platters. The turbot, filled with salmon mousse and glazed with chaud-froid and the lobsters en bellevue are very elegant showpieces.

The fish is followed by a selection of three meat dishes:
- (Red meat) Prime Rib with Young Vegetables
- Ham-which is sliced, reformed and decorated
- (Poultry) Galantine of Duck

The salads are served with the meats: the flavorful Taboulé which goes well with all the meats; " Cinderella " salad which combines asparagus and artichokes, and the Chinese salad which adds an exotic touch.

The cheeses are then passed by the servers and cut to order for each guest. They are accompanied by a variety of breads made with nuts.

Dessert Buffet

The principle dessert is the wedding cake. The classic choice is the traditional French croquembouche, made with small cream puffs and decorated with pulled sugar flowers and nougatine. Also appropriate would be a tiered decorated cake which is presented on a pedestal. Both can be presented if the client wishes.

The serving of the cake is followed by an assortment of individual desserts: petit fours, decorated and macerated fruits, butter cookies, almond macaroons, sorbet and ice cream cups, and fresh fruit.

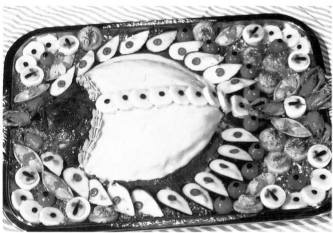

Preparation

This extensive menu involves many different preparations which must be well organized:

Assemble the various ingredients in advance and verify their freshness.

Items in the cocktail buffet menu that can be prepared in advance include: puff pastry, brioche, basic pie pastry, white bread, round loaves for surprise breads.

For the dessert buffet: sorbets and ice creams, cream puffs, sponge cake layers, nougatine, decorated and macerated fruits. The decorations for the wedding cake can also be made in advance.

Since there is a well-equipped kitchen, many of the final preparations will be done on-site. The " mise en place " (assembly of prepared ingredients) must be very well organized to ensure a smooth operation in the on-site kitchen.

Tables are set up in the garden of the château for the cocktail buffet.

Two rooms are used for the dinner buffet. One large buffet table is set up in the main room. A smaller table is prepared in the adjoining room where the dancing will later take place. Here, liquid refreshments are offered as well as some items at the end of the meal.

Tables for the guests are set with fine china, glassware, silverware and beautiful linen tablecloths. The elegant floral arrangements can include ones that have been sent by guests.

Other Considerations

The château is a perfect location for a reception with its large rooms and well equipped kitchen. However all rental; equipment, tableware, chairs, tables etc., must be procured by the caterer, delivered and set up.

For this occasion, the caterer is responsible for every detail; flowers, music, liquid refreshments, photographer, fireworks...

Other factors that make delivery for this reception a challenge is the long distance to the château and the warm weather.

When the event is over, clean-up and removal of all rental must be done as quickly as possible because another caterer has reserved the château the following day.

The caterer is totally responsible for every detail of this luxurious reception. Advance planning of each step of preparation, delivery and service is necessary for the event to run smoothly.

Organization (Example C++++)

Savory Items

Bouquet of Crudités

The vegetables are prepared one day in advance, covered with damp towels and refrigerated.

The bouquet is arranged on-site.

Mignonnettes and Hot Hors d'œuvres

The pastry bases and fillings are prepared one day in advance. Fillings are covered and refrigerated and pastry is stored in airtight containers.

Since the kitchen facilities at the château are ample, plan to assemble and reheat these hors d'œuvres just before serving.

Stuffed Crêpe " Hedgehog "

The crêpes are made and filled the day before the event, covered and refrigerated. The filled rolls are sliced, placed on toothpicks and attached to the base at the château.

Canapé " Hedgehog "

The canapés are made and refrigerated one day in advance.

They are sliced, placed on toothpicks and attached to the base at the château.

Surprise Breads

The breads are baked 2-4 days in advance which facilitates slicing. The sandwiches can be made and replaced into the bread " shell " 2-3 days in advance, wrapped tightly with plastic and refrigerated. In this case, it is recommended to not mix flavors in one loaf, so that the odors do not mix.

The crabmeat filling is always applied the day of the event to ensure freshness.

Canapés

The close-textured white bread, baked in rectangular loaves, is made 2-3 days in advance and sliced the day the before.

The various ingredients used to garnish the canapés are prepared one day in advance (monkfish is poached and chilled, butter is blended with flavorings and kept spreadable at room temperature).

The canapés are assembled the morning of the event, placed on sheets of moistened parchment paper to keep the bread moist, glazed once with aspic, covered with plastic wrap and refrigerated.

Shortly before delivery, the canapés are glazed a second time with aspic, placed in refrigerated containers and arranged on platters on-site.

Aspic Canapés

The bite-size aspics are made the day before and refrigerated to set.

The bread can be shaped and toasted and kept in air-tight containers (or preferably toasted the day of the event).

They are transported in the molds, turned out onto the toast rounds and arranged on platters at the château.

Apple Sorbet

The apple sorbet can be made several days in advance, scooped into the small cups and kept in covered containers in the freezer. Place in insulated containers for delivery.

The garnish of thin red or green apple slices should not be made too far ahead to avoid browning. During the event, the consistency of the sorbet should be checked so that the sorbet softens a little and is served " creamy " with a few drops of calvados and the apple garnish.

Cold Brochettes

The ingredients for the brochettes are prepared two days in advance and refrigerated.

Assemble the brochettes one day in advance, cover with plastic wrap and chill.

They are glazed with sauce the morning of the event then brushed with aspic just before delivery and arranged on platters on-site.

Fish in Aspic

The terrines and the turbot with salmon mousse are prepared two days in advance and refrigerated.

The lobsters are cooked and chilled one day in advance.

These dishes are glazed with aspic and arranged on platters at the château.

Elaborate Meat Dishes

Like the fish dishes, the meat is prepared two days in advance and refrigerated.

They are sliced, decorated and glazed the day of the event in the caterer's kitchen then arranged on platters on-site.

Salads

The separate ingredients are prepared one day in advance and refrigerated.

The salad ingredients are mixed shortly before delivery and the seasoning is done at the location so that the salads do not wilt.

Cheeses

The platters of cheese are arranged on-site or they can be ordered from a specialty cheese shop. The platters can be decorated with leaves, stalks of wheat etc.

The special breads made with nuts should be freshly baked and sliced shortly before service.

Sweet Items

Wedding Cake

A croquembouche must be assembled on-site. If the cake is made with filled spongecake layers, it can be prepared several days in advance and frozen or refrigerated.

The decorative base can be made several days in advance, made from molded sugar or carved styrofoam decorated with pulled sugar flowers, marzipan shapes, nougatine shapes etc.

Sorbets and Ice Cream Cups

The sorbet and ice cream can be made several days in advance. Scoop into the cups while still a little soft from being churned, cover and freeze.

Serve the sorbet and ice cream at a soft consistency.

Decorated and Macerated Fruits

The preparation of these fruits as well as the petit fours, butter cookies, and almond macaroons should be worked into the daily work schedule of the caterer.

They can be prepared in advance and kept in airtight containers.

Fruit Basket

The baskets can be ordered from a specialty shop or arranged by the caterer. Remember to order fruits in an attractive assortment of shapes and colors.

Spray the fruit with cold water just before setting the basket on the buffet table to make them look fresh.

Specifics

Discuss the various details with the client so you understand exactly what is needed: what kind of orchestra; duration, timing and theme of fireworks; what style of photographs etc.

Plan two deliveries:
• The first time, check the arrival of rental equipment and tables etc. (verify that ovens work..), set the tables, check the plants and flowers, set up the liquid refreshment table, put the decorative bases in place with supplementary lighting.
• Deliver the food closer to the time of the reception.

Meanwhile, the musicians arrive and set up their equipment and check the sound system and the fireworks are set up.

Four servers are scheduled; two to arrive with the food and two to arrive shortly before the reception. Assign specific duties during the reception and for the clean-up of the rooms when the reception is over.

Be present or designate someone to check the clean-up and check the rental to register any breakage or damage.

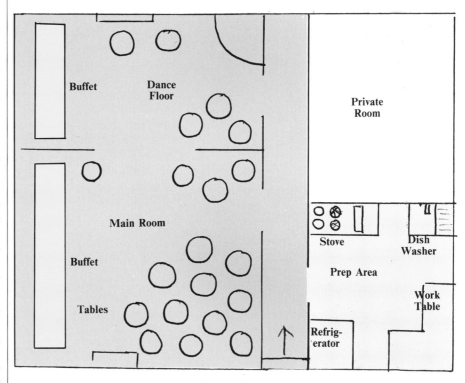

293

Inauguration of a New Gymnasium

The mayor of a small town has organized a reception to celebrate the completion of a new gymnasium. Prominent local figures have been invited to the event, which will also be attended by all the town residents. Invitations with R.S.V.P. envelopes were sent.

Details

The gymnasium will enhance the local sporting and cultural complex, and all of the concerned associations will be participating in the festivities. To mark the beginning of the event, the local marching band will give a parade.

Location

The buffet will be held in the main entrance hall, and a circus-style tent and a podium will be set up on the track.

CLIENT _Town Hall of St-Soupplets_ _June 28_ .... Dossier N° $\boxed{D+}$

If company
Person in charge ... _Secretary-Mayor's Office_ ....

Tel. .. _XX_ ....

Fax .. _XX_ ....

Address
for billing ..... _Town Hall of St-Soupplets_ ....

....

Number guests
_500_
Budget
Low

Method of payment .... _30 % in advance balance - 30/60 days_ ....

Place and address
of the reception ..... _St-Soupplets Community Center_ ....

....

Set-up and atmosphere of reception room	Preparation facilities
...... _Multipurpose hall_	.... _Small kitchen available_ ....

RENTAL EQUIPMENT ⌐‾⌐ Furnished by us
(Check)   (Dossier N° ------------------ ⌐‾⌐)

Rented ⌐ _X_ ⌐ from ... _Sterling Rental_ ....

BUFFET   Menu finalized
          by .... _June 1_ ....

BEVERAGES .... _Donated + back-up (we supply)_

....

Ice .... _250 lbs_ ....

TRANSPORTATION ... _Small delivery vans_ ......

RECEPTION SCHEDULE

Reception ---------- _5:30 pm_ ------------

Food
delivery ---------- _3:00 pm_ ------------

Food
pick-up ------ _Following reception_ ....

Rental
delivery .... _11:00 am_ ....

Rental
pick-up .... _Monday 8:00 am_ ....

(Other) ....

Flowers .... _Client will supply_ ....

Musique .... _Client will supply_ ....

Other ..... _Majorettes will provide entertainment_

PERSONNEL

..... _8 servers_ ....

..... _2 kitchen personnel_ ....

Additional information .... _Back-up supply of beverages_ ....

....

Suggested Menu: Example D+

Savory Items

Pastry Hors d'œuvres

50 of each of the following varieties: Almond, Hazelnut, Poppy Seed and Sesame Seed Matchsticks, Cheese Matchsticks, Cumin-Munster, Anchovy, Ham Crescents, Stuffed Olive, Chorizo, Mini-Pizzas

Total 500 Pastry Hors d'œuvres

Filled Rolls

- 100 Foie Gras Filled Rolls
- 100 " Fromage Frais " Filled Rolls

Total 200 Filled Rolls

Sandwiches

- 100 Ham Sandwiches
- 100 Lettuce-Cucumber Sandwiches
- 100 Egg Salad Sandwiches

Total 300 Sandwiches

Canapés

50 of each of the following varieties: Tuna, Shrimp, Bay Scallop, Anchovy, Salmon Mousse, Hard-Boiled Egg, Parma Ham, Dry Sausage, Andouille, Blood Sausage with Apple, Tomato, Sautéed Zucchini, Cucumber, Turnip, Asparagus Tip, Artichoke Bottom, Broccoli, Hearts of Palm, Parmesan, " Fromage Frais " with Paprika

Total 1,000 Canapés

Centerpieces for Buffets

- 4 Crudité Bouquets, each with 200 pieces
- 3 " Drakkars ", each with 100 pieces
- 3 Canapé " Hedgehogs ", each with 70 pieces
- 5 Stuffed Crêpe " Hedgehogs ", each with 100 pieces
- 14 Brioche Surprise Breads: 6 Louis XIV Brioches, each with 40 pieces
- 8 Brioche " Mousselines ", each with 40 pieces

Total 560 Pieces

Sweet Items

- 200 Assorted Tartelettes
- 200 Mini Cream Puffs
- 200 Petit Fours
- 200 Decorated Fruits
- 200 Macerated Fruits

Comments on the Menu Selection (Example D+)

This is a difficult menu to plan. The large number of guests demands a great deal of organization to prepare, deliver and serve these quanitities of food. In addition, the budget is not high.

The occasion is a cocktail celebration held at the city hall with many of the community's top citizens in attendance. It is an " open house " i.e. guests will arrive throughout the evening and stay for a short while. The food and service must be adapted to the situation.

Platters are replenished at regular intervals so that all the guests are served food that looks and tastes fresh.

Savory Items

To stay within the limits of the budget, a lovely assortment of 500 pastry hors d'œuvres are proposed that are easy to serve and eat and relatively quick to prepare.

Following are 300 sandwiches with three different fillings (ham, cucumber/lettuce, and egg salad) which are a filling item that is always well-liked.

Platters of filled rolls (foie gras and " fromage frais ") round out the sandwich selection.

An assortment of 20 canapés (1000 pieces) makes a beautiful display and are easy to prepare.

A lovely bouquet of crudités adds a fresh touch and is a very economical item.

To give dimension and a sense of volume on the buffet table, three impressive preparations are included in the menu (Drakkar, stuffed crêpe hedgehog and brioche surprise breads). Although these are more expensive items, the large number of easy-to-eat servings and the dramatic display makes them an important part of this menu.

Sweet Items

The sweet items include 1000 assorted bite-size desserts that are beautifully arranged on platters. The selection includes tartelettes in an array of colors, mini cream puffs with different flavored fillings, and decorated and macerated fruits.

Preparation

Due to the limited budget and large volume of food, the ordering of the various ingredients must be done with great care to procure top quality ingredients at reasonable prices.

Order the food in advance and plan each step of the preparation.

For the savory items, prepare the puff pastry, white bread and brioche in advance.

For the sweet items, prepare the pie pastry, cream puffs, cakes and decorated and macerated fruits in advance.

The final preparation takes place in the kitchen of the caterer, the items are then delivered in appropriate containers which are labeled with the contents.

The client will provide servers who must be instructed in advance so that the service runs smoothly.

This type of reception gives the caterer a great deal of local exposure so it is important that the event is well organized.

Other Considerations

This reception gives the caterer a great deal of exposure at the local level. It is therefore important to anticipate any problems in advance. The number of items per person should be enough to not run out, yet the caterer is working with a relatively modest budget. The caterer can have ready a back-up supply of several delicious but less expensive items in case of an emergency.

Proof of the caterer's skill and creativity can be shown by the display of a showpiece made especially for the event, a centerpiece in pastillage or other impressive work of culinary art.

For an event like this, the caterer is often in charge of coordinating the donations made by sponsors, who might supply a portion of the liquid refreshments, for example.

The caterer will work with volunteer servers who must be instructed in advance.

Specifics

Keep in contact with a representative from the city hall to confirm that the room has been set up and that servers have been scheduled. Be ready to supply additional servers if necessary.

Keep a list of the donations made for the event.

Confirm that liquid refreshments have been delivered and chilled the morning of the event.

Be present when the rental is delivered and verify that everything is in good working order.

Deliver the special centerpiece made for this occasion and set it on the buffet table with special lightling if necessary.

Schedule four servers to arrive when the food is delivered and four additional to arrive shortly before the reception begins.

Check the rental after the event to register breakage/damage. Inventory the liquid refreshments that were not consumed and have this list approved and signed by the client.

In this case, the bill will be not be paid by the same department that organized the event, which may cause complications.

Canapés

The close-textured bread (same as sandwiches) is made 3-4 days in advance and sliced the day before, wrapped in plastic and refrigerated.

The garnishes are prepared the day before (eggs are hard-boiled, ham and sausages are sliced, butter is blended and left at room temperature).

Organization (Example D+)

The occasion is a cocktail reception in honor of a city employee. The menu is composed of bite-size items that are arranged on platters which will be easy to serve in the large room where the reception is held.

Even though the menu is not complicated it involves the preparation of a large number of hors d'œuvres. The work must be organized so that the caterer's kitchen is not overloaded on any one day.

Savory Items

Pastry Hors d'œuvres

The puff pastry for the pastry hors d'œuvres is made in advance, cut into shapes and frozen unbaked 3-4 days in advance. The pastries are then baked fresh the day of the event shortly before delivery.

The canapés are assembled the morning of the event, brushed with aspic, placed on dampened sheets of parchment paper, covered with plastic and refrigerated.

If necessary, glaze with aspic a second time shortly before delivery.

They are transported in refrigerated containers and arranged on platters on-site.

Sandwiches

The close-textured white bread used to make the sandwiches is baked 3-4 days in advance, refrigerated then sliced the day before and wrapped well and refrigerated. The fillings can be prepared one day in advance. The sandwiches are assembled the day of the event and placed between damp sheets of parchment paper to keep the bread moist.

Filled Rolls

The small brioche rolls can be baked one day in advance. After they have completely cooled, fill and cover with plastic wrap and refrigerate.

Bouquet of Crudités

The vegetables are cut in bite-size pieces one day in advance and kept between moistened towels in the refrigerator. They are placed on toothpicks and attached to the base shortly before delivery.

Spray the bouquet with cold water just before setting it on the buffet table to make it look fresh.

Drakkars and "Hedgehog"

The surprise breads and filled brioches are made one day in advance as well as the cardboard boat. The canapés are prepared the day before, covered with plastic wrap and refrigerated.

The day of the event, the long strips are cut into even pieces, placed on toothpicks and attached to the base. The hedgehog is kept covered with a damp towel or aluminum foil until served.

Stuffed Crêpe " Hedgehog "

The crêpes are made and filled one day in advance, wrapped in plastic and refrigerated.

They are sliced into bite-size pieces the day of the event, placed on toothpicks and attached to a natural base (watermelon for example) or a base carved from styrofoam.

Brioches Surprise Breads

The brioche with the topknot and the richer " mousseline " which is baked in a cylindrical mold are made 1-2 days in advance. They are sliced, filled, and reformed the morning of the event, wrapped in plastic and refrigerated until delivery.

Sweet Items

The number of items is so great that the desserts for this event are not part of the daily work schedule of the caterer's shop but require the full attention of the baking staff.

Tartelettes

The pastry shells are shaped and baked 1-2 days in advance and kept in a cool, dry place. The cream and fruits are added the day of the event so the pastry remains crispy.

It is recommended to brush a little reduced apricot glaze on the bottom of the baked pastry before adding the filling to keep them from getting soft.

Mini Cream Puffs

The cream puff pastry can be made and baked then frozen one day in advance. It is also possible to freeze the dough, piped out on baking sheets to be baked the day of the event.

They are filled and glazed the day of the event.

Petit Fours

The cake layers are filled the day before and refrigerated. They are glazed, cut and decorated the day of the event.

Decorated Fruit

These dried fruit and marzipan desserts can be assembled several days in advance then dipped in sugar syrup (cooked to hard crack) the day of the event. It is possible to candy these preparations in which case they can be made entirely in advance and kept in a cool, dry place.

The macerated fruits are prepared one day in advance and finished the next day.

The platters are assembled on-site.

Organization and Layout of the Buffet

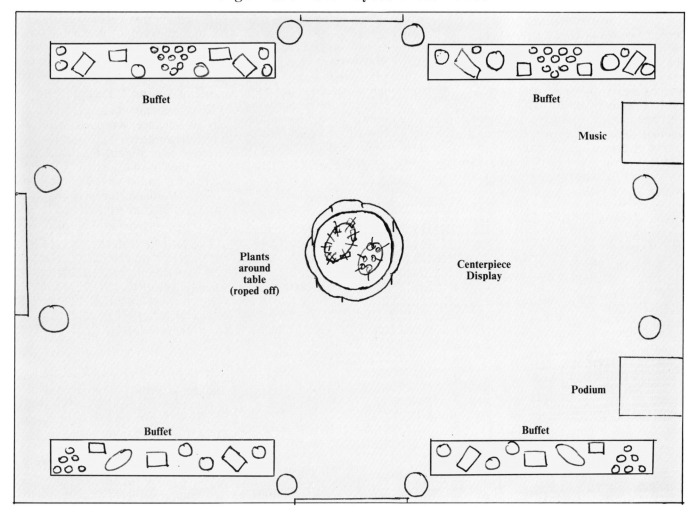

Buffet

Buffet

Music

Plants
around
table
(roped off)

Centerpiece
Display

Podium

Buffet

Buffet

General Information and Advice – Cheeses

Role

In France, cheese plays an important role in the meal. It is served after the main course and salad as a transition to dessert. At a family dinner the last sip of red wine from the main course marries perfectly with the full-bodied flavor of many French cheeses.

At a formal dinner a variety is usually offered with selected wines featuring specialties of the region along with the classic choice of a blue-veined, aged and fresh cheeses, chêvres, etc.

The cheeses can be chosen to reflect the theme or mood of the event (rustic, farmhouse cheeses for a less formal event, a well-rounded selection with labels for a wine tasting...).

Presentation

For a catered buffet, cheeses can be served in different ways to adapt to the situation.

At a stand-up buffet, cubes of hard cheeses on toothpicks is very practical. A small cube of bread can be included on each pick for convenience.

The toothpicks can be attached to a base like the " hedgehogs " described in this series or a block of cheese or even a round of Brie can be cut into bite-size pieces and reformed and served with toothpicks or small forks placed on the side.

For a dinner buffet, the platter of cheeses is placed on the buffet table and served by a waiter.

The breads that accompany the cheeses should be carefully chosen. Breads with walnuts marry well with hard cheeses and sourdough bread goes well with fermented cheese.

It is recommended to avoid cheeses that are too soft and runny and therefore hard to serve or cheeses that are too strong-smelling.

Transport and Storage

A hedgehog of cubed cheese on toothpicks can be assembled in the caterer's kitchen and covered with plastic wrap. Whole or large pieces of cheese should be kept enveloped in plastic or paper and assembled on platters on-site.

In France specialty cheese shops will prepare cheese trays to order.

The tray should remain covered until service to keep the odors from mingling with the other foods.

Cheeses should always be served at room temperature with wines selected to go with the taste of the cheeses.

The choice of cheeses is vast and the selection should reflect the personal tastes of the client.

Business School Dance

The school's social events committee has decided to throw a *particularly festive party this year. They have invited alumni, professors, and family members of enrolled students to join in the festivities.*

Details

Members of the social events committee have invited the alumni with the hopes that some of the students may be able to secure internships or summer jobs, and that graduating students may be able to find permanent jobs.

Location

The dance is held in the school gymnasium, which has been decorated for the event by committee members. Their will be a live band, and various school organizations will have stands on one side of the room.

CLIENT _Business School Alumni Association_ .... Dossier N° | _D++_ |

If company
Person in charge ......_Mr Alphonse BIROT_............................ Tel. _XX XX_ ....

Fax _XX XX_ ....

Address
for billing ...._B.S.A.A._..

............._11, rue du Commerce 21000 DIJON_....................

Method of payment .._50 % in advance, balance upon receipt of bill_.................

Number guests
_500_
Budget
...._Average_....

Place and address
of the reception ......_Same as above_...

Set-up and atmosphere of reception room

...._School gymnasium_..

Preparation facilities

........_Kitchen adjoining gymnasium_..............

RENTAL EQUIPMENT | _X_ | Furnished by us
(Check)   (Dossier N°.....................| _11_ |)

Rented| _X_ | from ..._S.L.M._..........................

BUFFET   Menu finalized
by ...._May 7_..................

BEVERAGES .._Champagne, whiskey,_............
.._fruit juices, Perrier_....................
Ice ...._6 x 40 lbs bags_...........................

TRANSPORTATION ...._3 vans (must rent one)_.......

Flowers ...._We supply_...........................

Musique ..._We supply disk jockey_..................

Other...

RECEPTION SCHEDULE

Reception ...._7:00 pm_...........................

Food
delivery............_5:00 pm_..........................

Food
pick-up ...._After reception_..................

Rental
delivery ...._11:00 am_.......................

Rental
pick-up ...._8:00 am next morning_.....

(Other)...

PERSONNEL

........._8 servers_.......................

........._2 kitchen personnel_.....................

Additional information ...._Service tapers off later in evening_..............................

Suggested Menu: Example D++

Savory Items

Pastry Hors d'oeuvres

100 of each of the following varieties: Walnut, Poppy Seed/Sesame Seed Matchsticks, Parmesan, Sliced Almond Hors d'oeuvres, "Chipolatas", Chorizo, "Croque Monsieurs", Mushroom Tartelettes, Mini Pizzas
Total 1,000 Pastry Hors d'oeuvres

Canapés

50 of each of the following varieties: Salmon, Smoked Eel, Pickled Herring, Mussel, Bay Scallop, Lumpfish Egg, Anchovy, Quail Egg, Tongue, Duck Mousse, Blood Sausage with Apples, Mixed Sausage, Tomato, Sautéed Zucchini, Radish, Cucumber, Corn, Green Peppercorn, Green Bean, Asparagus Tip, "Fromage Frais" with Chives
Total 1,000 Canapés

Aspic Canapés

- 100 Chicken Liver Aspics
- 100 Salmon Aspics
- Tongue Aspics
- 100 Lumpfish Egg Aspics
- 100 Chicken Aspics
Total 500 Assorted Aspics

Centerpieces for Buffets

- 1 "Hedgehog" of Stuffed Crêpes, with 500 pieces (lumpfish eggs, salmon mousse, Parma ham, "fromage frais", crab)
- Surprise Breads (foie gras mousse, tomato-lettuce, egg salad, salami, chicken, roquefort and walnut)
Total 500 Sandwiches

Terrines

- Rabbit and Hazelnut Terrine
  Chicken Liver Terrine
- Goose Rillettes
Total 500 Portions of Terrine (with condiments and country bread)

Sweet Items

- 500 Assorted Tartelettes
- 500 Mini Cream Puffs and Fours Glacés
- 500 Decorated Fruits and Macerated Fruits
- 500 Ice Cream and Sorbet Cups
Total 2,000 Servings
Grand Total 6,000 Servings

Comments on the Menu Selection (Example D++)

This menu is for the annual reception of the Graduate School of Business Administration which is always a grand affair with a guest list of 500 that includes professors and students.

The guests do not arrive all at the same time and the reception lasts quite a long time.

The menu must take into consideration the following factors:
• The budget
• The number of guests
• The distance of the reception from the kitchen (a small preparation area is set up near the gym where the reception is taking place, primarily to heat the pastry hors d'œuvres).

Savory Items

The first item to be offered are the pastry hors d'oeuvres (10 flavors/1000 pieces) which are lovely when arranged in neat rows on platters.

Stuffed crêpe hedgehogs (500 pieces) give dimension to the buffet table.

The surprise breads (500 pieces) are also decorative on the table and are a practical way of serving delicious sandwiches.

The canapés (20 flavors/1000 pieces) create a rainbow of colors and forms when arranged on large platters.

The aspic canapés are fresh tasting and the golden aspic glistens on the platters. Five varieties; chicken liver, salmon, tongue, lumpfish eggs, and chicken, make a wonderful assortment.

The remainder of the savory items are set out for the guests to serve themselves; terrine of rabbit with hazelnuts or with chicken livers and rillettes that are served with a variety of sliced breads and condiments. This is appropriate for this occasion where most of the guests are young and are well-acquainted.

Sweet Items

The selection of individual desserts is classic: 500 fruit tartelettes, 500 mini cream puffs and petit fours, 500 decorated fruits, 500 sorbet and ice cream cups.

Preparation

This is an important step due to the large number of items to shop for and prepare.

Order the ingredients to be delivered several days in advance and verify freshness.

For the savory items the following can be prepared in advance; puff pastry, basic pie pastry, white bread and loaves for surprise breads.

For the sweet items; sweet pie pastry, cream puff pastry, petit fours, decorated fruits, and ice creams and sorbets.

Once the preparation schedule is decided, it is important to not fall behind because there are so many items to prepare.

Everything is prepared in the kitchen of the caterer and transported in refrigerated or airtight containers, each labeled clearly with a list of the contents.

The service staff must also be well organized. The only items to be reheated are the pastry hors d'oeuvres which are warmed in batches and served throughout the reception.

Back-up platters of each item are prepared and brought out at intervals to replace the ones that have been on the buffet so that each arrival of guests sees and tastes the food at its best.

The terrines and breads are sliced a few at a time so that they are as fresh as possible when served.

Organization (Example D++)

There is ample room to set up the buffet on long tables so that the food is easily accessible to all the guests. Since it is not possible to finish many dishes on-site, the kitchen staff must be organized to produce the large numbers of items and have them all ready to be delivered at the designated time.

Savory Items

Pastry Hors d'oeuvres

The pastry hors d'oeuvres can be shaped and frozen unbaked several days in advance. If they are being reheated on-site they can be baked one day in advance and kept in airtight containers.

If the pastry hors d'œuvres are being served at room temperature they should be baked shortly before delivery so that they are fresh and crisp.

Stuffed Crêpe " Hedgehog "

The crêpes are prepared, filled, covered with plastic wrap and refrigerated one day in advance.

They are sliced into bite-size pieces, placed on toothpicks and attached to the base on-site.

Surprise Breads

Make the breads 2-3 days in advance. One day before the event, slice the breads and add the fillings (foie gras, salami, chicken, roquefort/walnut) replace the sandwiches inside the bread " shell " and wrap tightly in plastic and refrigerate.

The egg salad and tomato/lettuce fillings should be applied the day of the event because these fillings will make the sandwiches soggy if prepared too far in advance.

Canapés

Make the close-textured white bread 3-4 days in advance.

Slice the breads one day in advance, wrap (vacumn packing is ideal) and refrigerate.

Prepare the various garnishes (hard-boil the quail eggs, make the mousse..) the day before and refrigerate in covered containers.

The garnishes are arranged on the sliced bread, glazed once with aspic and refrigerated on damp sheets of parchment paper to keep the bread moist.

It is often necessary to glaze the canapés a second time just before delivery.

They are arranged on platters on-site.

Aspic Canapés

They are prepared one day in advance and refrigerated to set. They are unmolded onto toast rounds shortly before delivery and arranged on platters just before they are served.

Terrines and Rillettes

The terrines are made 3-4 days in advance and refrigerated in the molds. They are unmolded, sliced and glazed in the caterer's kitchen the day of the event and arranged on platters on-site.

The rillettes can also be made well in advance becasue they keep well if refrigerated in a mold and covered with a layer of fat.

Order or bake the specialty breads and assemble the condiments that go with the terrines and rillettes.

Sweet Items

Since the number of pieces to make is so large, this order is not worked into the daily baking schedule of the caterer's business but is given full attention by the baking staff.

Tartelettes

The pie pastry is made in advance and the shells are formed and baked one day in advance or preferably the morning of the event. To protect the pastry shells from the moist filling, it is recommended to brush a little egg glaze on the shells towards the end of baking and/or brush with a little apricot glaze when the baked shells have cooled.

The tartelettes must be garnished with the cream and fruit filling the day of the event to make sure that the pastry does not become soggy.

Mini Cream Puffs

The cream puff can be baked one day in advance and frozen or piped out and frozen unbaked to be baked the day of the event.

To better organize the work, the cream puffs can be filled and glazed 1-2 days in advance and frozen. In this case, they are filled with a mousseline cream and glazed with fondant mixed with 5% butter which solidifies the fondant for better freezing.

Decorated and Macerated Fruits

The decorated and macerated fruits are prepared several days in advance.

If the weather is not too humid they can be dipped in the clear sugar glaze (cooked to hard crack) the day before.

These desserts can be candied well in advance. The caterer can prepare large quantities at a time to fill many orders. For an event of this size, it is recommended to verify that the inventory is enough to fill this particular order.

Sorbet and Ice Cream Cups

The well-balanced assortment of ice creams and sorbets can be made several days in advance and scooped into the cups directly from the churn. The cups are frozen until delivery.

The sorbet and ice cream are best when they are soft and creamy. therefore they should be checked shortly before serving to ensure that they are at the right consistency.

Other Considerations

The kitchens of the university are too far away from the ballroom to be used for this event. A preparation area with a small kitchen is set up closer to the reception room.

Since the guests will be coming and going throughout the evening, the caterer must provide fresh platters of savory and sweet items at regular intervals.

Specifics

Meet with the service staff at the location of the event to instruct them on the placement of the tables and decoration of the room.

Set up the preparation area and install a refrigerated unit (and oven if necessary) and verify that all equipment is in good working order.

Verify that the disc jockey has arrived at the predetermined time and that the sound system is functional and adequate.

Plan the delivery in two stages: First deliver the liquid refreshments and chill them. Put the decorative bases in place and deliver platters and other serving pieces. Later in the day, deliver the food.

Schedule four servers to deliver the food, arrange platters and set up the buffet. Schedule four additional servers to arrive shortly before the reception to assist with the service. Four of these servers are scheduled to stay after the reception to pack up and clean.

Also schedule someone to inventory the rental and be present when it is picked up and to verify that the location was thoroughly cleaned.

Any breakage or damage of rental equipment must be added to the final bill.

Floral Decorations

Floral decoration is vital to the appearance of the buffet table, adding color, volume and grace.

The amount and type of flowers will of course depend on the client's budget and the type of party. A party for 50 would require a different floral arrangement than a party for 300. For a large party it is usually best to have one or two large floral centerpieces with many smaller arrangements bordering the tables.

The theme of the party will also determine the style of floral arrangement – a wedding calls for different flowers than does a business luncheon.

It is best to subcontract the flowers to a good florist, to whom the caterer will explain the size, theme and budget of the function.

Fresh Flowers

The main buffet table could hold a large arrangement of fresh flowers. At a wedding reception, for example, the bouquets sent by well-wishers

Organization and Layout of the Buffet

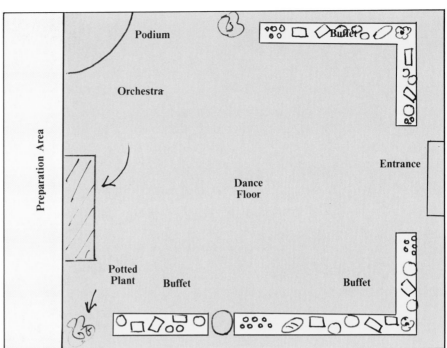

can be arranged around the central arrangement.

Artificial Flowers

Artificial flowers are rarely used, though the caterer may have some small tasteful artificial arrangements to use in cases where no fresh flowers are available.

Other Potted Plants

Potted green plants are used more as architectural elements than as real decorations: they are useful in framing entranceways and breaking up large spaces.

Again, a florist can be subcontracted to provide these items.

Presentation and Placement

Depending on which is most convenient, the florist can deliver the arrangements to the caterer, who in turn brings them to the event, or the flowers can be delivered directly to the party.

In either case, it is the caterer's responsibility to see to their placement and of course to bill the client.

With large plants, however, the florist should be the one to deliver, set-up and return the plants.

Introduction of a New Car Model

A local car dealership has organized an all-day reception in honor of the brand new model.

Details

The car manufacturer has organized the advertising campaign on a national level, with the hopes that it will increase orders for the new model.

Location

The dealership room is well-suited to a reception. Buffet tables will be scattered throughout the room, focusing on all the models, and the car dealers and their hostesses will be in charge of their replenishment.

CLIENT _ _ CENTRAL AUTO _ _ _ _ _ _ _ _ _ _ _ _ _ _ _ Thurs Oct 11 _ _ _ _ _ _ _ Dossier N° │D+++│

If company
Person in charge _ _ _ Mr DUCAPEAU _ Tel. _ _ XX XX _ _ _ _

Fax _ _ XX XX _ _ _ _

Address
for billing _ _ _ _ _ _ _ CENTRAL AUTO _

_ _ _ _ _ _ _ _ _ _ _ _ _ Avenue de l'Etoile _ _ _ 75116 PARIS _ _ _ _ _ _ _ _ _

| Number guests |
| 1200 |

Method of payment _ _ 30 % by check in advance, balance at 30 and 60 days _ _ _

Budget
_ _ _ _ _ _ High _ _ _ _ _

Place and address
of the reception _ _ _ _ _ _ Same as above _

Set-up and atmosphere of reception room   Preparation facilities

_ _ Main display room in car dealership _ _ _ _ _ _   _ _ _ _ _ _ Kitchen set up in stock room _ _ _ _ _ _ _ _ _ _

RENTAL EQUIPMENT   │ X │ Furnished by us
(Check)   (Dossier N° _ _ _ _ _ _ _ _ _ _ _ _ _ _ _ │ 10 │)

Rented │ X │ from _ _ _ OPTIONS _ _ _ _ _ _ _ _ _ _ _ _ _

RECEPTION SCHEDULE

Reception _ _ _ _ _ _ 11:00 am to 9:00 pm _ _ _ _ _ _ _ _

Food
delivery _ _ _ _ _ _ _ _ 9:30 am _ _ _ _ _ _ _ _ _ _ _ _ _ _ _ _ _

BUFFET   Menu finalized
by _ _ _ _ _ _ _ _ _ _ Oct 1 _ _ _ _ _ _ _ _ _ _ _ _ _

Food
pick-up _ _ _ _ _ _ _ 10:00 pm _ _ _ _ _ _ _ _ _ _ _ _ _ _

BEVERAGES _ Furnished by customer _ _ _ _ _ _ _ _ _ _

Rental
delivery _ _ _ _ _ _ _ 8:00 am _ _ _ _ _ _ _ _ _ _ _ _ _ _ _ _

Ice _ _ _ _ 6 x 40 lbs bags _ _ _ _ _ _ _ _ _ _ _ _ _ _

Rental
pick-up _ _ _ _ _ _ _ _ Monday morning 8:00 _ _ _ _ _ _

TRANSPORTATION _ Smalls vans and _ _ _ _ _ _ _

_ _ _ _ _ _ _ _ _ _ refrigerated truck _ _ _ _ _ _ _ _ _ _ _ _ _

(Other) _ Plan rotation of personnel _ _ _ _ _ _ _ _ _ _ _

Flowers _ _ _ We supply _ _ _ _ _ _ _ _ _ _ _ _ _ _ _ _ _ _ _

PERSONNEL

_ _ _ _ 8 servers _ _ _ _ _ _ _ _ _ _ _ _ _ _ _ _ _ _

Musique _ _ Client will supply _ _ _ _ _ _ _ _ _ _ _ _

_ _ _ 2 kitchen personnel _ _ _ _ _ _ _ _ _ _ _ _ _ _

Other _ EXTRAS : table cloths, mirrors, _ _ _ _ _ _ _
_ spotlights, silverware, elaborate centerpieces

Additional information _ _ Arrange several deliveries during the event so the food is always fresh _ _ _

Suggested Menu (Example D+++)

Savory Items

Pastry Hors d'œuvres
- 260 Stuffed Olive Hors d'œuvres
- 260 " Croque Monsieurs "
- 260 Mini Pizzas
- 260 Cheese Matchsticks
- 260 Pâté Hors d'œuvres
- 260 Anchovy Hors d'œuvres
- 260 Chorizo Hors d'œuvres
- 260 Ham Crescents
- 260 Cocktail Sausage Hors d'œuvres
- 260 " Chipolatas " Hors d'œuvres

Total 2,600 Pastry Hors d'œuvres

Filled Rolls
- 500 Foie Gras Filled Rolls
- 500 Ham Filled Rolls
- 500 Comté Cheese Filled Rolls

Total 1,500 Filled Rolls

Canapés
- 260 Fresh Salmon Canapés
- 260 Sole Mousse with Herbs Canapés
- 260 Monkfish Canapés
- 260 Bay Scallop Canapés
- 260 Lumpfish Egg Canapés
- 260 Quail Egg Canapés
- 260 Blood Sausage with Apples Canapés
- 260 Sautéed Zucchini Canapés
- 260 Asparagus Tip Canapés
- 260 Artichoke Bottom Canapés

Total 2,600 Assorted Canapés

Centerpieces for Buffets
1 " Hedgehog " of Assorted Stuffed Crêpes:
400 Lumpfish Egg Crêpes
400 Salmon Mousse Crêpes
400 Foie Gras Crêpes
400 " Fromage Frais " with Herbs Crêpes
Total 1,600 Crêpes

Sweet Items

1,500 Decorated Fruits
Grand Total 9,800 Servings

Comments on the Menu Selection
(Example D+++)

This is an " Open House " buffet in the showroom of a luxury car dealer who is promoting the newest model.

The most important consideration for this menu is the length of the event (11 am to 9 pm). The caterer must choose items that can be arranged on platters throughout the day.

Because the guests will come and go, it is not important to have a large assortment at any one time. However there must be an ample supply of each item kept fresh in refrigerated containers or even a refrigerated truck.

Savory Items

The four different savory items are presented together on the buffet table.

Some of each item should be available to the guests at all times. It is therefore important to replenish the platters in proportion to the number of guests that are present at any one time.

It is also important to not place too many items on the buffet at once so that the remainder stay as fresh as possible for presentation at the end of the event.

• The principle item is a selection of pastry hors d'œuvres; 10 different varieties/2,600 total pieces.

• The stuffed crêpes (1,600 pieces/-4 varieties) are arranged on small bases (grapefruits for example) which are lovely on the buffet table. The flavors include lumpfish eggs, salmon mousse, foie gras, and fromage frais.

• A beautiful assortment of 10 different canapés (2,600 pieces) are light and easy to eat and make an attractive display.

This portion of the menu is rounded out by 1,500 mini brioches filled with foie gras, ham and cheese.

Sweet Items

Decorated fruits are made in wide assortment of flavors and colors.

Preparation

Order the ingredients several days in advance and verify their quality.

Make the doughs in advance; puff pastry, white bread, brioche.

Advance planning is necessary for the kitchen to prepare and store the large number of hors d'œuvres. Everything is prepared in advance and delivered in refrigerated containers.

Two buffet tables are set up; one for liquid refreshments and another for the food. Since there will not be many people present at any one time, the buffet does not have to be large.

Other Considerations

Since there will be a non-stop flow of guests, often arriving in large groups, the serving staff must be organized to replenish the table quickly and efficiently.

Have a few back-up tablecloths on hand to replace any that are soiled so that the table always looks clean and neat. The table should always be well supplied with plates and napkins.

A refrigerated truck is recommended to keep the large number of perishable items fresh throughout the day.

Important Details

For this type of " open house " buffet it is not necessary to have a large assortment of items.

During the 10 hours, an estimated 1,200-1,500 people will come and go and will probably stay for no more than one hour.

For this length of stay, it is estimated that each person will consume an average of 5-6 hors d'œuvres.

The buffet is given to promote a luxury car, so it follows that the table and decorations are elegant; beautiful flower arrangements, silver platters and ornate presentation mirrors.

Specifics

Plan ahead to replace the tablecloths and have a back-up supply. Have plenty of platters in reserve so that they can be replenished efficiently.

Set up a preparation area as close to the buffet as possible and arrange

Organization (Example D+++)

This buffet is out of the ordinary because the food is served in small quantities over a ten hour period.

The assortment of items is elegant but small to facilitate the preparation and service.

The special theme centerpieces for each table should be made well in advance. For example, a vintage car can be fashioned from pastillage or nougatine and decorated with the emblem of the new model and used as a container to serve the decorated fruits.

Some of the canapés can also be decorated with the emblem (in piped out butter for example).

A refrigerated truck is needed to deliver the fresh items and can be used to store handy back-ups. It will probably be necessary to make several deliveries throughout the day to ensure freshness.

Savory Items

Pastry Hors d'œuvres

They are prepared, cut into shapes and frozen several days in advance.

It is best if they are baked fresh throughout the day and delivered in batches fresh from the oven. If this is not possible, bake at the last moment, allow to cool and store in airtight containers.

Stuffed Crêpe " Hedgehog "

The crêpes are made and filled one day in advance, covered in plastic wrap and refrigerated.

They are sliced, placed on toothpicks and attached to the base shortly before delivery. Cover the hedgehog with a damp towel until served or transport the slices on toothpicks and assemble on-site.

for the parking of the refrigerated truck close to the preparation area.

Have a telephone line close at hand to remain in contact with the caterer's kitchen in case of emergency and to order more items throughout the day.

Set up the tables well in advance.

Install supplementary lighting to spotlight the decorative centerpieces.

The server in charge is made responsible for the safety of the silver pedestals, candlesticks and platters.

Canapés

The bread is made 3 days in advance and sliced one day in advance, covered and refrigerated.

The garnishes are prepared one day in advance.

The canapés are assembled the day of the event and are best if assembled in several batches throughout the day to ensure freshness and variety.

They are glazed and delivered on sheets of damp parchment paper to keep the bread moist.

The canapés are arranged on platters on-site and the platters are replenished at regular intervals.

Mini Brioches

The rolls are made one day in advance and kept in air-tight containers.

They are best if filled at intervals throughout the day and delivered fresh.

They should be kept covered with plastic and refrigerated until arranged on platters.

Sweet Items

The decorated fruits in a variety of flavors can be assembled several days in advance. One day in advance, they are dipped in a glaze (sugar cooked to hard crack) or rolled in sugar and placed in small paper containers.

These desserts can be candied and stored for a longer period of time which allows the caterer to make large amounts in advance to fill many orders.

Schedule several shifts of servers, taking into account when the largest groups are expected to attend.

Locate a facility to clean the platters during the reception.

At the end of the event, designate someone to inventory the remaining liquid refreshments and check the rental for damage and breakage and to report this information before the billing.

After the event, verify that the location is perfectly clean and in good order.

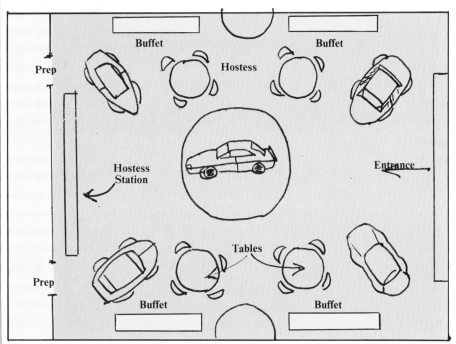

Decorations

The decorations are an important element in the success of any catered affair, adding life and beauty and providing an attractive setting within which to display the results of the caterer's hard work.

When planning the decoration, keep in mind the decoration of the rooms, the buffet tables, the serving pieces, the choice of tableware, and the flowers. Cold brochettes could be presented in a large styrofoam scallop shell covered with seaweed, or on a mirror.

• Pheasant ballotines could be displayed with colorful feathers attached and set in a birdcage.

• A wicker basket, wicker horn of plenty or even a small sedan chair could hold fresh or decorated fruit.

• Ice sculptures or shapes in sugar work could serve as bases for ice creams.

Factory Inauguration

This new factory will provide many jobs for the residents of the neighboring towns. Prominent figures from all over the area have been invited to the inauguration.

Details

Following the cocktail and buffet, the management will provide a tour of the new facilities.

Location

Due to the large guest list, the buffet will be divided between two locations. One buffet will be held outdoors, under a tent. Local business executives, politicians and journalists will attend the buffet given in the main dining room.

Denis Ruffel will personally oversee the buffet.

CLIENT _International Mobile Componants, Inc._ .... _May 24_ .... Dossier N° _D++++_

If company
Person in charge ..... _Mr. LOUFRANO_ ....

Tel. _XX XX_ ....

Fax _XX XX_ ....

Address
for billing .... _I.M.C., Inc._ ....

.... _Forest Industrial Park   77190 Ville-la-Nouvelle_ ....

Method of payment ... _40 % in advance, balance at 30 and 60 days_ ....

Number guests
_500_

Budget
Very high

Place and address
of the reception ..... _Same as above_ ....

Set-up and atmosphere of reception room	Preparation facilities
Reception hall in factory ;	_Kitchen adjoining reception hall_
Large tent	_indoor kitchen near tent_

RENTAL EQUIPMENT |_X_| Furnished by us
(Check)   (Dossier N° .... |_42_|)

Rented |_X_| from _OPTIONS_ ....

BUFFET   Menu finalized
by .... _May 2_

BEVERAGES _Champagne, whiskey_
Perrier, fruit juices

Ice ..... _4 x 40 lbs bags_

TRANSPORTATION ... _2 vans &_

.... _2 refrigerated trucks_

Flowers ..... _We supply_

Musique ..... _Customer supplies_

Other ..... _Tent, floor, lighting for tent_

RECEPTION SCHEDULE

Reception .... _4:00 pm to 8:30 pm_ ....

Food
delivery .... _12:30 pm_

Food
pick-up .... _After reception_

Rental
delivery .... _10:00 am_

Rental
pick-up .... _Next morning_ ....

(Other) ....

PERSONNEL

15 servers

7 kitchen personnel

Additional information ....

Suggested Menu (Example D++++)

Savory Items

Pastry Hors d'œuvres
Full Assortment of 35 Varieties (??only 28 in book)
Total 1,000 Pastry Hors d'œuvres

Canapés
50 canapés of the following varieties: Salmon, Tarama, Egg Salad, Boiled Ham, Garlic Sausage, Liver Mousse, Cherry Tomato, Turnip, Baby Corn, Mushroom, Sweet Pepper, Macédoine, Comté, Roquefort, " Fromage Frais ", Goat Cheese, Tongue, Sardine, Pickled Herring
Total 1,000 Assorted Canapés

Mignonnettes
100 of each variety: Cocktail Franks in Pastry with Mustard, Veal Sausages on Toasts with Apples, Spicy Blood Sausages in Pastry with Apple Mousse, Cocktail Franks with Bacon, Stuffed Prunes in Canadian Bacon, Banana Slices in Bacon, " Paupiettes " of Sole in Aspic, Belgian Endive Leaves with Smoked Salmon or Foie Gras, Stuffed Grape Leaves, Marinated Shrimp
Total 1,000 Mignonnettes

Hot Hors d'œuvres
Assortment of 10 Varieties
Total 500 Hot Hors d'œuvres

Centerpieces for Buffets
* 13 Surprise Breads, each with 40 pieces
* 2 Canapé " Hedgehogs ", each with 100 pieces
* 3 Stuffed Crêpe " Hedgehogs ", each with 100 pieces
Total 1,020 Pieces

Cold Brochettes
Assortment of 6 Varieties
Total 500 Cold Brochettes

Fish in Aspic
80 Portions Lobster

Elaborate Meat Dishes
* 80 Portions Cubed Ham with Pineapple
* 80 Portions Braised Beef " Bourgeoise "
* 80 Portions Stuffed Suckling Pig
* 80 Portions Tenderloin of Beef " Périgueux "
* 80 Portions Leg of Lamb with Mint
Total 400 Portions

Poultry in Aspic
* 80 Portions Turkey
* 80 Portions Chaud-Froid
Total 160 Portions – Grand Total 5,660 Savory Items

Sweet Items

* 500 Assorted Tartelettes
* 500 Assorted Mini Cream Puffs
* 500 Assorted Petit Fours
* Fours Sec and Macaroons
* 500 Decorated Fruits and Macerated Fruits
Total 2,500 Sweet Items

Comments on the Menu Selection (Example D++++)

Savory Items

A grand occasion such as this allows the caterer to present a stunning array of dishes on the buffet table.

Several considerations are made when choosing items for a luxurious menu such as this:
- Size and height of the presentations
- Color and shape
- Variety of ingredients
- Assortment of flavors

The large presentations which serve as centerpieces on the buffet account for approximately one serving per person in all.

It is interesting to note that the larger the group, the fewer items are consumed per person. So when counting on 7-10 pieces per person, the lower number is usually sufficient for large gatherings.

Sweet Items

The proportion of savory/sweet is the classic makeup of 2/3 savory/1/3 sweet.

The large number of pieces allows the caterer to offer a well-rounded assortment of desserts.

Preparation

The ordering of the food is a very important step as there is the following to consider:

- Large quantity of ingredients

- The high level of quality

- The wide variety

The food should be ordered and delivered several days in advance and checked for quality.

Prepare in advance: the white bread and round loaves, puff pastry, basic pie pastry and brioche.

For the sweet items prepare in advance: the decorated fruits, sweet pie pastry, petit fours, butter cookies, almond macaroons, and lastly the cream puffs and macerated fruits.

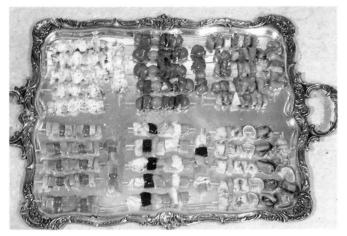

Other Considerations

This is a very important event for the caterer. The guest list includes a great number of influential people who are potential customers. The buffet should be absolutely impeccable to make a favorable impression.

Many of the details are worked out well in advance:

• Reserve the location and reserve a tent to be set up for the event.

• Rent all the equipment and other material needed for the tables.

• Select and order the flowers and other floral decorations that will play such an important role in the atmosphere of the event.

• Rent two refrigerated trucks and check the number of refrigerated containers belonging to the caterer and rent more if needed. These are important for storing the cold items on-site.

• Schedule the servers well in advance and designate one to be responsible for each buffet table. In all four servers are needed for the main table and eleven for the tables under the tent.

• Order the liquid refreshments in advance and arrange for a discounted price on the price of the Champagne which will be appreciated by the client.

• Contact the best person available to set up the lighting and sound system; important aspects of such a large event.

Specifics

Several days before the event, confirm the delivery times of the tent, rental, sound system etc.

The tent and floor should be in place 2-3 days before the event. The sound system and lighting should be installed at the same time.

Plan an easy-to-serve meal for the service staff and other personel.

The servers are scheduled so that half of them arrive early to set up the buffet tables and the second shift arrives just before the reception and stay after the event to disassemble the buffet and clean up.

The individual items are transported in well-marked containers and arranged on platters on-site by the servers.

Organization (Example D++++)

Large, elegant buffets demand a great deal of organization. All of the preparations that freeze well can be made several days in advance.

Each dish should be broken down into separate operations with notes made on which must be done at the last minute and so on. Once the schedule is laid out, it is important to follow the sequence closely to have everything prepared on time.

Savory Items

Cut out the puff pastry shapes and freeze unbaked. Bake them shortly before delivery.

Prepare the pastry bases and the fillings in advance, assemble and arrange on platters on-site.

Canapés

Make the close-textured white bread 2-3 days in advance. Slice the day before the event, wrap and refrigerate. Prepare the garnishes, sauces and flavored butters and store in covered containers. Leave the butter at room temperature and refrigerate the other preparations.

Canapé " Hedgehog "

Prepare the canapés in advance, wrap and freeze. Cut into bite-size pieces the day of the event. Assemble the hedgehog on-site.

Crêpe " Hedgehog "

Prepare the crêpes 1-2 days in advance, fill, wrap in plastic and refrigerate. Slice into pieces the day of the event and assemble the hedgehog on-site.

Cold Brochettes

Prepare the meats, vegetable and fruit garnishes and the sauces the day before the event. Assemble the brochettes and glaze them the day of the event.

Elaborate Meat Dishes

The meat is cooked 3 days in advance and refrigerated and the sauces can be made two days in advance. The day before the event, slice the meat, decorate and glaze. Store in the refrigerator and glaze a second time shortly before delivery.

Lobsters

Cook the lobsters two days in advance and refrigerate. Prepare garnishes and lobsters one day in advance and arrange on platters on-site.

Sweet Items

The preparation of the sweet items can be scheduled over three days.

The cream fillings should be made the day of the event.

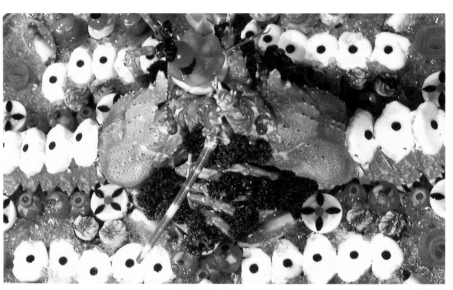

The elaborate dishes are finished at the last minute in the kitchens of the caterer mend arranged on platters on-site by an experienced server or the caterer.

Deliver in two stages: first deliver the liquid refreshments and ice, decorative bases, extra platters, and any food items kept on dry ice; later deliver the fresh items in a refrigerated truck.

An important detail: One server is in charge of distributing the right containers to the various tables. Each container is labeled clearly with its contents.

The buffet is disassembled by the servers and personnel sent from the caterer's kitchen. Verify that everything is in order and clean after the reception.

Organization and Layout of the Buffet

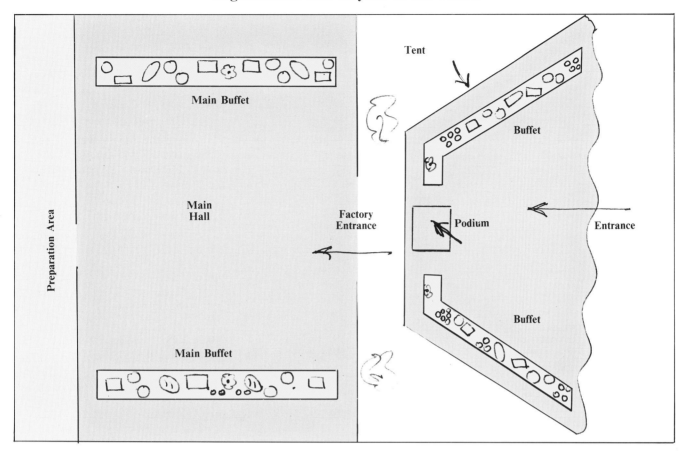

Croquembouche
and Other Dessert Centerpieces

Large dessert centerpieces are served in France to celebrate many occasions. The croquembouche is the most traditional and can be decorated in various ways to suit the event. This cone-shaped tower of filled cream puffs held in place with shiny caramel is a most elegant wedding cake. It is also served for first communions and baptisms in France. The decorations can be made of nougatine shapes, pulled-sugar flowers, spun sugar etc. and can be simple or fancy.

Depending on the size of the cream puffs, count on 3-5 per person. They are usually assembled on-site which requires advance planning.

Decorated layers of spongecake are served for gala occasions as well. For large groups, several cakes are arranged on a tiered base which is often augmented with royal icing piped in delicate patterns. The final assembly is done on-site (the cakes are kept refrigerated). A beautifully decorated cake set on an ornamental base makes a stunning centerpiece for the buffet.

Preparations in the Four Volumes

" + " Category: Low   " ++ " Category: Medium

Volume 1

Chapter 1 - Savory Hors d'Œuvres
Items in " + " Category
Almond Hors d'Œuvres
Walnut Hors d'Œuvres
Hazelnut Hors d'Œuvres
Poppy Seed and Sesame Seed Matchsticks
Cheese Matchsticks
Parmesan Hors d'Œuvres
Slivered Almond Hors d'Œuvres
Cumin-Munster Hors d'Œuvres
Paprika Hors d'Œuvres
Poppy Seed Hors d'Œuvres
Anchovy Hors d'Œuvres
Ham Crescents
Cocktail Sausage Hors d'Œuvres
" Chipolatas " Hors d'Œuvres
Mini-Pizzas Gougères
Croque-Monsieur
Salmon Tartelettes
Mini-Quiches
Pissaladères
Items in " ++ " Category
Pâté Hors d'Œuvres
Chorizo Hors d'Œuvres
Stuffed Olive Hors d'Œuvres
Items in " +++ " Category
Onion/Roquefort Tartelettes
Mussel Tartelettes
Tartelettes of Julienned Vegetables
Endive and Chive Tartelettes

Chapter 2 – Mini-Sandwiches and Filled Rolls
Items in " + " Category
Ham Sandwiches
Swiss Cheese Sandwiches
Lettuce and Tomato Sandwiches
Egg Salad Sandwiches
Lettuce and Cucumber Sandwiches
Chesse Rolls
Ham Rolls
" Fromage Frais " Rolls.
Items in " ++ " Category
Foie Gras Mousse Sandwiches
Salami Sandwiches
Chicken Breast Sandwiches
Roquefort and Walnut Sandwiches
Items in " +++ " Category
Mortadella Sandwiches
Crab Sandwiches
Roquefort Rolls
Foie Gras Rolls
Smoked Ham Rolls
Salmon Mousse Rolls

Chapter 3 – Canapés
Items in " + " Category
Hard-Boiled Egg Canapés
Egg Salad Canapés
Garlic Sausage Canapés
Dry Sausage Canapés
Tomato Wedge Canapés
Radish Canapés

Items in " ++ " Category
Sardine Canapés
Tuna Canapés
Lumpfish Egg Canapés
Quail Egg Canapés
Ham Canapés
Cucumber Canapés
Green Bean Canapés
Hearts of Palm Canapés
Mushroom Canapés
Macédoine of Vegetables Canapés
Comté Canapés " Fromage Frais " and Chive Canapés
" Fromage Frais " and Paprika
Items in " +++ " Category
Fresh Salmon Canapés, Pickled Herring, Shrimp, Mussel, Bay Scallop, Anchovy, Tarama, Smoked Trout, Andouille, Liver Mousse, Blood Sausage and Apple, Sautéed Zucchini, Turnip, Asparagus Tip, Artichoke Bottom, Broccoli, Sweet Pepper, Roquefort, Parmesan, Gorgonzola, Munster Cream, " Fromage Frais ", Walnut and Raisin, Aspic with Chicken Livers, Aspic with Salmon, Aspic with Chicken, Aspic with Lumpfish Eggs.
Items in " ++++ " Category
Canapé of Sole Mousse with Herbs
Smoked Salmon Canapés
Monkfish Medallion Canapés
Smoked Eel Canapés
Crab Canapés
Caviar Canapés
Salmon Egg Canapés
Parma Ham Canapés
Tongue Canapés
Foie Gras Canapés
Veal Sausage Canapés
Cherry Tomato Canapés
Baby Corn Canapés
Mini Goat Cheese Canapés
Aspic Canapés with Langoustine
Aspic Canapés with Tongue

Chapter 4 – Mignonnettes
Items in " +++ " Category
Cocktail Franks in Pastry with Mustard
Apicy Blood Sausage in Pastry with Apple Mousse
Cocktail Franks with Bacon
Stuffed Prunes in Canadian Bacon
Banana Slice in Bacon
Marinated Shrimp
Saltcod Fritters
Monkfish Fritters
Broccoli Fritters
Celery Sticks with Roquefort
Stuffed Grape Leaves
Items in " ++++ " Category
Veal Sausage on Toast with Apples
" Paupiettes " of Sole in Aspic
Langoustine Fritters
Belgian Endive Leaves with Smoked Salmon or Foie Gras

Chapter 5 – Hot Hors d'Œuvres
Items in " +++ " Category
" Croustades " Sweet Pepper Compote
" Croustades " with Curried Mussels
" Feuilletés " with Sole and Lime
Mini " Bouchées à la Reine "
" Croustades " of Chicken Livers with Raspberry Sauce
Items in " ++++ " Category
" Feuilletés " with Asparagus Tips
Quail's Eggs on Toast
Snail " Bouchées "
Mini Brioches with Crab
" Croustades " Bay Scallops Chervil Sauce
" Feuilletés " with Prawns
" Croustades " Sweetbreads Sherry Sauce

Chapter 6 – Centerpieces for Buffets
Items in " + " Category
Surprise Bread Walnuts and Raisins
Surprise Bread Ham and Swiss Cheese
Surprise Bread Chicken and Herbs
Surprise Bread with Boiled Ham
Surprise Bread with Dry Sausage
Surprise Bread with Garlic Sausage
Surprise Bread with Vegetables
Surprise Bread with Fish Mousse
Bouquet of Crudités
Items in " ++ " Category
Surprise Bread with Cumin, Roquefort and Walnuts
Surprise Bread with Salami
Stuffed Crêpe Hedgehog
Items in " +++ " Category
Surprise Bread with Country Ham
Bread Dried, Cured or Smoked Ham
Surprise Bread with Mortadella
Surprise Bread with Andouille
Bread Fish Eggs (Salmon/Lumpfish)
Bread Smoked Fish (trout/eel)
Louis XIV Brioche " Mousseline "
Canapé Hedgehog
The " Drakkar "
Items in " ++++ " Category
Bread with Olives, Crab and Watercress

Chapter 7 – Cold Brochettes
Items in " +++ " Category
Chicken Glazed with Herb Chaud-Froid
Ham and Pineapple Brochettes
Items in " ++++ " Category
Beef Stroganoff Brochettes
Curried Lamb Brochettes
Shellfish and Tropical Fruit

Volume 2

Chapter 1 – Individual Cold Dishes
Items in " + " Category
Eggs in Aspic with Ham
Eggs in Aspic " à l'Indienne "
Aspic Molds with Vegetables and Basil
Glazed Eggs Curry Chaud-Froid Sauce
Glazed Eggs Herb Chaud-Froid Sauce
Glazed Eggs with Tomato Sauce

Classified by Food Cost

"+++" Category: High   "++++" Category: Very High

Items in "++" Category
Avocado with Crab
Grapefruit with Crab
Artichoke Bottoms "St. Fiacre"
Seafood Aspic Molds
Glazed Eggs "Perigueux" Sauce
Items in "+++" Category
Eggs in Aspic "Luculus"
Smoked Salmon Aspic Molds

Chapter 2 – Pâtés
Items in "+" Category
"Pantin" Pâté
Tourte Lorraine
Items in "++" Category
Veal and Ham Pâté in Aspic
Ham and Spinach "Pithiviers"
Sausage in Brioche
Pâté of Duck à l'Orange in Aspic
Items in "+++" Category
Tourte of Rabbit with Hazelnuts
Salmon Koulibiac
Items in "++++" Category
Tourte of Sweetbreads and Morels

Chapter 3 – Terrines
Items in "+" Category
Terrine of Chicken Livers
Items in "++" Category
Goose Rillettes
Tricolor Terrine of Red Mullet
"Rainbow" Terrine
Items in "+++" Category
Duck Terrine Green Peppercorns
Terrine of Hare
Terrine of Bream
Vegetable Mousse Sweetbreads
Items in "++++" Category
Rabbit Terrine with Hazelnuts
Terrine of Foie Gras
Terrine of Pike with Asparagus Tips
Vegetable Terrine in Aspic

Chapter 4 – Galantines Ballottines
Items in "+" Category
Galantine of Chicken
Items in "++" Category
Galantine of Salmon
Items in "+++" Category
Guinea Hen Ballotines
Galantine of Duck
Items in "++++" Category
Ballotine of Squab

Chapter 5 – Aspics
Items in "+" Category
Aspic with Ham and Parsley
Items in "++" Category
Chicken Aspic with Sherry
Items in "+++" Category
Seafood Aspic with Vegetables
Items in "++++" Category
Aspic with Foie Gras
Aspic of Rabbit and Crayfish

Chapter 3 – Pizzas and Quiches
Items in "+" Category
Cheese, Mushroom and Olive Pizza
Anchovy, Olive and Green Pepper
Artichoke, Asparagus, Fava Bean
Zucchini, Corn, Broccoli and Olive
Hearts of Palm, Olive, Tuna Fennel
Zucchini, Mussel, Corn, Shrimp and Bay
  Scallop
Quiche Lorraine
Trianon "Croustade"
Onion and Roquefort "Croustade"
Leek "Flamiche"
"Croustade" of Vegetables and Basil

Volume 3 (*)
Chapter 1 – New Croustades
Items in "+" Category
Mussel Croustade with Pistou
Croustade with Eggs "Florentine"
Cheese Croustade
Items in "++" Category
Salmon Croustade Spinach and Sorrel
Seafood Croustade with Saffron
Items in "+++" Category
Croustade Asparagus and Frogs' Legs
Croustade Artichokes, Zucchini/Frogs'
Five-Mushroom Croustade
Croustade Poached Eggs "Benedic-
  tine"

Chapter 4 – Beignets
Items in "+++" Category
Beignets Peppers Stuffed with Cheese
Zucchini Beignets
Eggplant Beignets
Miniature Corn Beignets
Chicken Beignets
Beignets made with Brains
Squid Beignets
Mussel Beignets
Ground Meat Beignets
Items in "++++" Category
Gambas Beignets
Breaded Oyster Beignets
Breaded Red Mullet Beignets
Breaded Salmon Beignets with Green
  Beans

Chapter 6 – Mixed Salads
Items in "+" Category
Chef's Salad
Mediterranean Salad
Vegetables "à la Grecque"
Russian Salad
Taboulé
Items in "++" Category
Méli-Mélo Salad
Chinese Salad
Exotic Salad
Brazilian Salad
Japanese Salad
Country-Style Beef Salad
Items in "+++" Category
Cinderella Salad

Seafood Salad Pink Peppercorns
Haddock and Pine Nut Salad
Pasta and Seafood Salad
Duck Salad
Items in "++++" Category
Chicken with Sweetbreads Salad
Foie Gras Salad

Chapter 7 – Fish in Aspic
Items in "+" Category
Trout in Aspic
Salmon in Aspic
Items in "++" Category
Salmon Steaks in Aspic
Hake in Chaud-Froid
Items in "+++" Category
Stuffed Fillets of Sole Salmon
  Mousse
Sea Bass in Chaud-Froid
Items in "++++" Category
Turbot with Soufflé of Salmon
  Mousse

Chapter 8 – Lobsters
Items in "+++" Category
Lobster with Mayonnaise
"Manhattan" Lobster
Lobster with Vegetable Julienne Lob-
  ster "en Salpicon"
Items in "++++" Category
Platter with Two Lobsters
Lobster "en Bellevue"

Chapter 9 – Poultry in Aspic
Items in "+" Category
Chicken with Truffles
Items in "++" Category
Cubed Turkey in Aspic
Duck à l'Orange in Aspic
Items in "+++" Category
Chicken Chaud-Froid with Truffles
Items in "++++" Category
Quails with Foie Gras in Aspic

Volume 4
Chapter 1 – Elaborate Meat Dishes
Items in "+" Category
Pork Sirloin with Dried Fruit
Leg of Lamb with Mint
Items in "++" Category
Sliced Decorated Ham
Cubed Ham Pineapple and Cher-
  ries
Pork Loin with Dried Fruit
Braised Beef "Bourgeoise"
Items in "+++" Category
Stuffed Suckling Pig
Tenderloin of Beef "Perigueux"
Prime Rib with Young Vegetables
Breast of Veal with Dried Fruit
"Dodines" of Wild Boar
Ballotine of Pheasant "en Volière"
Items in "++++" Category
Noisette of Venison
Hare "à la Royale"

(*) Note: Quenelles (Chapter 2), Soufflés (Chapter 3), and Individual Hot Dishes (Chapter 5) are not presented in Buffets.

First published as *L'Artisan Traiteur* by Editions St-Honoré, Paris, France: copyright © 1990.

English translation copyright © 1990 by Van Nostrand Reinhold for the United States of America and Canada; by CICEM (Compagnie Internationale de Consultation *Education* et *Media*) for the rest of the world.

Van Nostrand Reinhold
115 Fifth Avenue
New York, New York 10003
Nelson Canada
1120 Birchmount Road
Scarborough, Ontario M1K SGH, Canada

ISBN 0-442-00143-6 (vol. 4)

CICEM, 229, rue St-Honoré
75001 PARIS (France)

© CICEM ISBN 2-86871-017-4
Dépôt légal 2ᵉ trimestre 1990
Imprimé en France par l'Imprimerie 🔲 Alençonnaise

Library of Congress Cataloging-in-Publication Data

Ruffel, Denis :

Collective title: The professional caterer series / by Denis Ruffel (Born in 1950)

Contents:

Vol. 1. Pastry hors d'œuvres, assorted snacks, canapés, centerpieces, hot hors d'œuvres, cold brochette's.
Vol. 2. Individual cold dishes, pates, terrines, galantines, and ballotines, aspics, pizzas, and quiches.
Vol. 3. Croustades, quenelles, souffles, beignets, individual hot dishes, mixed salads, fish in aspic, lobsters, poultry in aspic.
Vol. 4. Meat and Games, Sauces and Bases, Planning, Execution, Display and Decoration for Buffets and Receptions.

1. Quantity cooking. 2. Caterers and catering. I.
Title : The professional caterer series.
TX820.R843 1990 641.5'7--dc20 89-22600
ISBN 0-442-00143-6 (vol. 4)